CH00645668

Democratizing Global Justice

Deliberating Global Goals

The tensions between democracy and justice have long preoccupied political theorists. Institutions that are procedurally democratic do not necessarily make substantively just decisions. *Democratizing Global Justice* shows that democracy and justice can be mutually reinforcing in global governance – a domain where both are conspicuously lacking – and indeed that global justice *requires* global democratization. This novel reconceptualization of the problematic relationship between global democracy and global justice emphasizes the role of inclusive deliberative processes. These processes can empower the agents necessary to determine what justice should mean and how it should be implemented in any given context. Key agents include citizens and the global poor; and not just the states but also international organizations and advocacy groups active in global governance. The argument is informed by and applied to the decision process leading to adoption of the Sustainable Development Goals, and climate governance inasmuch as it takes on questions of climate justice.

JOHN S. DRYZEK is Centenary Professor and Australian Research Council Laureate Fellow at the University of Canberra. He is the author of numerous books on democracy and on environmental politics, including the prize-winning co-authored *The Politics of the Anthropocene* (2019). He is co-editor of *The Oxford Handbook of Deliberative Democracy* (2018).

ANA TANASOCA is a research fellow in Philosophy at Macquarie University. She is the author of *Deliberation Naturalized* (2020), *The Ethics of Multiple Citizenship* (2018), and recent articles in *Perspectives on Politics* and the *Journal of Political Philosophy*.

Democratizing Global Justice

Deliberating Global Goals

JOHN S. DRYZEK
University of Canberra

ANA TANASOCA
Macquarie University

CAMBRIDGE
UNIVERSITY PRESS

CAMBRIDGE
UNIVERSITY PRESS

University Printing House, Cambridge CB2 8BS, United Kingdom

One Liberty Plaza, 20th Floor, New York, NY 10006, USA

477 Williamstown Road, Port Melbourne, VIC 3207, Australia

314–321, 3rd Floor, Plot 3, Splendor Forum, Jasola District Centre,
New Delhi – 110025, India

79 Anson Road, #06–04/06, Singapore 079906

Cambridge University Press is part of the University of Cambridge.

It furthers the University's mission by disseminating knowledge in the pursuit of
education, learning, and research at the highest international levels of excellence.

www.cambridge.org
Information on this title: www.cambridge.org/9781108844987
DOI: 10.1017/9781108954167

© John S. Dryzek and Ana Tanasoca 2021

This publication is in copyright. Subject to statutory exception
and to the provisions of relevant collective licensing agreements,
no reproduction of any part may take place without the written
permission of Cambridge University Press.

First published 2021

A catalogue record for this publication is available from the British Library.

ISBN 978-1-108-84498-7 Hardback
ISBN 978-1-108-94934-7 Paperback

Cambridge University Press has no responsibility for the persistence or accuracy
of URLs for external or third-party internet websites referred to in this publication
and does not guarantee that any content on such websites is, or will remain,
accurate or appropriate.

Contents

Preface

The world has over the decades occasionally affirmed the need for global justice. Landmarks would include the Universal Declaration of Human Rights in 1948, the Millennium Development Goals (MDGs) in 2000, and – our major case here – the Sustainable Development Goals (SDGs) in 2015. But even as global justice is widely advocated in principle, it remains elusive in practice, and global injustice remains pervasive. Political theorists have grappled with the content of global justice, though they disagree as to its essence and on whether justice should be sought globally, rather than nationally or locally.

What then is the nature of our fresh contribution to thinking about global justice and why do we believe it matters? While we regard the pursuit of global justice as a moral imperative, we provide here no comprehensive normative theory as to what its precise content should be. Rather, we advocate inclusive deliberative processes to nourish agents who can determine what global justice should mean and how it should be implemented in any given setting, particularly those involving the setting of global goals such as the SDGs. The concept of formative agency is central. We will argue that formative agency, and its exercise through inclusive deliberative processes, are integral to the very concept of global justice. This is because any account of justice is incomplete without an account of the role of those formative agents who must jointly specify its meaning on the ground. We hope our argument will make sense to those currently exercising formative agency, be they located in advocacy groups, expert bodies, or international organizations, and not just to scholars interested in global justice, democratic theory, and global governance.

That argument entails a commitment to deliberative democracy, at the global level no less than elsewhere. But our case for the democratization of global justice does not depend on any prior commitment to deliberative democracy. Rather, this argument follows directly from contemplating the necessary role of formative agency in global justice, from the need to redeem its positive aspects as well as overcome its problematic ones. And if we are right, global justice and global democracy are mutually reinforcing. This in turn provides a fresh angle on the long-standing debate in political theory about the problematic relationship between democracy and justice.

Precursor papers and parts of the argument of the book (and in some cases its whole) have been presented at the Conference on New Frontiers of Global Justice at the University of California, San Diego; the Workshop on Poverty and Feasibility, Australian National University; the Conference on Developments in Deliberative Democracy, University of Westminster; in seminars at the Center for Global Ethics and Politics, Graduate Center, City University of New York; the Academy of Global Governance, University of Oslo; the Centre for Moral, Social and Political Theory, Australian National University; in the Political Theory seminar at Nuffield College, Oxford; the Political Theory Seminar at the University of Connecticut; the Canberra International Ethics Research seminar, convened by Toni Erskine; and at the 2014 Warrender Lecture in Political Theory, University of Sheffield. We thank audiences at all of these locations. Almost all of the writing was done in the Centre for Deliberative Democracy and Global Governance in the Institute for Governance and Policy Analysis at the University of Canberra, where our colleagues provided an excellent environment for thinking, research, and writing. The project was financed by the Australian Research Council, Laureate Fellowship FL140100154 awarded to John Dryzek for the project 'Deliberative Worlds: Democracy, Justice, and a Changing Earth System'.

For advice and comments, we thank Peter Balint, Wendy Conway-Lamb, Nicole Curato, Kari De Pryck, Ned Dobos, Toni Erskine, Robert Goodin, Carol Gould, Michael Morrell, Tomer Perry, Jonathan Pickering, Sanjay Reddy, Jensen Sass, David Schlosberg, Carole-Anne Sénit, Nicholas Southwood, Hayley Stevenson, Jan-Gustav Strandenaes, and two anonymous referees. We especially thank Sonya Duus for her work in locating and digesting relevant literature on the process that yielded the SDGs, interviewing some of the participants, and commenting on draft chapters.

At its heart, this is a work in international ethics and political theory. We also show how the theory can be applied to an analysis of the process that yielded the SDGs in 2015, and a more illustrative account of the history of climate governance as it takes on matters of justice, which has increasingly featured the normative force of global goals. We conducted twenty interviews with individuals with inside knowledge of the SDG process – not as a primary data source, but more to round out our knowledge of questions that are key to us, but not necessarily covered fully in official documents and in the extensive literature produced by academics, journalists, and activist groups on the process. We thank our interviewees for being so generous with their time.

In several chapters we have used some of the text from John S. Dryzek, Democratic Agents of Justice, *Journal of Political Philosophy* 23 (4) (2015): 361–84, by permission.

List of Abbreviations

AOSIS	Alliance of Small Island States
ATD	All Together in Dignity to Overcome Poverty
COPO	Conference of the Parties
CSO	Civil Society Organization
DESA	Department of Economic and Social Affairs
DGCA	Deliberative Global Citizens' Assembly
HLP	High Level Panel
HLPF	High Level Political Forum on Sustainable Development
ICC	International Criminal Court
IMF	International Monetary Fund
IO	International organization
IPBES	Intergovernmental Science-Policy Platform on Biodiversity and Ecosystem Services
IPCC	Intergovernmental Panel on Climate Change
IUCN	International Union for Conservation of Nature
LVC	La Via Campesina
MDGs	Millennium Development Goals
NGO	Non-governmental organization
OECD	Organization for Economic Cooperation and Development
OWG	Open Working Group
PPP	Purchasing Power Parity
SDGs	Sustainable Development Goals
SDI	Slum Dwellers International
SDSN	Sustainable Development Solutions Network
UN	United Nations
UNCSD	United Nations Conference on Sustainable Development
UNFCCC	United Nations Framework Convention on Climate Change

VNR   Voluntary National Review
WBCSD   World Business Council for Sustainable Development
WTO   World Trade Organization
WWF   World Wide Fund for Nature

1 | Introduction
Challenges, Agents, Cases

Global justice is an ethical imperative. Even those insisting that social justice should be pursued primarily within national borders have come to recognize the important obligations of justice that extend across national boundaries (see, notably, Miller 2008). And when international institutions do exist, surely they should be grounded in, and their practices informed by, principles of global justice. Yet global justice remains elusive in practice, as attested by the persistence of (among many other problems) extreme poverty and vast inequalities across the global rich and global poor. Our central point is that the practical pursuit of global justice will require global democratization, more precisely global *deliberative* democratization.

Our concern is with the *practical* pursuit of global justice through global democratization. Many of our chapters develop proposals to bring global institutions and practices more in line with democratic ideals and so render them better able to promote global justice. But there is nothing as practical as a good theory.[1] Our theory begins at the conceptual level with the idea of *formative agents of justice*, those (be they individual or collective agents) who shape what justice should actually mean in specific contexts and how it should be sought. Formative agents are always necessary because there are various competing conceptions of global justice and it is generally not obvious how each of them applies to a specific context or how they should be reconciled. We develop a normative theory about democratizing justice based on the idea that effective formative agency (involving citizens, states, international organizations, advocacy organizations, corporations, foundations, experts, etc.) is best exercised under deliberative democratic conditions. These conditions also involve empowering the poor and others who have long been marginalized. We apply the theory to the specific cases of the Sustainable Development Goals

---

[1] A maxim generally attributed to psychologist Kurt Lewin.

(SDGs) and climate governance. This application in turn yields insights that help us specify what democratization requires on the ground. The case analysis will also help refine the contours of the theory itself, notably by fleshing out the kind of deliberative institutions necessary to make justice and democracy work in synergy.[2]

The tensions between democracy and justice have long preoccupied political theorists (Gould 2004: 13–31). Theorists' conventional wisdom is that institutions that are procedurally democratic do not necessarily make substantively just decisions. In other words, there is no guarantee that more democracy means more justice.[3] In contrast, we argue that more inclusive deliberative processes can better promote justice. They do so by allowing a variety of individual and collective agents (most notably the poor) to act as effective formative agents and determine what justice should mean and how it should be pursued in any given context.

Deliberative democrats locate the essence of democracy in meaningful communication about matters of common concern linking those who exercise power and those who seek to or should influence that exercise.[4] Deliberation involves reflection upon preferences, interests, values, and identities, and striving to both reach and understand those with different frames of reference (be they religious, ideological, or philosophical). Ideally, democratic deliberation should be directly or indirectly inclusive of all those affected by (or subjected to) collective decisions, and consequential in determining the outcome of those decisions. Democratic legitimacy rests on the right, opportunity, and capacity of those affected by a collective decision (or their representatives) to participate in consequential deliberation about its content.

---

[2] This kind of refinement is not so unusual because pretty much all normative political theory relies on some empirical claims, if only in the minimal form of assumptions about human nature, or stylized facts. We simply go beyond such minimal use to deploy evidence gathered from real-world cases. However, ours is *not* an exercise in grounded theory, which constructs theory based on evidence gathered in cases. We begin our theorizing at the conceptual level, not the case level.

[3] See the discussions in Dowding, Goodin, and Pateman (2004). Several political theorists and philosophers have tried to overcome the separation of justice and democracy, but each attempt is normally accompanied by lament over the continued disjuncture between the two ideals (e.g. Shapiro 1999).

[4] For a history of thinking about deliberative democracy, see Floridia (2017). The term was coined by Bessette (1979). For the contemporary contours of the field, see Bächtiger et al. (2018a).

But can deliberative democracy be applied at the global level? Dahl (1999) and Keohane (2015) are among those who believe democracy can *only* exist within national boundaries, since the necessary bonds of political solidarity among citizens of different states are not present at the global level. Yet sometimes such solidarity bonds are hard to find within state borders as well, and this does not seem to negate the functioning of state democracy. Most pessimism about the feasibility of global democracy is premised on a narrow view of democracy. Democracy is not an all-or-nothing affair and elections are not the sole mechanism legitimating political authority. Even if global *electoral* democracy is hard to envisage, *deliberative democratization* is more readily applicable to the global level.

In this light, deliberative democracy can promote the realization of global justice by:

- enabling the more effective determination of what 'global justice' should mean, in general and in the context of particular challenges and practices;
- reconciling competing conceptions of justice (e.g. by deliberating the relative merits of national versus global ones);
- enabling different sorts of actors to become more effective in the implementation of global justice, by identifying the rights and duties, claims and liabilities that citizens, states, the poor, non-governmental organizations (NGOs), international organizations, corporations, the rich, foundations, experts, and public intellectuals have in the system of global governance;
- integrating different sorts of actors concerned with justice into a more effective global system of cooperation – a deliberative system; and
- enabling the recognition and effective political participation of the most disadvantaged groups and individuals.

Our inquiry contributes to the fields of international ethics, global justice, political theory and philosophy, deliberative democracy, and global governance.[5] Global justice is arguably *the* main question of

---

[5] Three of these fields are expansive enough to warrant a recent handbook. See Brooks (2020) for global justice, Bächtiger et al. (2018b) for deliberative democracy, and Levi-Faur (2012) for governance. There are several political theory and political philosophy handbooks, and a recent handbook of international political theory (Brown and Eckersley 2018).

international ethics (Nardin 2008). Justice in general is a central concern of political theory and political philosophy, with the relationship between justice and democracy a core question in these fields. As a contribution to deliberative democracy, our stress on agency contrasts with accounts that focus on formal and informal structures and processes (see e.g. Parkinson and Mansbridge 2012; Stevenson and Dryzek 2014), though in Chapter 8 we also analyse the integration of agents into the structures and processes of a deliberative system.

The theoretical arguments are informed by and applied to an analysis of two key vehicles of global justice: the process leading to the adoption of the SDGs in 2015 and climate governance inasmuch as it takes on questions of climate justice. We do not claim that either the SDGs or climate governance have delivered or will deliver global justice (in any substantive sense), simply that they operate in the domain of justice and so can be evaluated in this light. The cases will show that the problem is not that there is no justice in the current global order. Rather, the problem is that the order is dominated by some very limited notions of justice that should be questioned in a deliberative fashion, and if necessary replaced.

As well as being locations for the pursuit of global justice, the two cases we address manifest a new approach to global governance: 'governing through goals', as Kanie and Biermann (2017) describe it. The (potential) agents of justice we analyse (states, international organizations, advocacy groups, etc.) cover pretty much all the actors who together create global governance. Thus through the cases and agents we analyse, we contribute to the global governance field. While we look at only two cases, the framework we develop could be applied to other areas of global governance in the domain of justice (e.g. labour rights or trade) – not just global goals.

Before we say more about our cases, we will elaborate on how we will address two key challenges that face any attempt to further global justice: profound disagreement over the content of justice and the fact that theories of justice often say little about the agents who should put justice into practice.

First Challenge: Disagreement over the Content of Justice

Justice is a contentious issue. The first challenge to building a more just global order arises from reasonable disagreement over the content of justice, disagreement that is even more pervasive globally than domestically. Broadly, the domain of justice covers the allocation of rights, duties, benefits and burdens, and what members of a society owe each other. Different theories of justice prioritize different values (such as freedom, well-being, equality, or recognition). The scope or site of justice may also vary, with some scholars favouring justice among states (international justice), justice among all members of *different* political communities (cosmopolitan justice), justice within the *same* political community (national justice), justice among generations (intergenerational justice), justice between human and other sentient beings (interspecies justice), or finally justice between humans and ecological systems (ecological justice). We also see a plurality of principles of distributive justice (equality, sufficiency in the satisfaction of basic needs, and priority for the worst off) and a plurality of goods that can be distributed (welfare, material resources, opportunities, capabilities).

The same reasonable moral disagreement exists also (perhaps to an even greater degree) among political decision makers, bureaucrats, and lay citizens in trying to translate justice into law, policy, and practice. This means that we need some mechanism for coping with this disagreement. Moreover, the mechanism should be justifiable through reference to any political and epistemic (problem-solving) values that are more universally recognized. It should also be superior to other mechanisms we could think of (e.g. elections, lotteries, philosopher kings, technocracy). Building on suggestions from Amartya Sen, we argue that *deliberative democracy* represents such a superior mechanism for solving or accommodating moral disagreement about global justice (Sen 2009; Dryzek 2013a).

Deliberative democracy is especially valuable because it can move individuals to see past their narrow self-interest. In global governance and elsewhere, different actors can and do invoke theories and principles of justice strategically to serve their self-interest.[6] For example, wealthy actors will be more likely to invoke theories of justice in which private ownership, freedom from government, and procedural fairness loom large. Disadvantaged actors will more likely invoke the issue of historical responsibility for injustice (and compensation or reparations

---

[6] This invocation dominates especially debates about climate justice and is common in debates about international trade.

for the injustice), global equality, and the priority of their own material needs over non-material values. Since there are reasonable philosophical justifications for all sides, philosophical wisdom will not be able (by itself) to break this impasse. Yet deliberation among disagreeing actors might. Deliberation induces actors to try to put forward arguments and considerations that others can accept. If actors do still follow their self-interest, they must argue in a way that appeals to others' interests and perspectives as well as common interests if they wish to persuade others. Even in cases of deep moral disagreement, where participants initially reject the legitimacy of the values held by the other side, experience shows that deliberation can yield a mutual recognition of the legitimacy of competing values that makes collective decision making more tractable (see for example the deliberative forum composed of gay activists and fundamentalist Christians on the issue of HIV/AIDS policy described by Forester 1999).

Second Challenge: Who Is Required to Do What?

The second challenge is that theories and principles of justice often say little if anything about (1) what they require *on the ground*, in any given social, economic, cultural, and political context; and (2) *who* (states, global rich, NGOs, international organizations, corporations) is responsible for implementing them. The latter omission was identified long ago by Onora O'Neill (2001a) in her discussion of 'agents of justice', without which any theory of justice is incomplete.[7] Agents of justice are those who discharge the obligations justice requires, as well as enact the rights that justice bestows. However, O'Neill's account is itself incomplete. It neglects the fact that real-world actors might question the distribution of these rights and duties and the theory of justice behind it, and so the consequent need for considered political judgement to determine what justice means in specific contexts: in our words, the need for formative agency. Her account also neglects the limited guidance that theories of justice provide to agents in practical terms, when it comes to discharging or enacting rights. Just because we

---

[7] O'Neill does perhaps exaggerate the omission. States' agency is emphasized in the discussions of duties states have toward each other, and that rich states have toward poor ones (see e.g. Rawls 1999). Individual agency, especially that of rich persons, comes up in debates about duties to provide financial and other assistance to the global poor (see e.g. Singer 1972, 2015).

have established who exactly (e.g. states, international organizations, NGOs) bears an obligation (e.g. to end global poverty), doesn't mean we now know *how* agents should discharge the obligation and what the obligation requires in practical terms (e.g. what is poverty? How should the agent measure global poverty? By what means and in what ways should the agent try to reduce global poverty – monetary transfers, development programmes, etc.?).

Overcoming these limitations in the theory and practice of justice requires significant ethical and political work. We argue that deciding these issues constitutes a task that should involve not just the actors (such as the relatively wealthy and their states) bearing obligations, but also those towards whom obligations are directed – notably, the global poor. The global poor have often been treated merely as moral patients, objects of moral concern, or beneficiaries of others' duties. Most discussions of global justice (exceptions include Gould 2014) do not see them as playing any active role or having much input into their own rescue (see the critiques offered by Kuper 2002; Deveaux 2015, 2018). The few studies that discuss the global poor's involvement in development programmes leave underdeveloped the moral grounds of such calls for inclusion (Narayan et al. 2000). We will show how a much more active role for the poor in global justice can be envisaged.

All actors involved in the determination of what justice means on the ground are formative agents of justice. Formative agents give shape to the principles of justice that should be adopted in any particular situation. They can be individuals, or collectivities such as states, international organizations, and social movements. They can draw on general ideas about justice, for example that justice can be found above all in the respect for individual rights, or that justice is a matter of equitable distribution of resources, or that justice requires recognition of the full humanity and standing of all members of a society. However, formative agents must also recognize the specifics and circumstances of the issue at hand. Specific circumstances may require the interpretation of abstract and complex principles of justice – similar, for example, to how a court would have to interpret the more abstract principle of equal protection under the law in order to determine if discrimination on the basis of sexual orientation violates this principle.

Perhaps most straightforwardly, formative agency entails arguing effectively on behalf of some principles that should guide collective action. Sometimes rhetoric rather than argument alone can be very powerful in giving form to principles and advancing their adoption. Rhetoric is persuasion in all its forms. It includes arresting figures of speech, striking metaphors, appeals to emotions, exhibition of the virtuous character of the speaker. But formative agency does not have to be so explicit and conscious. By simply sharing their stories and experiences, particular groups can exercise formative agency and help shape the meaning of justice. Harrowing stories of discrimination and oppression can be important. Sometimes those who tell such stories can become international celebrities, for example Malala Yousafzai who survived her attempted murder and went on to win a Nobel Peace prize for her advocacy on behalf of girls' education. These stories also help communicate what marginalization and disadvantage feel like and what exactly needs to be remedied as a matter of (global) concern. Stories can also play a role in retreats from global justice, for example stories about crimes committed by asylum seekers that can lead to a hardening of borders.

In practice, argument, rhetoric, and storytelling all contribute to determining which sorts of actors or groups have claims to assistance and which do not; what kinds of knowledge (experiential, statistical, or ethical) are relevant in moral reasoning; and what are the historical origins of injustices. The meanings and interpretations of key concepts such as sustainability, poverty, or human development can be refined, disputed, validated, rejected, or adopted, and all this has consequences for our understanding of global justice.

Visual representation can also play a part in formative agency. Think, for example, of vivid depictions of the effects of drought, floods, the body of a Syrian refugee child washed up on a Mediterranean beach. In addition, the protests that are ubiquitous around global gatherings such as United Nations (UN) and World Trade Organization (WTO) negotiations can sometimes make a difference. Stiglitz (2002) suggests that anti-globalization protests led the World Bank to incorporate social justice concerns in its policies and practices. Leading by example can be a way to convince others of the virtues of one's principles. Think of the Fair Trade consumer movement hoping to influence the principles on which international trade more generally is conducted.

We will study the role of formative agency in global justice through the lens of deliberative democratic theory. The idea of a deliberative system in which agents interact is key. Any system is a set of differentiated yet linked elements that can be interpreted in light of some purpose(s). In a deliberative system, the elements might include citizens, legislatures, advocacy groups, social movements, citizen forums, international negotiations, international organizations, and expert bodies. The purpose we stress involves advancing global justice. To date, deliberative systems scholars (e.g. those collected in Parkinson and Mansbridge 2012) have said little about the proper division of labour among different agents in the system. In remedying this deficiency, we will explore the *democratic* and *deliberative rights* and *duties* individuals and other actors have in the system.

Let us now take a closer look at the two vehicles of global justice, both of which involve the setting of global goals that we will analyse in more detail.

Working through Cases: The SDGs and Climate Governance

History of the SDGs

Our major case is that of the SDGs. Our introductory discussion in this section will sketch the history of the process that yielded these global goals, explain why it is appropriate to treat them as a vehicle of global justice, and analyse the kinds of justice they proved to embody and ignore. The SDGs process was intended to be inclusive and participatory, and hence very different from the top-down, technocratic formulation of the Millennium Development Goals (MDGs), adopted by the UN in 2001. This means it is especially appropriate to analyse that former process through the lens of deliberative democracy. In subsequent chapters we analyse the degree to which the SDGs were actually formulated and adopted in deliberative and inclusive fashion, and to what effect when it comes to global justice (we do not pre-empt that analysis in this introductory discussion – suffice it to say that for the moment the deliberative glass is half-full). In Chapter 8 we will undertake a summary evaluation of the deliberative and democratic qualities of the overall system that yield the goals, and then develop prescriptions for how such a process could be improved. Our normative analysis has practical payoff insofar as these global goals still need to be implemented, and it will be relevant when the goals are revised or replaced by the UN before they expire in 2030.

The SDGs were adopted by the UN General Assembly in 2015 after over two years of consultations, dialogues, and negotiations, and they form the core of the larger 2030 Development Agenda. The SDGs embody an ambitious and detailed set of principles for action up to 2030, and each goal is accompanied by a set of more precise targets to benchmark progress. The SDGs are as follows:

1. End poverty in all its forms everywhere.
2. End hunger, achieve food security and improved nutrition, and promote sustainable agriculture.
3. Ensure healthy lives and promote well-being for all at all ages.
4. Ensure inclusive and equitable quality education and promote lifelong learning opportunities for all.
5. Achieve gender equality and empower all women and girls.
6. Ensure availability and sustainable management of water and sanitation for all.
7. Ensure access to affordable, reliable, sustainable, and modern energy for all.
8. Promote sustained, inclusive, and sustainable economic growth, full and productive employment, and decent work for all.
9. Build resilient infrastructure, promote inclusive and sustainable industrialization, and foster innovation.
10. Reduce inequality within and among countries.
11. Make cities and human settlements inclusive, safe, resilient, and sustainable.
12. Ensure sustainable consumption and production patterns.
13. Take urgent action to combat climate change and its impacts (acknowledging that the UN Framework Convention on Climate Change (UNFCCC) is the primary international, intergovernmental forum for negotiating the global response to climate change).
14. Conserve and sustainably use the oceans, seas, and marine resources for sustainable development.
15. Protect, restore, and promote sustainable use of terrestrial ecosystems, sustainably manage forests, combat desertification, halt and reverse land degradation, and halt biodiversity loss.
16. Promote peaceful and inclusive societies for sustainable development, provide access to justice for all, and build effective, accountable, and inclusive institutions at all levels.
17. Strengthen the means of implementation and revitalize the global partnership for sustainable development.

The SDGs had one root in the plan for the Post-2015 Development Agenda that was initiated at the Millennium Development Goals

Summit in 2010. The MDGs were to expire in 2015. There were only eight MDGs and the longest of them is stated more briefly than the shortest of the SDGs. The MDGs are as follows:

1. Eradicate extreme poverty and hunger.
2. Achieve universal primary education.
3. Promote gender equality and empower women.
4. Reduce child mortality.
5. Improve maternal health.
6. Combat HIV/AIDS, malaria, and other diseases.
7. Ensure environmental sustainability.
8. Global partnership for development.

The focus of the MDGs was relatively narrow: alleviate poverty and its associated conditions in developing countries. The SDGs in contrast are universal: they apply to all countries of the world and are much broader in scope. (They are, however, still skewed in places toward developing countries, for example including a target for ending malnutrition, but not for obesity.) The MDGs were grounded in a discourse of human development based on ideas about individual human capabilities, as measured, for example, in the UN's Human Development Index (Hulme 2007). There was considerable success in these terms over the ensuing fifteen years, though the amount that can be ascribed directly to the MDGs is debatable (much of the world's poverty alleviation came from China's economic growth). An even larger contrast can be found in the way the two sets of goals were formulated. In some (slightly exaggerated) accounts, the MDGs were written by a small group of UN experts ('in the basement of UN headquarters'; see Ford 2015), before being finalized by the UN Secretariat, then presented in a report by the secretary general to the UN General Assembly. In contrast, the process that produced the SDGs contained a huge range of forums and consultations over several years (many of which will be visited in the chapters that follow) – it is the most inclusive and participatory process in the history of the UN. The focus on inclusive participation and especially on the participation of developing countries is well captured by the two mantras of the process: 'no one left behind' and 'nothing about us without us' (a popular slogan for groups representing indigenous peoples, the poor, women, people with disabilities, and others). The title of the 2030 Agenda – *Transforming Our World* – indicates the scope of the ambition.

Universality and focus on sustainability were the two biggest substantive advances of the SDGs. The environmental dimension is significantly stronger in the content of the SDGs than in the MDGs. 'Environmental sustainability' appears as Goal 7 in the MDGs, but mostly as an afterthought. The idea of sustainable development is in contrast central to the SDGs, not least in their name. This points to the other ancestry of the SDGs: global environmental governance. The discourse of sustainable development has dominated global environmental governance since 1987 when the Brundtland report, *Our Common Future*, was published (World Commission on Environment and Development 1987). The essence of the Brundtland report was that environmental conservation, economic development, and social justice both within and across generations could be mutually reinforcing. The report asserts the compatibility with great rhetorical force and flourish.

The second root of the SDGs, and indeed the idea that the successors to the MDGs should be *Sustainable* Development Goals, can be located in the process leading up to the 2012 UN Conference on Sustainable Development (UNCSD) held in Rio de Janeiro (twenty years after the landmark UN Conference on Environment and Development, also in Rio). Colombian negotiator Paula Caballero Gomez was a leading proponent of SDGs being a key outcome of the Rio event. In a Colombian government proposal the SDGs were conceived of as being 'modelled on the Millennium Development Goals (MDGs), to help define the post-2015 [development] framework' (Kamau, Chasek, and O'Connor 2018: 41). Negotiations about the process for developing the goals resulted in statements in the UNCSD outcome document *The Future We Want* that emphasized 'an inclusive and transparent intergovernmental process' for developing the goals and the establishment of an open working group that would try 'to ensure the full involvement of relevant stakeholders and expertise from civil society, the scientific community and the United Nations system in its work, in order to provide a diversity of perspectives and experience' (UN 2012: 19, 64). The principle of participatory engagement was also stressed in the opening section of the document:

13. We recognize that opportunities for people to influence their lives and future, participate in decision-making and voice their concerns are fundamental for sustainable development. We underscore that sustainable development requires concrete and urgent action. It can only be achieved with a

broad alliance of people, governments, civil society and the private sector, all working together to secure the future we want for present and future generations. (UN 2012: 3)

Prior to 1987, sustainable development was often associated with radical grassroots challenges to dominant models of development. Brundtland introduced sufficient ambiguity into the idea of sustainable development to make it acceptable to global economic and political elites. With time, 'development' became more easily equated with 'growth', such that at its worst, sustainable development could be taken to mean continued growth. Corporations and business groups became increasingly active in promoting partnerships for sustainable development with governments and NGOs. The internal deradicalization of the discourse was reinforced by encounters with the neoliberal discourse that has dominated global economic and financial affairs (see Dryzek 2013b: 150–5 on the history of sustainable development).

Thus by the time the sustainable development discourse came to inform the creation of the SDGs, it was in deradicalized form. Even in this form it encountered resistance, in particular from some development agencies and influential non-governmental aid organizations that have long dominated the UN's development policies and who did not want the anti-poverty focus to be compromised by the addition of an environmental sustainability agenda. At the same time, sustainable development was not the only conceivable partner for the anti-poverty agenda coming out of the MDGs. It is conceivable that the successors to the MDGs could have partnered instead with the global trade regime or global financial governance and their supporting discourses – much more well developed, more embedded in the policies of governments, and with much greater enforcement capacity than anything associated with sustainable development. In this light, the partnering of sustainable development and the post-MDG anti-poverty agenda was itself the result of a significant exercise of formative agency, mostly on the part of those active on the sustainable side of the equation, coming out of the 2012 UNCSD.

By 2012, the discursive landscape for negotiation of the SDGs was in place, based on the human development discourse of the MDGs and the by now deradicalized discourse of sustainable development. The next three years involved a flurry of activity involving multiple national and global bodies, civil society interactions, forums, and public consultations, many of which were only loosely coordinated. Eventually all this activity converged on multilateral international negotiations between representatives of governments (Kamau et al. 2018). The key body here was the Open Working Group (OWG) convened in 2013 (whose title, but not composition, was inherited from *The Future We Want* document coming out of the 2012 UNCSD that we mentioned earlier). The OWG was composed of representatives of seventy national governments who shared thirty seats. In 2015 the OWG agreed on the terms of the larger 2030 Agenda in which the SDGs were embedded, which was adopted unanimously by 193 states at a UN summit in September of that year. It is striking that the negotiations of the OWG yielded consensus in two years. This can be contrasted with the UNFCCC, which took twenty-three years (1992–2015) to reach anything approaching a comprehensive agreement.

The processes that converged on the SDGs illustrate formative agency in action, as meanings of both sustainability and development get advanced, contested, deliberated, negotiated, changed, and established. This in turn influences how global justice is conceptualized in global governance and how it can be pursued by individual states (and others) on the ground, as we'll discuss later in the chapter.

Along with the earlier MDGs, the SDGs represent the best examples of 'governing through goals' in the international system: 'governing through goals . . . is a new governance strategy that has emerged at an opportune time under the novel conditions of the twenty-first century' (Kanie and Biermann 2017: ix). The SDGs lack any 'hard' mechanism for compliance. No legally binding agreement was enacted in 2015 and no formal organization (analogous to say the World Trade Organization) was established to oversee implementation of the goals (though the High-Level Political Forum established by the UN was charged with reviewing progress). States are called upon to voluntarily endorse and pursue the goals and targets through the specific policies they adopt. The UN did not institute any formal penalties for non-compliance with the goals or their associated targets and states need only *voluntarily* submit their reports to the UN. Despite the SDGs being universal on paper, the UN lacks any mechanism by which it can keep track of the progress made by every state,[8] though it does publish an annual SDGs report that is an overview

---

[8] Some twenty-two states submitted reviews in 2016, forty-three states in 2017, and forty-seven states in 2018. Important countries like the United States, China, and Russia had not submitted any reviews at the time of writing.

of global progress. The operationalization of some targets and their relevant indicators took time, and some states' national statistical agencies complained that they simply lacked the resources to monitor so many targets and indicators.

In a way, the lack of hard compliance mechanisms is not surprising since many of the goals are aspirational and their implementation is not obviously feasible, or foreseeable, in the near future (e.g. the eradication of poverty). The SDGs rely instead on 'soft' compliance mechanisms that leverage off states' reputations insofar as all states can, if they so choose, periodically report to the UN on their progress towards the implementation of the goals. This also means that each state can be aware of how well it fares in that respect by comparison to other states. Other soft mechanisms include the convergence of expectations around goals so that they become taken for granted by policy makers, as well as the assimilation of the norms embodied by the goals in the commitments of key actors. The SDGs can be used as ammunition by advocates for policies within both countries and international organizations. They can be used as benchmarks to evaluate the performance of governments by insiders, as well as by outsiders. It is also possible (but by no means guaranteed) that subsequent international treaties may embody some of the goals, which would give them more legal bite.

The Goals and Global Justice

But what justifies our view of the SDGs as a vehicle of global justice? Their title suggests they are about sustainable development rather than global justice. However, an examination of their content reveals that sustainable development covers only a small fraction of what they do. The SDGs are comprehensive in their aspirations for a global order that is improved on many dimensions, including the vast majority of dimensions that might factor into global justice.[9] They have no competition from any other global process when it comes to the range of global justice questions they cover.

If we take no position ourselves on the exact substance of justice, how can we be so confident in describing the SDGs as a vehicle of

---

[9] In specifying some targets for states to pursue, the SDGs also have implications for justice within countries, so they are not *solely* about global justice.

justice? The answer is that we can define the *domain* of global justice (in terms of the allocation of benefits and burdens such as rights and obligations, along with factors such as recognition or oppression that either facilitate or inhibit such allocations), even if we take no position on the precise substantive *content* of global justice. In this light, it is straightforward to say the SDGs are indeed a vehicle of global justice because their domain is clearly the same as that of global justice.

Accordingly, we stress here that 'justice' should not be understood solely or even primarily in terms of redistributing a *fixed* amount of goods among parties. Justice can also be a matter of development, concerned with increasing the amount of goods available to those parties. Redistribution and development might both aim, for example, to promote global equality. Redistribution will do so by taking from wealthier people (or countries) and giving to poorer people (or countries). Development will try to bridge the gap between developing and developed countries and their peoples by encouraging the former to grow their economies faster than the latter countries.

Global *equality* is just one conception of global distributive justice. Global *sufficientarianism* is another, in the form of the 'basic needs' or 'capabilities' approach. Here the idea is to ensure that all people achieve a sufficient basic set of capabilities, pertaining to their health, freedom, agency, security, reasoning capacity, and so forth (Sen 1999; Nussbaum 2011; Robeyns 2017). This kind of approach to human development was at the core of the MDGs and does not in principle require global redistribution (though it well might in practice). Human development as it appears in the MDGs and sustainable development are not necessarily in conflict (Sengupta 2016). However, human development is more individualistic and anthropocentric, while sustainable development could, in its stronger forms, imply greater emphasis on ecological systems, other species, and the condition of the planet as a whole. Yet the SDGs do not reject the human development approach; indeed, they embody it. Any contradictions between human development and sustainable development was resolved by the weakly ecological way in which sustainability is treated in the SDGs.

A glance at the list of SDGs shows that the word 'sustainable' (or 'sustainably') appears in eleven of the seventeen goals. In contrast, the word 'justice' appears in only one of them (Goal 16) and even then only in terms of 'access to justice', meaning access to the procedural justice of the legal system. Yet on closer inspection the goals are largely about social justice. As we noted earlier, a sufficientarian idea of justice emphasizing basic needs and capabilities is prominent (notably in Goals 1–8). As Cimadamore (2016) points out, the SDGs can be interpreted as a compass to a more socially just world. Those involved in the process invoked the language of social justice. For example, the Global Call to Action Against Poverty campaign, active in trying to shape the 2030 Development Agenda, 'supports people in their struggles for justice and brings individuals and organizations together to challenge the institutions and processes that perpetuate poverty and inequalities. Together, we defend and promote human rights, gender justice, social justice, climate justice and the security needed for the dignity and peace of all'.[10]

The SDGs specify who exactly should be the objects of concern in matters of global justice (and justice at other levels such as the national and local). Mostly the objects of concern appear to be individuals, although Goal 10 involves reducing inequality across countries (as well as within countries), suggesting (controversially) that justice involves comparing the well-being of whole nations with each other. Thus Goal 10 furthers international justice of the sort that Brown (2006) believes has been dominant in thinking about global governance in general. Elsewhere in the goals, international justice seems to have been displaced by a more cosmopolitan emphasis on individuals irrespective of where they live. Feminist theorists of justice would approve the commitment to gender equality and female empowerment in Goal 5 (which does mean that all feminists would consider the SDGs adequate in gender terms).

The goals also specify the metrics by which justice should be assessed: not just income (which indeed is not explicitly mentioned), but also in access to goods such as health, education, empowerment, nutritious food, reliable energy, water, sanitation, and 'decent' employment. As such they are consistent with the capabilities approach that was embedded in both the UN's Human Development Index and the MDGs, and whose driving idea is that poverty is not just a matter of inadequate income, but also of lack of education, being subject to discrimination, poor health, poor housing, an unhealthy environment, and lacking control over the circumstances of one's life.

---

[10] See www.whiteband.org/en/book/export/html/631.

The fact that the first goal involves ending poverty suggests a special concern for the least advantaged in a way that should gladden the heart of Rawls (1971) and others for whom the condition of the least advantaged is much more important to justice than the average condition of everyone – which is what utilitarian approaches to justice would stress. While there is no reference to average well-being in the goals, Goal 8's commitment to 'economic growth, full and productive employment, and decent work for all' does perhaps reflect this sort of utilitarian concern; while Goal 3's aim to secure healthy lives and promote well-being 'for all at all ages' involves a nod to intergenerational justice (which appears much more explicitly in the preamble to the 2030 Agenda than in the goals themselves).

Also instructive is what is missing from the goals. Despite the fact that the UN document establishing the SDGs is called *Transforming Our World*, there is no reference to any need for transformation of the global political economy in directions that would undermine its domination by neoliberalism, for example in establishing more effective public or participatory control over the economy (Carant 2017: 34). This need becomes acute to the degree that neoliberalism's commitment to markets, deregulation, and the free flow of capital has exacerbated the problems of inequality that Goal 10 says must be countered. Furthermore, the commitment to protect the environment, to fight climate change (Goals 12, 13, 14), and to ethical consumption potentially compete with neoliberal values and might support increased regulation. Neoliberalism is not of course a conception that scholars and advocates for global justice would generally endorse. But it does minimally fulfil the logical requirements of a theory of justice in that it contains principles about how benefits and burdens are to be distributed: they should be determined in processes of free exchange and benefits secured by private property rights.

There is no reference in the SDGs to *democracy* (though again, democracy is mentioned in the 2030 Agenda document, paragraph 9). Goal 16 refers to 'accountable and inclusive institutions at all levels', which could be interpreted as pointing toward democracy, but need not make authoritarian governments too nervous. The indicators associated with Target 16.7 to 'develop effective, accountable, and transparent government' are very weak, referring only to the need for different social groups (defined by age, sex, etc.) to be proportionally present in government positions. There appears to be a retreat here from the 1948 Universal Declaration of Human Rights, which stated in Article 21 that 'everyone has the right to take part in the government of his country, whether directly or through freely chosen representatives' and that 'the will of the people shall be the basis of the authority of government; this will shall be expressed in periodic and genuine elections which shall be by universal and equal suffrage'. In the 1948 Declaration, the word 'democracy' was not used, but the meaning is fairly clear. By 2015, democracy was too controversial to serve as a goal, as it seems autocrats successfully exercised their formative agency in the adoption process. However, we also note that in referring to 'institutions at all levels' Goal 16 could be read as supporting the (weak) democratization of global governance and of international organizations. If so, Goal 16 would have a meta-quality in that it sets principles of legitimacy for global governance that would include the very institution that created the goals – the UN – an institution that has long been criticized for its democratic deficits.[11] There is no explicit reference in the SDGs to *justice across generations* (beyond the nod to 'across all ages' we noted), unless the word 'sustainable' is taken to imply intergenerational justice (as it did in the 1987 Brundtland report). Ecosystems are mentioned in Goal 15, but mainly as objects of 'sustainable use'; there is no recognition that justice might be truly *ecological*, including a concern for the intrinsic value of ecosystems and non-human species. The goals do not recognize the possibility that the integrity of the Earth system may be under threat from unrestrained economic growth[12] or that treatment of the Earth system in its entirety can be a matter of justice. The SDGs assume that growth is good for everyone and fail to incorporate (for example) the idea of planetary boundaries, a concept pushed by Earth scientists (see Steffen et al. 2015) in the very years that the SDGs were being formulated. Taken seriously, planetary boundaries could provide the context for the pursuit of all the other goals (Hajer et al. 2015).

---

[11] Like most of those who have contemplated global democracy, but in contrast to some insiders, we do not consider democracy within the UN as simply a matter of all states having an equal and effective say, especially given that many states are not internally democratic and they vary massively in the size of their populations.

[12] Notice that Goal 8 refers to both 'sustained' growth (which can be unrestrained) as well as 'sustainable' growth.

There is no mention of *property rights*, which may presumably disappoint libertarian theorists of justice for whom property rights are central. Nor is there any mention of individual rights and liberties of the sort mainstream liberal theorists of justice would seek. The SDGs are surprisingly weak when it comes to *rights in general*, including, for example, rights of access to clean air and water, the rights of children, and the rights of disadvantaged groups such as indigenous peoples. Yet the *Transforming Our World* UN document that announces the goals does recognize rights. Its principle 8 says: 'We envisage a world of universal respect for human rights and human dignity'. So there is a commitment to rights in the abstract in the 2030 Development Agenda, but specific rights are harder to find in the SDGs. One of the few mentions is in Target 8.8, which, amid a neoliberal celebration of economic growth, says 'protect labour rights'. There are several explanations for this notable absence. One would be that not all states are equally willing to recognize the same categories of rights. The second would be that other UN documents and treaties – such as the Universal Declaration of Human Rights – are already authoritative in that regard.

Social justice can be a matter of *recognition* as well as distribution (Honneth 1995; Fraser and Honneth 2003). Recognition means validation of the full standing and identity of all, but especially those who have in the past been victims of oppression; it is an antidote to humiliation. Claimants for recognition might include ethnic minorities, indigenous peoples, oppressed social classes, minorities based on sexual orientation, disability, or refugee status. In the goals themselves, explicit recognition goes only to women and girls (Goal 5). Otherwise, the language 'for all' is more prevalent, appearing in five of the goals. Resolution 68/261 of the UN General Assembly might seem to move in the direction of recognition when it says: 'Sustainable Development Goal indicators should be disaggregated, where relevant, by income, sex, age, race, ethnicity, migratory status, disability and geographic location, or other characteristics'. But then the Resolution says this is to be done 'in accordance with the Fundamental Principles of Official Statistics', suggesting a statistical accounting exercise rather than validation of identity. Recognition is not just a matter of a category of people getting a fairer share of resources or having their material condition improved, which is all that Resolution 68/261 implies. Overall, beyond the case of women and girls, justice as recognition is at best only weakly reflected in the SDGs. Again, it is much stronger in the 2030 Agenda document, whose paragraph 23 refers to the empowerment of 'children, youth, persons with disabilities, people living with HIV/AIDS, older persons, indigenous peoples, refugees and internally displaced persons and migrants'.

In light of what we said earlier about the need for any theory of justice to have a strong account of agency, what is missing in a big way from the SDGs is any strong specification of the *duties* that are incumbent on any set of actors, such as states. So while we can read both cosmopolitan and international conceptions of redistributive justice into specific places in the goals, there is no specification in the goals and targets themselves (as opposed to the more expansive 2030 Agenda) of the duties that affluent states and individuals have to poor states or individuals. Justice is by definition about the allocation of burdens as well as benefits. Yet the goals themselves are silent as to upon whom exactly the obligation to promote justice rests; that is, the primary agents of justice in O'Neill's terms, the implementing agents or effectors in our terms (see Chapter 2 for more detail). Who exactly should bear the main responsibility to end poverty and hunger, ensure healthy lives, quality education, and so forth? The SDGs (and 2030 Agenda) are silent on this question (Pogge and Segupta 2016).[13] The SDGs therefore constitute an incomplete theory of justice, for the reasons we set out earlier when the idea of agents of justice was introduced. There is, in addition, no ascribing of liability for any of the problems that the goals address, which might point to who exactly should now be responsible for remedying the problems (in contrast to the global climate regime, as we will see shortly).

Despite the lack of explicit specification of primary or implementing agency, there are some implicit assignments of responsibility in the targets associated with the goals. In failing to specify any new or unusual kind of governance, the goals and targets implicitly assume that the existing structure of governance in the world – dominated by states – will do most of the work. Principle 41 of *Transforming Our*

---

[13] It would be possible to read into the goals an implicit allocation of burdens: it is incumbent on all actors in the global system to pursue the goals and targets, in proportion to their power to do so. This would not be so different from the implicit burdens or duties in Rawls's famous theory of justice, in which 'individuals have a duty to conform to the rules of just institutions, if they exist, and if they do not exist, to strive to bring them about' (Arneson 2006: 47).

World says, 'We recognize that each country has primary responsibility for its own economic and social development'. This emphasis on each state's responsibility for its own population undermines any calls for cosmopolitan or global justice, or indeed international justice. Goal 17, which is about revitalizing the partnership for sustainable development, points in the opposite direction. This partnership is designed to benefit developing countries and involves multiple stakeholders, with explicit reference to the private sector and civil society. Target 17.18 is about building the governance capacity of states in developing countries and so presumably their capacity to exercise primary or implementing agency. But even the targets under Goal 17 do not identify which actors are jointly responsible for leading the partnership or who are the most important kinds of primary or implementing agent.

To summarize, the SDGs constitute a statement of some key meanings that justice should take in global affairs. Prominent in the goals we can find conceptions of justice that reflect:

- a weak universal concern 'for all';
- an ambiguous concern with international justice (between states);
- a Rawlsian concern for the least advantaged;
- a feminist concern for women and girls;
- a sufficientarian concern for capabilities;
- the global neoliberal order.

Conflicts between different conceptions of justice were not resolved in the content of the goals. The interactions of formative agents would normally require some way to adjudicate across different conceptions of justice (e.g. between generations, across persons, across nations, those that emphasize the interests of the least advantaged, those that stress universal human rights). In the case of the SDGs, different conceptions of justice could be accommodated at different places in the long list of goals and targets. Disputes were resolved largely by multiplying goals and targets, which is one reason why there are so many of them.

Largely missing from the goals are ideas about justice that involve:

- any need to question the existing structure of the global political economy and other root causes of poverty and oppression;
- intergenerational justice;

- an ecological concern with the rights and interests of non-human nature;
- human rights;
- a libertarian commitment to the primacy of private property rights;
- justice as recognition;
- an explicit commitment to international and cosmopolitan distributive justice that reaffirms the duties affluent states have towards less affluent states, or that rich individuals from some states have toward poor individuals from other states;
- an explicit statement of who is responsible for implementing the goals – at most there is implicit recognition of the role of national governments.

While some conceptions of justice fared much better than others, it is hard to point to any conception of justice being *explicitly* rejected in the process – though there was certainly implicit rejection of any conception of justice that involved radical critique of the international political economy. The fact that the goals were conditioned by the deradicalized discourse of sustainable development arguably meant they were in no position to engage such a critique, or indeed help move the world away from its highly unsustainable developmental trajectory. Let us now take a brief look at a case where different conceptions of justice have clashed more visibly, where explicit rejections of others' ideas about justice are common, and where the duties associated with justice are front and centre.

Climate Governance

Climate governance is our minor and more illustrative case (and as such will not receive sustained attention in all chapters). Again, this introductory discussion will explain why it is appropriate to treat climate governance as a potential vehicle of global justice, sketch the relevant history, and analyse the kinds of justice climate governance embodies or sidelines. Unlike the SDGs, there has never been any coordinated attempt by the UN to advance participatory and inclusive norms, but it is still instructive to look at climate governance in deliberative terms because justice *arguments* are pervasive there. We leave the deliberative analysis for subsequent chapters.

Our focus on *global* justice can be extended to *climate* justice insofar as: the global poor are often especially vulnerable to climate change, while the causes of climate change can mostly be traced to the global rich; some causes of poverty are environmental and thus climate-inflected (think, for example, of how desertification can affect subsistence agriculture in Africa); and the distribution of the benefits and burdens of climate change mitigation and adaptation can have massive differential effects across rich and poor.

Climate justice covers the allocation of burdens, benefits, rights, responsibilities, and obligations associated with the mitigation of and adaptation to climate change.[14] A concern with justice has been present in the global governance of climate change from the outset. The agreement at the UN Conference on Environment and Development at Rio in 1992 that established the UNFCCC embodied the foundational principle of 'common, but differentiated responsibilities' of states for reducing greenhouse gas emissions. The 'differentiated' qualifier means that wealthy countries that built their prosperity on a history of fossil fuel use have greater responsibility to reduce emissions than poorer countries whose contribution to anthropogenic climate change has been much smaller. In 1997, this principle was codified in the Kyoto Protocol, under which a list of developed 'Annex 1' countries received legally binding targets for emissions reduction, while all other countries had no legal obligation to curb emissions. The 1992 idea of justice was therefore *international* in that it applied to relationships among states and *backward-looking* in establishing states' future duties according to their past contributions to climate change (though their current capacity was also factored in).

The 'common but differentiated responsibilities' principle fails, however, to recognize that there are poor people in rich states and rich people in poor states whose obligations and rights may not be the same as the average for the state of which they happen to be a part. So, for example, rich consumers and producers in India and China have built their prosperity on a history of fossil fuel use no less than have rich consumers in the United States or Western Europe, and so should perhaps have an obligation to reduce emissions on a par with rich consumers in those more developed states. Suppression of this kind of concern showed that, at the global level, justice largely remained conceptualized in international terms, addressing the privileges, rights,

---

[14] For philosophical analyses of climate justice, see Shue (1993), Gardiner (2011), Page (2011), and Caney (2012).

and obligations that *states* have in relation to each other, rather than those that individuals have towards other individuals.

However, there is much more to the story of climate justice than the adoption of the 'common but differentiated' principle. Since 1992, the UNFCCC process has been engaged by states, civil society organizations, various sorts of activists, public intellectuals, and occasional new claimants for recognition (such as indigenous peoples). Prominent arguments have concerned the following:

- Whether or not a country's history of fossil fuel use really should have any bearing on its future obligations. The G77 group of developing countries plus China has been adamant that historical responsibility is decisive in determining future obligations. The United States has often been vociferous in rejecting this argument, on the grounds that for most of its industrial history there was no awareness of the impact of emissions on the global climate.
- Whether or not fairness in terms of the competitive position of the economies of different countries should have any bearing on differentiated responsibilities (at an extreme, should override the principle of differentiation). This idea has been implicit in the reluctance of the United States (and of other developed countries) to accept expensive emissions reductions that would make their industries less competitive in comparison to developing countries.
- How much is 'common' and how much is 'differentiated' when it comes to responsibilities and obligations. Differentiation tends to be stressed by poorer actors, commonality by wealthier ones.
- Whether commonality and differentiation should apply across states, or across categories of persons. For the most part, the UNFCCC negotiations have proceeded in terms of international justice, across states. More cosmopolitan alternatives have been proposed by ethicists, think tanks, and some advocacy organizations.
- The extension of the 'common but differentiated' principle to adaptation to the effects of climate change. For a long time talk of adaptation was widely seen as defeatist, but now communities that will suffer most from climate change (e.g. those living in low-lying deltas in poorer countries) make demands for compensation and for assistance to adapt from the big emitters.
- How vulnerability to the impacts of climate change should be recognized when it comes to having a voice as well as in claims for

assistance. The Alliance of Small Island States (AOSIS) has influence less in virtue of the size of the populations and economies it represents and more in virtue of representing communities that are on the front lines of climate change.

On the face of it, the sheer volume of arguments about climate justice suggests that climate governance might be a promising place to look for deliberation; but closer inspection reveals a different story (which we shall elaborate in subsequent chapters). For arguments have been intertwined with power politics, strategizing, attempts to offload responsibility for action on to others, attempts by fossil fuel producing countries and companies to block progress (including by asserting the injustice they will suffer if they have to cut back on oil or coal production), and other unsavoury practices. Like it or not, the meaning of climate justice in political practice at any time depends not just on how compelling different justifications or principles prove to be, but also upon the balance of political forces and the power plays mobilized by different sides.

By 2015 it became clear that the vast number of competing financial and material interests had rendered any legally binding global climate treaty a remote prospect. The fact that each of those interests could be backed by arguments about justice only led to their adherents becoming still more dogmatic and entrenched in their positions during negotiations. As a result, the landmark 2015 Paris Agreement did not impose legally binding greenhouse gas emission reduction targets and timetables on states. All it required was that individual countries should pursue mitigation measures, develop their own 'nationally determined contributions' to greenhouse gas emissions reductions, and then periodically report on progress in this light. NGOs are enlisted to monitor governments and continue lobbying them to meet their obligations and improve their performance. The Agreement also provides for a periodic 'global stocktake'. Unlike the 1997 Kyoto Protocol, the Paris Agreement envisages mitigation pledges from all countries, not just developed ones, thus tipping the balance away from 'differentiated' and toward 'common'. Climate justice gets an explicit mention (but no definition) in the preamble to the Agreement. In a sense, just like the SDGs, the Paris Agreement envisages 'governing through goals'. The global goal is the stabilization of the average global temperature at 1.5°C (or at most 2°C) above pre-industrial levels, while countries establish their own national goals to help meet the global goal. (As the years pass after 2015, the goal looks increasingly out of reach.)

Preview

Chapter 2, 'Agents of Justice', develops the theoretical framework of the book and its conceptual categories. Agents of justice face considerable challenges when trying to choose across and apply abstract theories and principles of justice in the real world. We conceptualize the agents involved in this essential moral task as 'formative agents' of global justice and argue that formative agency is best channelled through democratic deliberation. The chapter also introduces a distinction between different kinds of agents (formative agents of justice, global justice entrepreneurs, and effectors of global justice) and discusses the roles that they should play in global governance.

States and international organizations are of course central to global governance, and in practice are significant formative agents of justice (and injustice), in advancing, sifting, or undermining principles. In Chapter 3, 'Democratizing Formal Authority: States and International Organizations', we discuss reasons why states and international organizations cannot be relied upon to determine the content of global justice. In this light, they should primarily act as *effectors of global justice* whose main task is to make sure the outcomes determined in more extensive deliberation are implemented. Rather than simply dismiss their formative role, however, the chapter also explores whether their problematic features can be corrected. We show how their problems can indeed be ameliorated by some democratic mechanisms and deliberative engagements, hints of which are on display in the process that yielded the SDGs. International organizations for their part are not immune to prioritizing their own material self-interest over global justice. International organizations such as the International Monetary Fund (IMF) and WTO can also be rigid adherents to dominant discourses, for example in enforcing neoliberal conceptions of justice. Engagements with global civil society (of the sort we now see in global climate governance) can help here.

Money talks, when it comes to global justice no less than elsewhere. But what does money say? And does that have any legitimate role in realizing global justice? The persistence of injustice in a world dominated by the wealthy suggests that their discretion should not be relied upon to secure justice, though that does not preclude them playing a role in ameliorating injustice. Chapter 4, 'Democratizing Money: The Rich, Corporations, and Foundations', discusses the formative agency of the global rich, corporations, and foundations. The formative agency of the rich is exercised in both their political influence and in choosing who should be the recipients of their largesse, on what terms. Justice requires the democratic extension of formative agency beyond the rich and toward the poor. The political influence of corporations is felt in the SDGs, which treat business as a potential force for good – as opposed to a source of many of the problems the SDGs are designed to solve. So long as corporations are hard-wired for profit, their formative agency should be kept in check on questions of justice. Foundations for their part are increasingly prominent in global governance; the Gates Foundation distributes more than \$4 billion per year. Embedding foundations in deliberative democratic relationships would advance democratic legitimacy, as well as yield substantial epistemic benefits by bringing different sorts of knowledge about real-world contexts to bear. Deliberative accountability should extend to all wealthy actors, with major implications for their democratic duties. Wealthy actors' capacity to decide what global justice means and requires should be counterbalanced by an active role for citizens, the global poor, civil society, and international organizations.

Global governance is transacted through the medium of language. Chapter 5, 'Democratizing the Power of Words: Experts, Public Intellectuals, Advocacy Groups, and the Media', scrutinizes the standing of formative agents of global justice who rely most heavily on words: experts, public intellectuals, advocacy groups, and the media. Democracy and expertise exist in tension. Experts have played significant roles in both the SDGs and climate governance, where the experts of the Intergovernmental Panel on Climate Change were joined in its Fifth Assessment Report by moral philosophers to cover climate justice. There are benefits in the integration of lay and expert perspectives that deliberative democratization would enable. Public intellectuals for their part by definition already engage with publics, and are prominent in climate change and on the SDGs. The partial perspectives that public intellectuals offer ought to be reconciled in deliberation involving a broad public whose situated knowledges may increase the quality of outcomes. NGOs, advocacy groups, and activists have important roles in representing different discourses on the global stage, providing essential grist for deliberation. But when they implicitly claim to represent categories of people they become democratically problematic – potentially bending the content of global justice in questionable directions. We reflect on the special duties advocacy groups (such as Oxfam) have toward the poor they claim to represent, in order to embed unelected representation in deliberative democracy. The role of old and new media alike has been highly problematic on matters of global justice, for example in contributing to polarization and the rise of organized climate change denial. In the context of the expressive overload that now pervades new media, it is necessary to cultivate deliberative spaces of reflection, be it in the media itself, or beyond.

Citizens of course ought to be central in any account of democracy. In Chapter 6, 'Empowering the Many: Citizens and the Poor', we show how any limitations on the capacity of citizens to exercise formative agency can be overcome in inclusive, deliberative settings. In this light, we assess the extensive but imperfect citizen consultations conducted for the SDGs. We show how citizen deliberation could be promoted through transnational and global forums – most ambitiously, a deliberative global citizens' assembly. We then argue on both ethical and epistemic grounds for the participation of the poor in democratizing global justice. Currently the poor are often missing in global governance, though again the SDGs process did more to try to reach them than any previous global process. It is possible to think of the agency of the poor in terms of poor-led social movements and institutional design to enable the poor to act as a global community of interest. The poor from different parts of the world should deliberate together on what global justice requires on the ground, in contrast to state-based exercises (such as the national dialogues conducted for the SDGs) that are limited in both democratic and epistemic terms.

How can we include the affected interests of future generations and non-humans in deliberations about global justice given that they cannot exercise formative agency themselves? Starting from the role moral imagination plays in moral reasoning, and hence formative agency as well, Chapter 7, 'Democratizing Intergenerational, Interspecies, and Ecological Justice: The Role of Moral Imagination in Deliberation', looks at ways in which deliberations can be enhanced to promote the inclusion of these neglected interests. Visual and experiential prompts should complement talk-centric deliberative processes. This would expand the deliberators' moral imagination, enabling them to internalize the interests of future generations, animals, and the Earth system, and reach decisions reflecting all affected interests, even those bound to be silent (though that seeming silence itself may reveal a human incapacity to listen). Currently these frontiers of justice are only weakly present in the SDGs (which look ahead only to 2030), turned down the chance to incorporate planetary boundaries, and say nothing about non-humans (beyond a vague reference to 'ecosystem and biodiversity values' in Target 15.9).

No single category of agents holds the key to the effective formation of global justice. Chapter 8, 'Global Justice in the Deliberative System', gives a systemic account of deliberative governance that shows how formative agency can be productively distributed across multiple sites, actors, and institutions. It is the deliberative capacity of the entire system that matters most, rather than that of any given unit, actor, process, or site within the system. In a way, the process that yielded the SDGs recognized this by establishing multiple venues, decision-making groups, and negotiation tracks, all infused with participatory norms. However, there was no logic to their interaction and links were often simply absent. We supply the logic and the links in (for example) the integration of tracks engaging experts, citizens, and the poor. This analysis does not gainsay the importance of cultivating the formative agency of citizens and the global poor, which should always receive proper recognition in nodes and sites of the system. Deliberative systems in global justice governance no less than elsewhere should develop reflexive capacity in order to reflect on and improve their own performance.

Chapter 9 reflects critically on the feasibility of democratizing global justice, especially when it comes to the practical proposals for institutional design developed in some of the earlier chapters of the book. An important shift toward more inclusive global governance processes has occurred in recent years and this may pave the way for a more defensible global order. Current processes, while still far from deliberative and democratic ideals, have become more inclusive and participatory over time, as we have seen in the case of the SDGs. Promoting global deliberative democracy would be the natural next step.

Conclusion

The cases of the SDGs and climate governance show how formative agency is currently being exercised. They also reveal its present limitations and problems: implicit ideas about justice embedded in the dominant global economic system can dominate more considered contemplation of alternatives, some conceptions of justice may get sidelined for no good reason, there can be impasse across competing views of justice that blocks progress, and powerful actors (such as corporations) can successfully bend the language of justice to their own interests. These problems and limitations can, however, be mitigated. Throughout the following chapters we discuss how the exercise of formative agency in global governance can be improved through deliberative democratization and how the SDGs framework (and any successor featuring global goals) in particular could benefit from this in the coming years. Thus the next chapter takes a closer look at how formative agency can be redeemed, especially in inclusive processes of democratic deliberation, and how we can begin to think about the roles of different sorts of agents in more effectively promoting global justice.

2 | *Agents of Justice*

Politics and morality can hardly be kept apart.[1] Through their laws and policies, domestic political institutions decide not only on matters of fact but also on matters of value. In having to decide how to allocate limited resources among competing claims, states must decide on a daily basis what justice is and what it calls for. And just as state institutions cannot operate entirely outside the area of justice, so too will global governance institutions have to navigate the treacherous waters of global justice. They too will have to decide what justice requires, from both states and individuals, at the global level.

This chapter elaborates the theoretical and conceptual apparatus standing behind and driving the following chapters. Here we expand on the concept of *formative agents of justice*, the cornerstone of this book. First, we point out how the concept contributes to existing discussions of agency in global justice. Second, we argue that formative agency is best channelled and expressed through democratic deliberation. Democratic deliberation, defined as the inclusive and equally participatory exchange of reasons, allows individuals and collectives to act more successfully as formative agents involved in the articulation and realization of global justice. And finally, third, we distinguish between the different roles agents can play in the specification and implementation of justice: pure formative agents, global justice entrepreneurs, and global justice effectors. We point out how different actors (states, individuals, international organizations, non-governmental organizations (NGOs), corporations, and others) can fit into these different roles.

---

[1] We start from the assumption that moral principles should apply equally to the political domain. Our entire book is thus premised on the antithesis of realism as understood by international relations scholars.

Agency and Justice: Concepts Clarified

Before we proceed to discussing formative agency, we will briefly explain first what we mean by 'agency' and 'justice', since we centrally employ these concepts whenever referring to formative agents of justice. There is an extensive literature in the philosophy of action and metaphysics devoted to the first of these concepts, and in ethics and political philosophy to the second. We will not delve too much into those debates – just enough to ensure that readers understand what's at stake when using these terms. Discussions of global justice often miss their mark because they neglect some basic, but key, philosophical distinctions that serve to circumscribe 'agency' and 'justice'. Without these distinctions in place, there is a real risk of both logical and moral slippage.

What Is 'Agency'?

Generally, an agent is a being with the capacity to act, and agency is the exercise of the capacity to act (Anscombe 1957; Davidson [1963] 1980).[2] Under the standard theory of action, an 'act' is conceived as being necessarily 'intentional', and agency therefore refers to the performance of intentional acts. This focus on the existence of particular mental states has led some authors to claim that being an agent requires one to *reflect* about one's motivations (e.g. Frankfurt 1971). To be an agent is 'to deliberate, decide, and act' (Schlosser 2015, citing Mele 2003 ch. 10). To be an agent requires 'self-governance': 'to take a stand in favor of or against certain motivations, a stand that can itself be subject to reexamination and revision' (Bratman 2000: 50–1; see also Velleman 1992). There is thus a sense in which *reflection* as the capacity to *deliberate internally* over one's reasons is a pre-requisite for agency. On such a view, agency becomes essentially a *human* capacity (Schlosser 2015).[3]

---

[2] We draw on Schlosser (2015) for this brief review of the most prominent accounts of agency.

[3] While some authors are happy to accept that (e.g. Davidson 1982), other authors have proposed a minimal account of agency that does not require the possession of representational mental states (Varela, Maturana, and Uribe 1974; Barandiaran et al. 2009). In this book we discuss agency primarily as a human capacity, However, in Chapter 7 we discuss the place of non-human animals and

Furthermore, we can distinguish *individual* and *collective* (or shared) *agency* where the latter is the exercise of the capacity to do something together. Some authors (e.g. Bratman 1993, 2007) argue that collective agency requires certain mental states as well ('we' desires, 'we' intentions, etc.), on the part of individual agents. Others query whether unorganized groups can truly be agents because they necessarily lack mental states. Still others point out that at least organized collectives can, through their established collective decision procedures, form intentions and make and act on plans to serve their agreed goals.[4] We address the implications of these views for global justice in Chapter 6, where we discuss how and why the global poor should be empowered collectively to act as a global community of interest.

What should we take away from this discussion of agency when discussing global justice? First, we should remember that one's exercise of agency does not always succeed in realizing one's intentions. This means that the capacity to act (the input) and the outcome (the output) should not be conflated. In other words, just because they do not always succeed in realizing their goals, it does not follow that people *lacked* agency or that their agency was thwarted. The satisfaction of people's preferences is quite separate from their capacity to act.[5]

As we will discuss later, many political theorists couch their arguments in favour of 'empowering the poor' in terms of overcoming their 'lack of agency'. The point of empowering the poor is to bring about a certain outcome that is presumptively desired by the poor themselves (global justice, global equality, etc.). But having the capacity to act (to exercise agency) is quite different from having the capacity to actually achieve any given outcome (to exercise agency *effectively*). We should better draw a distinction, perhaps, between 'enabling' someone to act at all and 'empowering' them to have the desired impact. The former speaks of people's possession of agency, the latter to the effectiveness

the environment in global justice, and how their interests might be advanced even if they cannot directly engage their agency in global governance.

[4] For a discussion of collective agency, see List and Pettit (2011) and Collins (2019).

[5] For example, at auctions, people make losing bids all the time. In making the bids they were all exercising their agency, even though only one of them (the winning bidder) succeeded in obtaining the thing for which they were all bidding. More schematically: I might do x in order to bring about my preferred outcome z. Even if I fail in securing z, I have nonetheless exercised my agency in doing x.

of their agency. These are two wholly separate issues that must not be conflated. In this book we're concerned, first, with enabling the exercise of formative agency in global governance, through deliberative-democratic processes. Second, we argue that such processes can also make such an exercise of agency more effective in promoting global justice. That is to say, such processes can lead to those formative agents' 'empowerment'.

What Distinguishes 'Justice' from Other Moral Domains?

Likewise, it is important to clarify what we mean by 'justice', as this term can also be prone to loose usage in well-intentioned but philosophically inept ways. What distinguishes the domain of justice from other moral domains is that it is concerned with moral *rights* and *duties* and with what we 'owe' one another (Hohfeld 1917; Rawls 1971; Valentini 2011, 2013, 2017). Rights morally empower the right-holder, but also impose moral constraints on the duty-bearer's behaviour.

When people stand in a relationship of justice with one another, one party's right correlates to the other party's duty. One party's duty is thus 'directed' or owed to the other party, the latter having a right against the former. Rights can thus specify what we can legitimately demand of others as a matter of justice (Feinberg 1973: 58–9; Darwall 2006: 18). It is also commonly said that rights override other moral considerations and that only rights can trump other rights (Dworkin 1977).

Duties of justice are *perfect* duties. They are specific as regards both the content of the duty and to whom it is owed, the latter having a *right* against the duty-bearer to discharge her duty. In this regard, duties of justice are different from duties of beneficence or charity, which are *imperfect* ones, leaving the duty-bearer with some latitude in those respects. Imperfect duties do not specify when the duty should be discharged, how, or to whom. In this case, no party has a right against the duty-bearer to discharge her imperfect duty of beneficence or charity.

Some scholars argue that the duties we have toward the global poor are perfect duties of justice, while others claim that they can only be imperfect duties of charity (Pogge 2002). Because we discuss the Sustainable Development Goals (SDGs) as a vehicle of *global justice* and argue that the poor should be enabled to exercise formative agency in global governance, it may look like we are taking a position in this debate. This is not necessarily the case, however. As we'll point out next, these two seemingly irreconcilable positions about the nature of duties toward the global poor can both be accommodated. Reconciling these two positions does, however, point to the importance of *global institutions* in improving the fate of the poor.

Those who argue that duties toward the poor are duties of justice often point that the rich have either contributed to causing the poor to be in the position they're in, or are benefitting from their being in this position. But most often, we cannot blame any single individual rich person for global poverty.[6] Nor do the benefits of the current global situation accrue to any single individual. Rather, we can say that the global rich are *collectively* responsible for the fate of the poor or are collectively benefitting from others being in a disadvantaged position as a result of various global practices and institutions. In virtue of this, we can say that the rich, as a collective, have a duty of justice to help or 'compensate' (for past harms) the global poor.

The same conclusion follows for those who start from the other side and argue that our duties toward the poor can only be imperfect duties of charity.[7] One reason they give is that (perhaps with the exception of some unimaginably wealthy people) we individually simply *cannot* make any appreciable difference to the alleviation of global poverty: no individual has the resources to effectively do this.[8] Or they may argue that our duties toward the global poor must be imperfect ones because helping all of the world's poor would come at an unreasonable cost to us individually. These are, however, only arguments against the existence of *individual* duties of *justice* to help the poor. They are not

---

[6] Indeed, especially since it may be the outcome of global structures. On structural injustice, see Young (2004, 2006, 2011).

[7] Of course, the fact that they are imperfect does not make those duties less morally binding or weighty than the perfect ones (Campbell 1974; Goodin 2017). For example, in many ways, my individual duty to help those in need (although imperfect and thus underspecified) is more important than my (very specific content- and temporal-wise) perfect duty to repay the ten dollars I borrowed from a friend who is in so little need of money he probably forgot I borrowed it.

[8] We may be unsure where to draw the line between 'rich' and 'poor'. Even so, the existence of some borderline cases does not negate the existence of clear cases of poverty or wealth, just like the existence of dusk does not negate the existence of night and day. Our argument here applies to such clear cases.

arguments against the rich *collectively* having such a duty of justice, because by working together, the rich of this world can help alleviate global poverty.[9] Indeed, they may even do so without that coming at an unreasonable cost to themselves and their welfare.

Duties that are imperfect at one level can be perfect duties at another level. While our duties toward the poor might not be perfect duties of justice at the individual level, they can be so at the collective level.[10] The global rich may collectively have a perfect duty of justice toward the global poor as a collective, even though any given individual rich person has only an imperfect individual duty of charity toward the poor in general.

The rich can discharge the duty of justice that they collectively have toward the poor as a group by collectivizing. Through domestic and especially global governance institutions, the rich can coordinate and effectively discharge these duties at no excessive costs to themselves. So too should the poor be able to exercise formative agency collectively. As we argue in Chapter 6, the poor should be allowed to exercise formative agency as *a global community of interest*. Furthermore, through deliberative-democratic processes allowing them to exercise formative agency in global governance, the poor can constitute themselves and act as a collective agent and right-claimant.

[9] We are talking about 'alleviating' rather than 'eradicating' global poverty because the causes of global poverty are multiple and complex – some (e.g. corrupt, incompetent, or unaccountable governments, weak institutions and weak rule of law) might indeed find themselves outside of the rich's control. Long-term solutions to global poverty require more than rich countries simply pouring aid into poor countries. They require circumventing their corrupt or incompetent governments as much as possible. Empowering the poor vis-à-vis their governments, holding those governments to account on the world scene, and helping local communities develop informal local economies are ways in which we can robustly alleviate poverty in the long term.

[10] Notice that to say that the rich have *collective* duties of justice does not mean that they must already be constituted as a collective agent to discharge those duties. All that is needed is that they be *able* to constitute themselves as such (Collins 2019). To a great extent the rich already exercise such collective agency through their domestic governments and then one level up, through intergovernmental organizations. Domestic governments are responsive to the median voter, but because of disparities in voter turnout, the median voter's income is above the median income (not to mention the other ways in which the rich can intervene in the political process, e.g. through campaign financing). These rich-biased domestic governments can then coordinate at the global level and make collective decisions through intergovernmental organizations like the United Nations.

Agents of Justice: Genealogy and Lacunae

Having defined the two key terms, we now turn to the concept of 'agents of justice' itself. We examine first the existing claim that global justice theories are incomplete without an account of agents of justice. We immediately go on to show how such existing discussions of agents of justice are themselves lacking in one important respect.

Implementing Agents of Justice

The concept of 'agents of justice' was first introduced by Onora O'Neill when discussing who is responsible for securing the human rights recognized by the Universal Declaration of Human Rights (O'Neill 2001a). In her view, any theory of justice is incomplete without identifying agents of justice: the agents who must discharge those duties, as well as the agents who must give legal force to the rights that justice morally bestows on people. Let us call these 'implementing agents of justice' to distinguish them from other categories of agents we discuss next.

O'Neill thus identifies two categories of implementing agents of justice. 'Primary' agents have 'capacities to determine how principles of justice are to be institutionalized within a certain domain' (O'Neill 2001a: 181). They have the coercive powers required to enforce and enact rights and duties. Primary agents of justice can set up or control the activity of other, 'secondary' agents (collective and individual). These secondary agents then contribute to justice mainly by 'meeting the demands of primary agents, most evidently by conforming to any legal requirements they establish' (O'Neill 2001a: 181). States are, in O'Neill's view, the main primary agents of justice, bearing a duty to comply with international human rights law and enforce it within their borders. But non-state agents, such as corporations or NGOs, can also act as agents of justice (or injustice) especially where state institutions are too weak to enforce human rights or deliver basic goods to their populations. However, in O'Neill's view, they are neither primary nor secondary agents, but rather occupy a different, unspecified, category (O'Neill 2001a: 191, 192–4).

It is obvious that O'Neill's conception of global justice is mostly inspired by international law – mainly the Universal Declaration of Human Rights. While binding on the states, the Declaration has nonetheless an aspirational character. In positing such abstract rights, the Declaration leaves open the question of what such rights actually require on the ground, in the context of any given state and its local (stronger or weaker) institutions.

It is perhaps surprising, therefore, that O'Neill overlooks some important obstacles encountered by her implementing agents of justice. First, O'Neill's account neglects the fact that theories of justice provide little guidance to agents of justice as to *how* exactly duties and rights should be discharged and enacted on the ground. Second, O'Neill's account neglects the fact that in the context of pervasive moral disagreement surrounding matters of justice, real-world actors can always question any particular distribution of rights and duties as well as the general theory of justice chosen by those agents implementing justice.

Hence while we may have established (per O'Neill) that a certain agent (state or NGO) has an obligation (to end poverty, to enact human rights), that doesn't mean that we also know *how* that agent should *practically* discharge that obligation, or what priority *that* obligation should have relative to other existing obligations. This is in part because judgements about what justice requires on the ground are context-relative. They must take into account the social, economic, political, and cultural circumstances that impose feasibility constraints on the implementation of different conceptions of justice in any particular setting.

Furthermore, realizing justice requires *precisifying* abstract rights and duties, as well as other morally relevant concepts people may disagree over. For example, while we may agree that a certain agent has a duty to end global poverty, discharging this duty in practice requires deciding what 'poverty' is, how to measure it, and by what means and ways the agent should reduce it (monetary direct transfers, development programmes, etc.). Not only do agents of justice face a multitude of abstract principles and theories of justice to choose from (which is no simple moral task in and of itself), they must also fill in the gaps left by these abstract principles and theories.

In recognition of the special moral work required to implement abstract principle of justice on the ground, we label those who do this work 'formative agents of justice'.[11] We label the special type of moral

---

[11] Notice that they can do this without engaging in, or engaging with, abstract thinking themselves.

agency involved in this type of moral reasoning 'formative agency' (following Dryzek 2015).

Formative Agents of Justice

To be a formative agent of justice means to be able to act toward influencing the scope and content of justice, as well as its realization. Formative agents can be individuals or collectives. In practice the same actors (e.g. states) can serve both as primary implementing agents of justice (in O'Neill's terms) and as formative agents of justice. For example, states act as formative agents when they negotiate the content of an international treaty and as primary agents when they enforce the obligations imposed by that treaty. Here we just make the analytic distinction between these two categories of agents of justice, between the two different functional roles actors can serve in global justice.

In a looser sense, individuals and organizations act as formative agents by defining justice through their behaviour and interactions, whether or not they are motivated by ethical principles. What justice means in practice is thus socially constructed and encoded in social norms of behaviour.[12] It is not just philosophers who get to operationalize what justice is in social reality. Rather, multiple individuals and political actors collectively operationalize justice through political practice. For example, if we examine the process that yielded the world's two greatest global poverty alleviation agendas – the Millennium Development Goals (MDGs) and SDGs – we see highly political processes in which different actors bring different conceptions of justice to bear on these agendas, with the eventual content of the goals being sensitive not just to different arguments, but also to rhetorical appeals, negotiating ploys, and the exercise of political power.

But formative agency can also be exercised in a more *reflective* and reasoned way – indeed, this is how it *should* be exercised, as we will centrally argue in this book. Formative agents of justice can reflect upon and decide how abstract principles of justice translate into particular policies or political decisions. Drawing on general principles of justice, they can decide how justice should be pursued on the ground,

---

[12] Defined as regularities of behaviour that have a prescriptive force. See Brennan et al. (2013).

by taking into account the context-sensitive factors that are usually bracketed by abstract theories and principles of justice.

If abstract principles of justice operate at the level of ideal theory,[13] formative agents can interpret how these apply to *non*-ideal contexts. They do this by examining how the options available in a specific context should be evaluated against the yardstick of ideal principles of justice.[14] Formative agents of justice act like moral arbiters when deciding: whether justice is best conceived as a matter of distribution, recognition, or both, or neither; whether the units of concern and obligation when it comes to global justice should be individuals, states, or other entities; how domestic and global justice should be weighed against one another; and whether justice should take into account the interests of future generations, and if so what weight should be given to these interests.

Thus at least in some sense (if not in others) formative agents act similarly to judges who must decide how the letter of the law should be interpreted and how it bears on any given specific case brought before the court. Their job is to 'fill in' the details left unspecified by laws that must be general enough in their character. At the same time, judges must also address any potential conflicts of laws that might bear on the same case. Similarly, formative agents accomplish two moral tasks. First, they must arbitrate between different conceptions and principles of justice and bring a *resolution* to the conflicts that might exist between different justice principles (e.g. an intergenerational equity principle, the Rawlsian difference principle that prioritizes the interests of the worst off, or a libertarian principle maximizing freedom and prioritizing property rights). Second, they must precisify abstract conceptions and/or principles of justice by *specifying* what they require in any given context, for example by specifying: the relevant units of moral concern (individuals versus collectives, humans versus non-humans, present versus future generations, etc.); the key duty-bearers (individuals, states, corporations, generations); what kind of

---

[13] Ideal theory rests on assumptions about the state of the world as creating favourable social conditions for realizing and complying with justice. Among them, the assumption that people are not afflicted by hunger and poverty, human rights violations, civil war, environmental degradation, or corrupt state institutions.

[14] On ideal and non-ideal theory, see Valentini (2009), Simmons (2010), and Steiner (2017).

considerations and knowledge should bear on moral judgements about justice; what sort of justice should be prioritized (historical, distributive, or retributive);[15] and what is the appropriate currency of distributive justice in any given socio-economic, political, and cultural context.[16] Focusing on the implementation of justice by primary implementing agents of justice, as O'Neill does, might lead us to neglect the prior and essential step of *specifying* justice through the exercise of formative agency.

To illustrate, consider the case of climate justice. The original terms were set in the 1992 agreement establishing the United Nations Framework Convention on Climate Change (UNFCCC). It referred to 'common but differentiated responsibilities' for action when it comes to reducing greenhouse gas emissions. Since 1992, states, civil society organizations, various sorts of activists, and occasional new claimants for recognition (such as indigenous peoples) took part in the UNFCCC process. They debated, among other matters: what is 'common' and what is 'differentiated'; whether commonality and differentiation should apply across states, or across categories of persons; whether the principle should apply also to adaptation to the effects of climate change or whether another principle should be preferred for the latter; what sorts of knowledge should bear on the allocation of duties and entitlements in climate change mitigation; and how special vulnerability to the effects of climate change creates an entitlement to voice as well as ameliorative action.

---

[15] Historical, distributive, and retributive refer to three different kinds of justice. Historical justice is concerned with the apportionment of responsibility for past wrongdoings and compensations (reparations) for those wrongdoings. Distributive justice is concerned the (re)distribution of various goods required by any given principle of distributive justice (e.g. egalitarianism, sufficientarianism, prioritarianism). Retributive justice is concerned with the distribution of sanctions and punishment for wrongful acts.

[16] Of course, all that we will be discussing here as 'abstract' principles of justice are actually 'mid-level abstractions'. Rawls's difference principle, for example, does not simply say 'distribute primary goods justly' but rather, more concretely, says 'distribute primary goods in such a way as to make the worst off as well off as possible'. The point of these mid-level abstractions is to be general enough to make them applicable in that form pretty much everywhere (but not necessarily at all times, or literally everywhere, even at the present moment: see Rawls 1971: 542ff.). Our argument is that those mid-level abstractions must be further precisified to be fully applicable to any particular place at any particular time – and that is the task of our formative agents of justice.

The UNFCCC and its surrounding decision processes have created a kind of community of inquiry that allows the reflective exercise of formative agency. At the same time these processes have featured power plays, evasions, distortions of language, dubious assertions of victimhood (e.g. when fossil fuel producers lament their loss of future income), attempts by countries to avoid obligations, lack of participation by the most vulnerable, bending of the language of justice to serve one's self-interest, as well as the strategic deployment of justice claims to block progress in the negotiations. Ironically, the most fervent critics of these shortcomings were those actors working *without* reference to any well-defined conception of justice, but concerned about the costs or benefits to special groups of people (e.g. poor farmers evicted as a result of reforestation programmes or traders and rich consumers benefitting from offsetting schemes).

This just shows how what climate justice means in the real world is, for better or worse, the provisional outcome of complex processes engaging a myriad of formative agents with their own agendas that may be more or less narrow. The natural step is to inquire how we can *improve* such decision processes that channel the exercise of formative agency, constantly reconstructing what global justice means on the ground. We discuss this in the section on formative agency and democratic deliberation later in the chapter.

Formative Agency and Practical Reasoning

The concept of formative agency resonates with a rich tradition in the philosophy of practical reasoning.[17]

Practical reason is the capacity for deciding, through reflection, the question of what one should do (Wallace 2014). It is 'practical' in that it is concerned with action and generating new intentions to act a certain way. Practical reason refers to a 'distinctive standpoint of reflection'. Mainly, 'in practical reasoning, agents attempt to assess

---

[17] Philosophically, 'practical reasoning' stands in contrast to 'theoretical reasoning'. Theoretical reasoning deals with the deliverances of pure reason, a priori propositions that are non-contingently true everywhere and always. Practical reasoning, in contrast, deals with contingently true propositions and is contextually sensitive to opportunity sets and feasibility constraints. Practical reason is paradigmatically instrumental reasoning, telling you what are the best means for achieving your chosen goals.

and weigh their reasons for action, the considerations that speak for and against alternative courses of action that are open to them'. But they do so 'from a distinctively *first-personal* point of view, one that is defined in terms of a practical predicament in which they find themselves' (Wallace 2014, emphasis added).[18] Practical reason allows individuals to identify not only the right means for accomplishing any given end, but also ways to ensure that all their ends harmonize in the process (Wallace 2014). One task of practical reason thus concerns the *specification* of ends: before we even think about what is the best means for any given end, we need to ensure the end in itself is not too indeterminate (Wiggins 1975–6; Wallace 2014).

While moral principles and norms govern practical reasoning, they do not, by themselves, provide any clear answer to the question of how one should act. That is in part because moral principles are too general in form to be action-guiding in any given context. They leave individuals some 'latitude' in their interpretation and implementation. Hence individuals must exercise additional judgement when trying to apply moral principles in everyday life. Agents engaged in practical reasoning may draw on abstract moral principles (such as Kantian ethics or consequentialism), but they must also 'fill in' the gaps left by these principles, paying specific attention to features of context in which they act (O'Neill 2001b). There are various ways to conceptualize this process. Some see this process as entailing the creation of mid-level norms that can bridge the more general moral principle and the concrete cases requiring our attention (Richardson 1990: 284). Or as merely 'specifying' the abstract moral norm by 'adding clauses indicating what, where, why, how, by what means, by whom, or to whom the action is to be, is not to be, or may be done' (Richardson 1990: 295–6).

Another problem that practical reasoning must solve is the potential conflict that might arise among the different moral principles bearing on any given situation (Richardson 1990: 295–6). In practical reasoning individuals and collectives must find the proper action or policy that can satisfy a plurality of moral principles in any given socio-economic, political, and cultural context of choice. In other words, the highest practical wisdom is achieved by those who 'bring to bear upon a situation the greatest number of pertinent concerns and relevant

---

[18] In the following section we discuss the problems this 'first-personal' standpoint raises in moral judgement and hence also for the exercise of formative agency.

considerations commensurate with the importance of the deliberative context' (Wiggins 1975–6: 45).

Practical reasoning, just like any other type of judgement, can be more or less reliable. Irrationality can affect people's judgements, in which case their practical reasoning will not be 'automatically practical in its issue' (Wallace 2014). Formative agency can be vulnerable to the same pitfalls. Fortunately, there are ways in which its exercise can be made more reliable.

Formative Agency in Democratic Deliberation

In the previous section we showed that processes of moral deliberation and reflection are part and parcel of practical reasoning. Furthermore, practical reasoning entails the *specification* of ends and choosing means appropriate to the pursuit of those ends, just as formative agency does in our earlier discussion. The exercise of formative agency requires some form of practical reasoning. Yet in another respect, the exercise of formative agency should be importantly different from mere practical reasoning. Philosophers of practical reason ordinarily conceive such moral deliberation as a *solitary* form of moral inquiry taking place inside each person's head. We, on the other hand, argue in what follows that formative agency concerning matters of justice is best exercised through collective, group deliberation, allowing individuals to *interact discursively* with one another.

Formative agents can be *more or less* successful when determining what abstract principles of justice require on the ground and how conflicts between different principles of justice should be resolved. If they get it totally wrong, their actions will promote injustice rather than justice. The argument here is that they are more likely to promote justice (according to some external standard imposed by the abstract principles of justice) if they exercise their formative agency in a democratic fashion, and in particular if their formative agency is channelled through processes of democratic deliberation.

There are two fundamental reasons why democratic deliberation will make formative agents more likely to track the truth in their judgements about how abstract principles of justice should be pursued on the ground. The first concerns the *ends* to be pursued. Those ends will be more defensible when the multiple competing interests of all affected parties are given due consideration and are reconciled as best

as possible depending on the context. Democratic deliberation, a process by which the interest-based claims of all these parties can be
carefully examined and reconciled, is valuable in that respect. The
second reason concerns the *means* by which to pursue those just ends.
We may of course be unsure which means will best promote any given
just end. Democratic deliberation, a process that enhances actors'
epistemic competence, helps to ensure that the best option is identified
and chosen. We elaborate on each of these claims in turn in the
subsections that follow.

Neutralizing Self-Interest

One first advantage of democratic deliberation is its capacity to neutralize biases that might affect the quality of collective outcomes.
Earlier in the chapter we analogized formative agents to moral arbiters
or judges who must adjudicate between different principles and conceptions of justice and decide what weight each should have in any
given case. One virtue of judges and arbiters is of course *impartiality*,
by which we mean the disinterested consideration of all affected
parties' interests. Arbiters and judges don't have personal interests in
the decisions they make; they can thus act as Hume's and Smith's
impartial spectator (Smith [1759–90] 1982; Hume [1751] 1998;
[1739–40] 2007). For Hume and Smith, and many following in their
footsteps, moral judgement itself requires adopting an impartial standpoint that takes into account all affected parties' interests (Nagel 1970;
Parfit 1971). Ideally, we would want formative agents – those casting
judgements about how justice should be pursued on the ground – to be
impartial as well in their judgements.

As we have pointed out, most practical reasoning is done from a
first-personal standpoint. Judgements about how *one* should act are
unavoidably self-referential. Yet to make things worse, actors exercising formative agency in global governance also have *stakes* in the
decisions they make. They are *self-interested* actors enjoying more or
less influence in decision making. There is thus a danger that, when
exercising formative agency, they may only reach a *partial, one-sided*
judgement about what justice requires, and 'bend' justice to fit their
interests. That one should not be judge in her own cause (*nemo iudex
in causa sua*) is a well-known principle of natural justice (see Coke
1610; Hobbes 1651: chs 15, 23; Locke [1690] 1960: ch. II) for a good

reason. But, of course, in global governance actors will be able to act as judges in their own cause. (In the following chapters we discuss in more detail how different actors – e.g. states, corporations, or even NGOs – may use the language of justice in self-serving ways.) If we want to promote justice in global governance, then we need to find ways to ensure that decision making and the exercise of formative agency are infused with impartiality.

Fortunately, impartiality can be ensured in several ways. The first requires agents to be impartial and have no stakes in the judgements they make. This is obviously not an easy option in global governance. The second ensures impartial outcomes by *procedurally neutralizing* agents' partiality. For example, by giving all equally affected parties (or their representatives) equal power in decision making we can ensure the affected parties' interests cancel one another, and what emerges from the process will better advance the common good. The outcome thereby achieved is *impartial* across the affected parties, although the inputs into that process remain partial. Notice, however, that ensuring that *all* affected parties (directly or through their representatives) participate in decision making and that all have *equal* influence on the collective outcome is crucial in guaranteeing such impartiality. Special arrangements, enabling the respectful engagement and equal deliberative input of all these parties, are thus required to ensure that partial formative agents will promote justice through their collective judgements. As we will see in the following chapters, global governance processes often fail in this respect.

Of course, one advantage of this second way of ensuring impartiality is that it is *democratic* as well – it allows affected parties to exercise decision power and thus to self-rule (Dahl 1979: 108–29; Goodin 2007). In Chapter 1, we pointed out that it is difficult to square democracy (which ordinarily involves the pursuit of self-interest[19]) with justice (which requires impartially setting aside one's self-interest). To be sure, we want collective decisions to be democratic. Yet when it comes to decisions about matters of justice, while all affected parties have a claim to formative agency in virtue of the stakes they have in the decision, they all are at the same time (because of those stakes)

---

[19] Or merely expressing one's identity, as some political scientists (e.g. Achen and Bartels 2016) remark.

vulnerable to promoting injustice (or partial views of justice) when exercising this formative agency on their own, *independently* of one another.

This problem can of course be overcome by making decisions together, with one another, collectively, in an inclusive and equally participative way – whether by voting or deliberating.[20] Either mode of democratic decision making can neutralize bias by ensuring the equal participation of all affected parties, and through it, that multiple, partial conceptions of justice counterbalance and complement each other. However, democratic deliberation that also enables the interactive, discursive engagement among those parties – the free and open exchange of arguments and reasons (Habermas 1990; Dryzek 2000) – has *additional, in-built* safeguards against partiality that voting by majority rule alone does not. This third way of countering partiality is thus unique to democratic deliberation.

In trying to persuade others of their positions, deliberators must appeal to reasons and arguments others can accept. Hence they cannot so easily appeal to self-interested reasons for action that others do not necessarily have any reason to accept. Arguments framed in terms of the common good, however, are more likely to strike a chord. In consequence, democratic deliberation can 'launder' the actors' preferences: people can reformulate their preferences in the course of the deliberation such that 'instead of working with a fixed set of preferences the social decision machinery changes them in the process' (Goodin 1986: 86–7).[21]

Publicity, in particular, as a feature of democratic deliberation encourages the 'civilizing force of hypocrisy'. Even if actors are initially hypocritical in advancing common interest-oriented reasons, under the

[20] Sometimes the deliberative engagement may promote a consensus or at least 'non-opposition' (Urfalino 2014) – a situation where not all deliberators agree on a position, but where some are willing to stop opposing it and accept it as the group's standing decision. Other times, however, disagreement may endure even after all the parties' reasons have been exchanged and examined. In this case voting might be used to bring deliberation to a conclusion.

[21] 'There is a deeper dynamic ... which induces people to launder systematically their own preferences, and to express only a subset of their preferences in the form of political demands ... "an individual" response depends on the institutional environment in which the question is asked. Certain kinds of argument, powerful though they may be in private deliberations, simply cannot be put in a public forum' (Goodin 1986: 87).

pressure of public scrutiny they may later on end up acting on those reasons to keep face or even believing them (Elster 1986).[22] In consequence, actors' attempts to bend the language of justice to serve their self-interest are thwarted.

This shows how deliberation can act on the very nature of the *inputs* into decision making in a way that voting cannot. It can ensure the *individual* inputs themselves become more impartial and less self-interested through the deliberative process. Because of this *transformative* effect (or 'laundering'), formative agents will also be more likely to promote justice through their individual judgements. Deliberation thus limits the formative agents' capacity to advance self-serving understandings of justice even if *at the start* they are acting as judges in their own cause, trying to promote their very own partial interpretation of justice. As deliberation progresses, and they appeal to shared reasons others can accept, those partial interpretations also expand, becoming more inclusive and thus more impartial across all the affected parties. These transformative effects of deliberation will matter especially when collective decision making has a strong moral component and thus calls for the exercise of formative agency. This will be the case in many areas of global governance, whether we are talking of sustainable development, poverty, or climate change – they all represent 'perfect moral storms' (Gardiner 2006).

Of course, the pursuit and expression of self-interest may be democratically defensible – especially when one risks danger or severe disadvantage by the collective decision (Mansbridge et al. 2010). It is easy to see that acting in one's self-interest is not necessarily bound to clash with justice. For example, it is in an actor's self-interest not to have his or her rights violated or basic material conditions of life undermined. It may be in the interest of a small island state not to disappear as a result of rising sea levels caused by climate change. It is only proper that one draws one's co-voters' or co-deliberators' attention to these injustices to enter a plea (even though it is a plea on one's *own* behalf) that those injustices be avoided. Still, the pursuit of self-interest in such ways 'must be curtailed both by the universal constraints of moral behavior and human rights and the specifically

---

[22] A similar argument has been made in favour of 'unveiling the vote' (Brennan and Pettit 1990): public (as opposed to secret) voting would provide citizens additional incentive to take into account the public interest when casting their votes.

deliberative constraints of mutual respect, equality, reciprocity, fairness and mutual justification' (Mansbridge et al. 2010). Actors can be, and are, tempted to advance false or morally unwarranted rights claims. Public deliberative decision making can guard against such disingenuous claims by simply allowing formative agents to challenge each other's claims.

To sum up, democratic deliberation can reduce the tendency of stakeholders acting as formative agents to interpret and advance justice in terms that serve their own self-interest. It can restrict the sheer pursuit of naked self-interest as well as the masking of self-interest by the language of justice.

Improving Epistemic Competence

The second reason why formative agency in global justice is better exercised in democratic deliberation is *epistemic*. Even after we have identified, through democratic deliberation including all affected parties, the ideally just ends to be pursued, we still need to deliberate on the best means for practically achieving them. The inclusive and open exchange of reasons and arguments will make formative agents more likely to be correct in their judgements regarding the right means.

Epistemic democrats have long hailed the advantages of democratic decision making, both majoritarian and deliberative. They have also stressed the importance of the number and cognitive profiles of the decision makers. For a collective decision to track any truth or, more practically, locate effective solutions to collective problems, it is essential that those making the decisions hold *diverse* information and assess it *independently* from one another (Landemore 2012; Goodin and Spiekermann 2018). This means that global governance processes should try to include the largest possible range of *diverse* stakeholders – stakeholders whose agendas are set *independently* of one another's, who represent *different* constituencies of interest, and have access to *different* sources of knowledge.

Deliberative processes will facilitate the discovery of generalizable interests and integrate diverse perspectives on complex social problems (Dryzek 1990: 57). Participatory deliberative processes involving a wide range of formative agents will thus be more likely to solve complex problems such as climate change or global poverty. This is in part because subsets of formative agents can focus on different facets of the same problem, reducing thereby the cognitive burden on each formative agent (Dryzek 1990: 70–5; Goodin and Spiekermann 2018: ch. 8). Yet by coupling this cognitive division of labour with communication between different sets of formative agents, the entire group of formative agents can grasp the connections between the different aspects of the same problem. As a result, the entire group's capacity to finding appropriate solutions to complex problems increases (Goodin and Spiekermann 2018: ch. 9).

Deliberation involving *diverse* and *independent* formative agents allows the free exchange of information and expertise among these agents and hence the calibration of beliefs ('dynamic belief updating' in Bayesian terminology) in real time – something voting by majority rule cannot achieve. Another way by which deliberation increases the formative agents' capacity to promote justice in their judgements is by enabling them to find 'integrative solutions' – third-way, win–win solutions that emerge from the exchange of ideas among deliberators (Follett [1925] 1942; Walton and McKersie 1965; Warren and Mansbridge 2013). Such solutions are more likely to surface in an environment of *mutual trust and respect*, where deliberators 'will not anticipate threat and therefore behave defensively, which will then create defensive postures in others; will not try to "control information"; will be able to hear more accurately what others are saying; and will be able to experiment with attitudes and ideas, and test and retest perceptions and opinions' (Walton and McKersie 1965: 141–3).

Some of the biggest problems states face today are *global* problems that cannot be solved without sustained coordinated action among state governments, NGOs, and citizens. While national sovereignty is a cornerstone of international law and international relations, states must recognize that many of their domestic policies have important externalities. States are no longer (if ever they were) self-contained units capable of achieving and sustaining the same levels of development and welfare for their citizens in the long run and independently of other states. Yet in a world of sovereign states, successful collective action in global governance cannot exist without some broad resolution among all those actors (or at least the biggest contributors to those externalities) regarding what they all should do.

Some of the disagreements about how best to deal with these world problems have important moral dimensions. Formative agents of justice may have trouble promoting justice in a climate of moral pluralism and disagreement. It is not enough for actors to agree on who has a duty (who is, in Onora O'Neill's terms, a primary agent), if they cannot agree on *what* that duty requires in practice and *how* exactly it should be discharged.

The scholarly community is to some extent plagued by the same disagreements.[23] There we can find multiple theories of justice prioritizing different *values* (freedom, well-being, or equality) (Rawls 1971; Nozick 1974; Dworkin 2000). Each is persuasive on its own. Furthermore, what *principle* of distributive justice should we follow at the domestic and global level: equality, sufficiency, or priority (Rawls 1971; Scheffler 1982; Walzer 1983; Frankfurt 1987, 2000; Miller 1995)? And *what* exactly should be distributed as a matter of justice towards achieving equality, sufficiency, or priority: welfare, material resources, opportunities, or capabilities (Rawls 1971; Arneson 1989, 2000; Cohen 1989; Dworkin 2000)?

Some philosophers have argued in favour of universal duties we owe to all humans, while others have pointed out the importance of special relationships between those who are members of the same state (Goodin 1985; cf. Scheffler 1982; Miller 1995). Others prefer to emphasize the importance of duties toward future generations (Barry 1977; Feinberg 1980; Gosseries 2001). How we should weigh the duties we have toward our countrymen, our cosmopolitan duties toward the rest of the world, and the duties we have toward future people remains an unsolved puzzle. How much weight should we place on each, especially when these duties conflict? To complicate things, some philosophers argue that we have duties toward the environment and non-human animals as well; they disagree on the extent and strength of these duties.

If such disagreements persist even in the ivory tower, it's no wonder that citizens, representatives, and bureaucrats acting in the much messier real world may encounter the same moral disagreements (and perhaps some additional ones as well) when acting as formative agents of justice. Collective action toward solving global problems cannot exist until they find a way of moving past this disagreement. *Global deliberative democracy* is an instrument for solving moral

---

[23] Although dispute at the level of abstract principles often gives way to agreement on more practical questions (MacIntyre 1988).

disagreement about global justice in a way that can allow formative agents to more successfully promote justice on the ground (Sen 2009; Dryzek 2013a).

A Typology of Agents of Justice

We have argued that justice needs not only *implementing* agents of justice, but *formative* agents as well, tasked with specifying what justice calls for on the ground.

Although those two categories are analytically distinct, in practice the same actors can often play both of these roles, to a greater or lesser extent. Agents implementing justice often end up specifying justice prior to and in the process of implementing it, thereby exercising formative agency. And formative agents who specify justice can end up implementing it as well, on a larger or smaller scale.

Hence there is a *continuum* between agents *specifying* and *implementing* justice. At one end of the continuum, we have agents whose exclusive role is to specify justice. We label them *pure formative agents of justice*. At the other end of the continuum, we have agents whose exclusive role is to implement justice. We term them *global justice effectors*. They are the 'implementing agents of justice' that O'Neill was discussing. In between we have agents who exercise both formative agency and implementation agency in differing combinations. *Global justice entrepreneurs*, to be discussed next, are a prime example of such a mixed case.

As we will see in the following chapters, different actors (states, individuals, international organizations, NGOs, charities, corporations) can fit into these categories and indeed, in practice, the same actors can play multiple roles. Here we define these categories through their functional roles in global justice. In the chapters that follow we discuss how exactly different actors exercise their agency and what factors influence this, how they interact with other agents of justice, and what democratic and deliberative duties should apply to them.

Global Justice Entrepreneurs

Global justice entrepreneurship may be considered a special kind of formative agency involving primarily *advocacy* for a particular conception or principle of justice. Global justice entrepreneurs[24] promote a certain vision of what global justice requires in any given context; they try to persuade other actors to adopt, advocate, and implement that vision. Insofar as they frame and advocate a particular vision of justice, they serve as formative agents of justice. But insofar as they are successful in their advocacy, global justice entrepreneurs can also promote the implementation of justice (albeit indirectly, by others rather than themselves).

NGOs, for example, act as global justice entrepreneurs every time they aim to convince states and international organizations to devote their resources to particular programmes – whether it's famine relief and direct aid programmes or renewable energy infrastructures. The functional role of global justice entrepreneurs is to advocate concrete views of justice and policies and programmes, and persuade other agents (especially states and international organizations) to implement those. Some (developing) states themselves act as global justice entrepreneurs when trying to convince, through their advocacy in international fora, other (developed) states to support certain solutions to global problems such as global poverty or climate change. Columbia's advocacy for universal and sustainable goals over the course of the SDG process is just one example.

Important from a deliberative-democratic perspective is the fact that such global justice entrepreneurs advocate certain conceptions of justice *on behalf of* certain constituencies of affected parties. In other words, global justice entrepreneurs sometimes claim to 'speak for' and 'represent' the interests of a certain constituency (e.g. the global poor, children, non-human animals, workers in general, or certain professions in particular). Through such representative claims (Saward 2010; Rubenstein 2014, 2015), the global justice entrepreneurs assume the power to exercise formative agency in global justice on others' behalf.

In the case of NGOs, this is often done in the absence of any accountability mechanism that would allow the affected parties themselves (who have a primary moral claim to exercise formative agency directly) to influence their activity. In the case of states (if these states

---

[24] In choosing this term, we were inspired by the concept of 'norm entrepreneurs' (Finnemore and Sikkink 1998).

are democracies), it is done under a legitimate democratic mandate: states have a right to speak on *their* citizens' behalf. Even so, democratic elections represent a basic and imperfect accountability device. It should be supplemented by other (deliberative) means of democratic participation that allow citizens to have direct input into state laws and policies. In Chapter 6, we will raise a number of concerns about states exercising formative agency on behalf of the global poor.

To be sure, those global justice entrepreneurs who advocate particular visions of global justice on others' behalf represent a solution to the problem of scale. After all, it would be impossible for *all* primary claimants to formative agency to exercise this formative agency directly. Yet their functional role in global justice, insofar as they claim to speak on others' behalf or represent others' interests, should be circumscribed by particular deliberative-democratic duties toward the primary claimants to formative agency who cannot exercise this formative agency directly. We elaborate these duties in the chapters that follow.

Implementing Agents: Global Justice Effectors

Nearer the other end of the specification-implementation spectrum, we find agents who play primarily 'implementational' rather than 'formative' roles. Onora O'Neill (2001a) calls agents with the material, legal, political, and symbolic resources and capacities to implement justice on the ground 'primary' agents in this regard, but we think that 'primary' is a misleading term when we think of what these agents do in the larger scheme of things. *Logically*, the task of specifying justice precedes that of implementing justice. What formative agents and global justice entrepreneurs do is logically prior to any action taken by the implementing agents that O'Neill calls 'primary'. Hence we use the label 'global justice effectors' to refer to those agents in charge of the resources needed to ensure global justice takes effect on the ground.

Putting into a temporal sequence the division of labour among different agents of justice, it would look like this: (1) General principles (be they abstract or practical ones) are first *specified* by *pure formative agents of justice*. These agents can then also be involved in the conversion of principles into *concrete actions* (policies, programmes, plans). (2) Those concrete actions meant to promote global justice and the more general principles standing behind them are then *advocated* by the *global justice entrepreneurs* with the purpose of persuading the *effectors of global justice* to (3) use their resources to pursue these actions – that is, to realize global justice on the ground.

Governments, NGOs, international organizations, governments in collaboration with NGOs and corporations, or international organizations in collaboration with NGOs and transnational governance networks, can act as effectors of justice. Sometimes international NGOs themselves have the material and social resources to implement different programmes on the ground. Foreign aid goes to governments directly, who then should use the resources to promote global justice.

Of course, as we have said, in practice those actors fulfilling the role of global justice effectors (e.g. state governments) also typically end up exercising formative agency to a greater or lesser degree. In other words, they end up further specifying what justice requires in any particular context before (or better yet, *through*) implementing justice in that context.

As we said at the beginning of this section, the same actor (whether it is a state or an NGO) can act in multiple capacities. For example, an NGO can act as (1) a formative agent of justice when it decides to what causes, policies, communities, or individuals to dedicate its agenda; (2) a global justice entrepreneur when it engages in advocacy to persuade other agents to endorse a particular course of action or set of principles meant to advance global justice; and (3) a global justice effector when the NGO uses its own material resources to implement particular programmes on the ground. As we will see in the following chapters, both global justice entrepreneurs as well as global justice effectors exercise a fair amount of formative agency.

In the next chapter we focus on the role of states and international organizations as agents of justice. States and international organizations are essential in global governance not just for their capacity to implement justice, but also because they can effectively shape the practical meaning of global justice when acting as formative agents. An obvious example is the way states can, through international law as well as global policy, expand or restrict the scope of duties they have towards their own citizens and other states and their citizens. However, the formative agency of states and international organizations can be problematic. States are inclined to define justice in self-interested ways, and the SDGs negotiations are no exception to that. Nonetheless, through the adoption of democratic mechanisms promoting a wide deliberative inclusion of affected parties, states and international organizations can become more legitimate formative agents of justice.

3 | *Democratizing Formal Authority*
States and International Organizations

States and international organizations at first glance largely constitute global governance. For what else is global governance but international organizations (such as the United Nations (UN), World Trade Organization (WTO), and International Monetary Fund (IMF)) set up by states, who then interact within these organizations, and agree (to greater or lesser degree) to abide by and implement collective decisions? While there is in fact quite a lot more than this going on in global governance (which we will examine in the next four chapters), these sorts of formal processes and structures remain central. They largely (though not completely) constitute what in Chapter 8 we will analyse further as 'empowered space' in global deliberative systems. Thus their capacity to exercise moral agency (of the sort we outlined in Chapter 2) matters enormously in securing global justice.

States and international organizations thus play crucial formative roles in advancing, undermining, and sifting principles for collective action in the domain of global justice. In this chapter we will show that these roles are problematic, but can be corrected by inclusive deliberative democratic mechanisms. There are glimpses of these mechanisms in the process that yielded the Sustainable Development Goals (SDGs), especially in the interactions of states in the Open Working Group (OWG) that finalized their content, and in the engagements of international organizations with global civil society. But there are limits to these mechanisms, which suggest that however important they may be as potential effectors of global justice, states and international organizations should be embedded in larger systems of formative deliberation that grant key roles to other actors that we will visit in subsequent chapters.

In playing formative roles, states and international organizations are rarely the sources of ideas relevant to justice, and so are not *pure* formative agents (in the terms we established in Chapter 2).

Rather, what they do affects the relative weight of competing principles on the world stage, as advocates (global justice entrepreneurs) as well as opponents of specific principles. An example of advancing principles would be the effective solidification of neoliberalism that highlights the centrality of free exchange and investment, and private property rights, by international economic organizations such as the IMF and WTO. Or consider the way the UN Development Programme (UNDP) mobilized principles of human development for the Millennium Development Goals (MDGs; see Chapter 1). An example of undermining would be the long-standing US attitude to the International Criminal Court (ICC), which the United States treats as an appropriate instrument to hold leaders of (especially) African countries to account for wrongdoing – but refuses to subject itself to the ICC, thus undermining the principle of universality in the application of criminal justice and the rule of law (Bosco 2014). An example of sifting competing principles would be controversies involving different states in the UN Convention on Biological Diversity. Some state representatives emphasize the monetary valuation of ecosystem services, treating the non-human world in instrumental economic terms; others emphasize reverence for the non-human world and its intrinsic value, so itself is a subject of justice. At the time of writing the balance has moved slightly with the 'nature's contribution to people' terminology becoming more widely used than 'ecosystem services', though this shift still falls short of intrinsic value (Pascual et al. 2017). Beyond any formative or entrepreneurial role, states and international organizations are also the crucial effectors or implementers of any actions to promote global justice that are collectively determined.

Important though it may be, the formative role played by states and international organizations can be highly problematic. This chapter will show how and why this is the case, and explore what might be done about it. Despite the formal authority that they possess, states and international organizations cannot be relied upon to promote global justice. But given their centrality to global governance, we cannot simply dismiss their formative role. It is more productive to explore whether, and if so how, their problematic features can be corrected through deliberative-democratic means. This correction proves only to go so far, which justifies looking more closely at other formative agents in global governance in the chapters that follow.

The Main Problem with States: Veiling Material Self-Interest in the Language of Justice

Ethicists (acting as pure formative agents of justice) like to propose all kinds of things that states should do in, for example, protecting their vulnerable citizens, transferring money to poorer states and societies, or protecting human rights. But we cannot of course assume that states will pursue justice simply because morally they should. States are not straightforwardly free to produce justice, still less justice beyond their borders; and a glance at history shows that justice (however described) may be low on their priority list. Early modern states existed mainly to keep order internally, compete with actual and potential enemies, and raise the funds necessary for these first two tasks (Skocpol 1979), though such states might sometimes claim a concern with justice (for example, in 1609 Hugo Grotius wrote his *Mare Liberum* in part to justify the Dutch claim to the right to travel for trade to the East Indies). Contemporary states also prioritize creating the conditions for economic growth, and if they do promote income security and a social safety net within their borders, it has often been for the sake of social stability, though that does not rule out a more principled commitment to justice.

Matters become more tricky when it comes to justice toward those who live beyond a state's borders. They remain tricky when it comes to states' participation in international processes ostensibly designed to deliver (or at least promote) justice, or indeed any social values. Here states reveal a ubiquitous propensity to define justice in terms that serve the state's material self-interest, especially when the stakes are high. Note that it is not the mere pursuit of self-interest that is problematic here (however undesirable that may be in obstructing justice as impartiality), but rather the veiling of material self-interest in the language of justice. Deliberative democratic theory can alert us to this problem by providing standards for meaningful communication, including sincerity and the attendant need to avoid the combination of deception and self-deception that facilitates using the language of justice as a cover for material self-interest (though sometimes agents making such claims may truly believe them, in which case it is psychology rather than deliberative theory that alerts us).

This kind of veiling is especially problematic when it pervades the formative sphere – which we will show has sometimes clearly happened in the history of global concern with climate justice, especially when it is states that have dominated discussion and decision making. Examination of the process that yielded the SDGs reveals similar problems, even if they turn out to be less consequential and paralysing than has often been the case with climate justice.

This tendency to interpret and advance justice in terms that serve material self-interest is not confined to states, and subsequent chapters will show how it can arise for other actors and agents ranging from corporations to the poor and vulnerable. Sometimes this interpretation is justifiable. As we pointed out in Chapter 2, It may be in an individual's self-interest to have his or her rights protected and basic needs of life secured, which can defensibly be claimed as matters of justice. The material interests of poor states need to be protected against devastating climate change, which again is also clearly a matter of justice. These sorts of arguments could survive deliberative and democratic scrutiny (see Mansbridge et al. 2010). However, this does not obviate the need for such scrutiny, which is still more pressing in the case of arguments drawing dubious connections between self-interest and justice, which as we will now see haunt global climate governance.

States and Climate Justice

The multilateral negotiations held under the auspices of the UN Framework Convention on Climate Change (UNFCCC) offer a good example of how claims about justice can be used as covers for material self-interest. As noted in Chapter 1, the UNFCCC has been pervaded by the language of justice since its establishment in 1992 on the agreed basic principle of 'common but differentiated responsibilities', which is essentially a principle of justice. But exactly what is common and what is differentiated became a matter of dispute. For the G77 group of developing countries plus China, for a long time it was differentiation that dominated. This meant that their conception of justice was historical, in the sense that the industrialized countries that built their wealth on a long history of fossil fuel use should now bear the main and perhaps sole responsibility for the burden of cutbacks in greenhouse gas emissions. In other words, industrialized countries have incurred a 'climate debt' as a result of their past emissions that needs to be repaid. Accordingly, the 1997 Kyoto Protocol imposed greenhouse gas emission reduction obligations only on developed countries –

which eventually proved unacceptable to some of them, led by the United States, which withdrew from the Protocol in 2001. By the time of the 2015 Paris Agreement the G77 position had changed substantially and most developing countries accepted they had a role to play in reducing future emissions. However, in Paris, Indian prime minister Modi could still say 'climate change ... is not of our making' and reiterated the principle that it is developed countries that should take the lead in fighting climate change.[1] In the past, Indian negotiators had done much better in protecting the high emissions lifestyle of the Indian elite than in representing the poor Indians most vulnerable to climate catastrophe (Ananthapadmanabhan, Srivinas, and Gopal 2007).

The United States has remained vociferous in rejecting any 'climate debt' approach to justice. As their chief negotiator in the UNFCCC put it in 2009: 'I actually completely reject the notion of a debt or reparations or anything of the like ... Let's just be mindful of the fact for most of the 200 years since the Industrial Revolution, people were blissfully ignorant of the fact that emissions cause the greenhouse effect' (Samuelsohn 2009). Blissful ignorance only goes so far: the theoretical possibility of a greenhouse effect was recognized in the nineteenth century, and the likelihood of its practical realization was flagged in US government documents in the 1960s. Still, the United States sets history aside, and sees justice in terms of fairness in the area of trade: for rich countries to bear the sole burden of emissions reduction would unfairly benefit their competitors such as China. Despite their differences, it is noteworthy that the arguments of both the G77 plus China and the United States serve the material self-interest of those making them. In addition, both take nation states as their unit of analysis, concern, and obligation, thus reinforcing the idea that justice should be international (between nations), rather than between persons (reflecting the fact that there are poor people in rich states, and rich people in poor states) or concerned with vulnerable communities wherever they happen to live.

This veiling of self-interest in justice claims long impeded the ability of the UNFCCC to promote climate justice – on any definition of justice. The tactics pursued by states in negotiations often suggested that their public proclamations of concern for the global climate

---

[1] See http://climatesouthasia.org/climate-change-is-not-of-our-making-modi-at-paris-summit.

masked the pursuit of economic self-interest (Winkler and Beaumont 2010: 643). The fact that states (and blocs of states, such as the G77) could convince themselves that justice was on their side added to their intransigence. In 2015 the UNFCCC's Paris Agreement seemed finally to have broken the impasse and opened the door to obligations being taken on by all countries. Rather than a treaty with legally binding emissions reduction targets and punishment for non-compliance, the Paris Agreement lets countries set their own targets and timetables and requires that they periodically report upon progress. Much remains to be seen in how this will play out. In the past, as Stevenson (2013) shows, states have used any kind of leeway to reinterpret their obligations in ways that undermine the spirit of global climate agreements. For example, developed countries have used transnational carbon trading (buying emissions permits from poorer countries) and technology transfer to avoid tackling emissions at home or decarbonizing their own economies.

In short, despite the progress signalled by the Paris Agreement, the fact that the inter-state politics of climate change long featured the language of justice has not meant that climate justice (beyond versions of justice that affirm the status quo) has been advanced – and for a long time meant that justice on pretty much any defensible definition was impeded. These sorts of problems lead some commentators to suggest that progress on climate change would be facilitated by dropping all talk of justice (Posner and Weisbach 2010). We believe in contrast that justice claims can be productive – provided they are addressed through deliberative-democratic means, which we will detail later in this chapter. As we will now see, the situation when it comes to the SDGs is a bit different from climate change: it converged on a global agreement embodying a variety of views on global justice and related issues very quickly, such that there are some positive lessons to be drawn (though its task was made easier by the fact that not only does it specify no legally binding targets, but reporting too is entirely voluntary).

States and the SDGs

The adoption of the SDGs can, as noted in Chapter 1, be interpreted as an exercise in formative agency, given these global goals are a set of principles for subsequent global and national (even local) action. The OWG that was crucial in finalizing the seventeen goals and associated targets was made up of representatives of states. The goals, and the *Transforming Our World* 2030 Agenda of which they were a part, were eventually adopted by the UN General Assembly, which is of course an assembly of states. However, the fact that all states have now signed off on the SDGs does not mean they are going to try to achieve the goals. One negotiator suggested to us that if their head of government had actually read the 2030 Agenda, they would not have signed up to it. And leaders in some developed states (including the same head of government we just mentioned) have not internalized the idea that the SDGs apply to them as well, not just to poorer countries, failing to recognize that the SDGs are different to the MDGs in this respect. (This also explains why many developed states did not see the need to organize public consultations on the SDGs.)

Before the OWG swung into action, the process that eventually yielded the goals featured many disparate kinds of debates, forums, and consultations, involving states, international organizations, and others. The very idea that there should be a set of SDGs combining the anti-poverty agenda of the MDGs and the equally established sustainability discourse owes a lot to the efforts of Colombia (supported by Guatemala) at the 2012 UN Conference on Sustainable Development (Rio+20). Colombia thus played an important early role as an entrepreneur in getting this particular global justice agenda off the ground (Kanie et al. 2017: 14–15), in the face of opposition from many governments (including the G77 group of developing countries as well as some wealthy states and anti-sustainability petrostates) that did not want the economic development and anti-poverty remit of the MDGs compromised by expansion toward sustainability. The shift from the specificity of the MDGs on developing countries to the universality of the SDGs was then pushed by some low- and middle-income states. Low-income states wanted to see obligations put on wealthy states to change, not just upon themselves. Middle-income states wanted the SDGs to speak to their own interests (bearing in mind substantial poverty within these states), not just those of the poorest states.

How, then, did the material interests of states play out in the SDG process? State material self-interest had played a role in the predecessor MDGs. Notably, as Hulme (2009: 14) points out, wealthy countries managed to get the goals and targets specified such that there were no strong, specific, and time-bound obligations imposed on themselves.

The same might be said for the SDGs, which have no legally binding obligations attached to them.

In relation to the SDGs, there is no assertion of naked material self-interest of the sort that can sometimes be found in aggressive nationalist interventions in global governance. Think, for example, of President George H. W. Bush's declaration that 'the American way of life is not negotiable' at the Rio Earth Summit in 1992. Or Donald Trump's 'America first' renunciation of the Paris Agreement on climate change in 2017. In the context of the SDGs and the 2030 Development Agenda more generally, states do not advocate for any specific goal or target on the grounds that it will protect their own excessive level of consumption, or enable them to receive more aid money, or let them avoid any responsibility to offer financial support for a programme, or help them benefit from a particular kind of economic development. What goes on is much more subtle than that.

For example, when it came to inequality, developed Western states emphasized inclusion and non-discrimination within countries – thus trying to avoid any commitment to redistribution across national boundaries, which is opposed by the United States in particular (Langford 2016: 171). This emphasis is not because these states necessarily intend doing anything about their own internal inequality, but serves rather to deflect attention from international redistribution that they would have to pay for. Developing countries (including the G77) in contrast believed that inequality should be addressed in international terms, be it in relation to aid, trade, or in representation in international organizations dealing with economics and finance (Langford 2016: 171). In the end both groups got what they wanted. Goal 10 is to 'reduce inequality within and among countries'. If we examine the targets associated with Goal 10, the first four refer to the internal affairs of states. When it comes to international targets, there is a commitment to 'enhanced representation and voice for developing countries in decision making in global international financial economic and financial institutions'. The closest commitment to global redistribution comes in Target 10c, but this is only about ensuring that aid and investment go to the countries that most need it, rather than suggesting any need to increase the total quantity of aid.

Another good example of thinly veiled material interest can be found in Saudi Arabia's attempt to stop energy being associated with the climate change goal; instead, Saudi Arabia wanted energy to be addressed in the context of the energy needs of the poor and sustained economic growth (Kamau et al. 2018: 84 and 114). In the end energy was not mentioned under climate change, but received its own goal (Goal 7), 'affordable and clean energy', which is primarily about access to energy. While Target 7.2 is 'increase the share of renewable energy in the global energy mix', the targets avoid saying anything about the damage caused by fossil fuels and the need to transition away from them.

States could often veto anything that threatened their material interests. Wealthy states managed to avoid committing themselves to anything that would change their established bad practices (such as excessive consumption). China kept any explicit mention of democracy out of the SDGs (Langford 2016: 173) and impeded consideration of peace, security, and (along with Brazil and India) the rule of law (Kamau et al. 2018: 110 and 203). However, the rule of law did eventually make it in as Target 16.3, and democracy receives a positive mention in the *Transforming Our World* document adopted by the UN, containing the SDGs. Radical challenge to neoliberal discourse was effectively sidelined throughout the process (Carant 2017).

Powerful states could also avoid commitments that would apply to themselves specifically. The 2030 Development Agenda does set out procedures for national, regional, and global review of how the goals are working out in practice, but allows flexibility in national implementation (UN 2015: paras 72–91). This flexibility arguably reflects the formative agency of powerful states reluctant to see binding commitments imposed on themselves.

In looking at the behaviour of states, ideology can be intertwined with self-interest. In 1995 the United Kingdom argued for a single MDG – income poverty reduction – because it would validate the Conservative government's neoliberal market-oriented growth commitment (Hulme 2009: 14). However, ideology does not have to reduce to a cover for material self-interest: after a 1997 change of government, the United Kingdom changed its position on the MDGs poverty measure, though the material interest of the state was unchanged. Ideology may loom particularly large when it comes to goal-setting exercises like the MDGs and SDGs because they do not set up any institution, still less give it a mandate. They do not bind any state to doing anything specific, or even set in train a process for the generation of such commitments (as found in, for example, the 2015 Paris Agreement on climate change).

In the climate change negotiations, the clashing material interests (and corresponding conceptions of justice) of states managed to block any substantial progress for over two decades. In contrast, only two years elapsed between states getting involved in the OWG and the SDGs being finalized. So on the face of it, the problem of pervasive veiling of material self-interest in the language of justice was overcome and negotiators could be observed changing their positions on issues, seemingly persuaded by arguments, just as a deliberative process requires. However, the material stakes were of course lower in the SDGs, meaning the United States in particular did not initially feel the need to exert its weight in the OWG negotiations in a big way (though that changed toward the end of the process). And many of the negotiators in the OWG did not begin with well-formed, let alone entrenched, positions on many of the questions they were negotiating. Negotiators were therefore relatively free to contemplate the shape of the goals as a whole, rather than just bargain for their own state's interests, and they could change positions in response to good arguments – again as good deliberation requires.

Chasek and Wagner (2016) explain the difference between the climate change and SDG negotiations in terms of institutional design. The UNFCCC negotiations have always been multilateral, with up to 194 states all needing to sign off on anything significant. In contrast, the OWG that finalized the SDGs had only thirty seats (seven for Asia-Pacific, five for Western Europe and 'others' (Anglosphere and Israel), five for Central and Eastern Europe, six for Latin America/Caribbean, seven for Africa). Though Chasek and Wagner (2016) do not use the word, the OWG practised an innovative form of 'minilateralism' as opposed to multilateralism (as advocated by Naím 2009, among others). The thirty seats were in turn shared among seventy states. This meant 'troikas' of states had to share a seat; the number in each troika varied from one to four. Some troikas were very unusual in their composition (e.g. Iran, Nepal, and Japan). Each troika had to come to a common position on all points.

The OWG managed to avoid the prolonged impasses that characterized the UNFCCC and its discussions were more civil and measured than has often been the norm on climate change, where organized climate change denial has been accompanied by vicious personal attacks on climate scientists (Dunlap and McCright 2011). Before getting to negotiation about the content of the goals, there was a stocktaking phase geared toward shared understandings. The membership of each troika in some cases cut across – and so undermined – entrenched and often cohesive negotiating blocs such as the G77 group of developing countries or the European Union (EU). Agreement proved much more easily achieved across 30 rather than 194 parties. Paradoxically, all those 30 parties also agreed that their list of goals and targets was too long, but found themselves unable to shorten the list, because that would have unravelled the entire agreement. If a group of states was tenacious enough, it could ensure its preferred goal (or target) was somehow incorporated, even in the face of continued opposition from other states (such as the Saudi opposition to Goal 5 on gender equality). The African countries insisted on the need for Goal 17 on effective institutions (needed to facilitate investment), and small island states were successful in securing Goal 14 on oceans (Kamau et al. 2018: 117–18).

There was no need to constitute small contact groups as often happened in the UNFCCC negotiations (except until the last days of the OWG); such groups tend to exclude under-resourced and non-English speaking parties. In addition, the OWG adopted a number of procedures that facilitated agreement and flexibility. The process was transparent and there were opportunities for input from global civil society that were actually welcomed by negotiators: as a US delegate said, 'they helped us learn' (Kamau et al. 2018: 125). However, civil society was present mainly in the form of the Major Groups recognized by the UN, which constitute a privileged group of insiders. The OWG developed an ethos of common purpose that did not reflect entrenched blocs and an openness to ideas from different sides. Chasek et al. (2016) lament the fact that after the OWG had run its course and the SDGs were adopted, negotiations on the Development Agenda returned to traditional polarized blocs. Yet what the OWG produced was decisive in determining the content of the SDGs.

The OWG did, then, move to decisive outcomes much more quickly and in more deliberative fashion than could a multilateral process such as the UNFCCC. Rapidity does not necessarily equal effectiveness in promoting global justice. As we have seen, the content of the SDGs and their associated targets is substantively imperfect, and constitutes too long a list even from the perspective of those who finalized it (the OWG). But perfection is never realistic in global governance.

Democratizing the Engagements of States

The history of the role of states in both climate justice and the SDGs contain hints of how deliberative democratic innovation can promote progress toward global justice.

In the case of climate justice, the 2015 Paris Agreement suggested that pervasive state intransigence was beginning to crack, and formally at least the vast majority of the world's states could now be enlisted in the control of greenhouse gas emissions. In the absence of any formal compliance mechanism, the agreement relied on what international relations scholars call 'orchestration' (Abbott et al. 2015). Orchestration involves enlisting civil society intermediaries in the role of monitoring and evaluating the performance of states in terms of their emissions reduction pledges, and exerting pressure on states to ratchet up their commitment. As such, orchestration enhances the accountability of states – which is a democratizing move (as we will see later, however, it may detract from other democratic roles that civil society organizations can play).

This accountability aspect of orchestration suggests one way in which the problematic aspects of states as agents can be ameliorated by deliberative-democratic means. Accountability here means that state practices and performance have to be justified publicly, not in terms of the material interest of the state, but in terms of some more general conception of the (transnational) public interest. Even if they lack public interest motivation, states here can be subject to what Elster (1998: 12) calls 'the civilizing force of hypocrisy', which could eventually induce states to behave in ways consistent with their public expressions – as opposed to underlying material interests. Moreover, these material interests are not immune to deliberative reformulation: for example, if it can be argued that a shift from coal to renewable energy is good for the economic growth of the state in question.

The general point here is that expanding their deliberative engagements can help correct for the problematic aspects of states as formative agents of justice by making it harder to manipulate the language of justice to serve material interest. (As we have noted, there can also at times be defensible congruence between material interest and justice, which itself can be revealed in deliberation.) In a deliberative setting, other actors will have the opportunity, ability, and incentive to scrutinize and expose such manipulation. Deliberative engagements can be with other states – and with many other actors, including civil society organizations and citizens. Deliberative engagements with civil society can be difficult because some states in international negotiations (especially undemocratic states) resist the idea that non-governmental organizations (NGOs) have any legitimate standing – and developing countries can be very wary of liberal NGOs based in wealthy countries (Anderson 2017). This means that the standing of civil society organizations in deliberative terms needs to be thought about very carefully (we will address this question further in Chapter 5).

In actual engagements between states, there can sometimes be a modicum of deliberation and persuasion – a 'logic of argumentation', as Risse (2000) puts it. But this logic is often crowded out by more strategic behaviour. What might shift the balance toward mutual justification and deliberation? Here, an important deliberative credibility mechanism can help regulate the propensity of states in their international interactions to define justice in terms that serve material self-interest. Actors in general become more credible (and eventually more legitimate) formative agents of justice to the degree they abide by deliberative democratic principles of reciprocity (striving to communicate in terms that can be accepted by those who do not initially share one's framework) and mutual justification, even as they advance notions of justice consistent with their self-interest (Mansbridge et al. 2010). In this light, states could enhance credibility by accepting that the principles they urge upon others should also apply to themselves. So China, for example, could increase its credibility by accepting that the responsibility for historical emissions argument that it applies to developed states also applies to its own sub-population of rich consumers (see Harris 2009). The same might be said for India. The United States for its part could allow that fairness in the terms of trade means accepting that it should not be able to embed more emissions in the goods and services it produces than countries at a comparable level of development (such as Germany and Japan). States that urge principles on others that they are not willing to accept themselves lack credibility and so lose (soft) persuasive power.

Turning to the SDGs, the procedural innovations of the OWG described earlier have much to commend them in deliberative terms.

First and perhaps most obviously, face-to-face deliberation is (just about) possible when there are thirty participants – but not when there are 194 parties. Face-to-face deliberation can only work in small groups. Thirty is the very upper limit to effective group size here. This is why most designed deliberative processes either feature small numbers of participants (the typical number for a citizens' jury is around twenty) or divide larger numbers into smaller groups for face-to-face deliberation, meaning deliberative polls and citizens' assemblies can have up to several hundred participants. (In Chapter 8 we will address how much larger numbers of participants can be linked in a deliberative system.) Parliamentary chambers can have several hundred members, but any real deliberation in parliaments generally occurs only in small committees. Communication on the floor of parliament is mostly ritual performance whose point is not to persuade one's opponents to shift their position (Tanasoca and Sass 2019).

Aside from being enabled by its small size, deliberation in the OWG was promoted because its composition meant that any positions taken were not entrenched as markers of national or bloc identity. Thus participants could be more open to persuasion by others and more able to be creative in finding ways to meet different concerns (though simply multiplying goals and targets was one easy way to do this). The prolonged information-gathering 'stocktaking' prior to the actual negotiation meant that there was plenty of time for participants to reflect before taking positions on anything. The stocktaking phase highlighted common interest concerns and public goods – rather than the strategic interests or positions of different states and blocs (Kamau et al. 2018: 75). There were also sustained engagements with civil society representatives.

Chasek and Wagner (2016), among others, suggest that the OWG comes off looking better than most global governance processes in democratic terms. Whatever its imperfections in terms of both deliberative process (which could, for example, not completely overcome the obstructive behaviour toward renewable energy of some fossil fuel producing states) and justice outcomes, it did perhaps enable states to be more effective formative agents of justice than in most international negotiations. Observers commented that the OWG differed from many UN processes in the critical questioning and openness among participants, as opposed to the re-stating of entrenched positions (Kjørven 2016), and noted the highly effective role of the chairs in facilitating such interchange. Many of the states involved did change positions in the course of the OWG proceedings. So China did allow the rule of law to be included; developed states did allow Goal 12 on sustainable consumption and production to be adopted, despite initial resistance to it; the United States did not veto inequality across countries being addressed; the G77 and China did retreat on their initial insistence that the principle of 'common but differentiated responsibilities' should pervade all the goals; and many developing countries did rethink their resistance to any suggestion that industrialization should prioritize environmentally friendly technologies. The dynamics were complicated and involved a mix of deliberation and bargaining, and as we noted earlier, simple tenacity could ensure that a goal or target was included in the final list. China's reluctant acceptance of the rule of law is not because China was convinced of its virtues, but rather in return for getting concessions on other goals and targets (Kamau et al. 2018: 203). Not all members of the OWG supported every goal and target in the final set. But in deliberative terms, the SDGs constituted a workable agreement that all of the members could live with. Any continued objections to specific goals or targets were set aside in the interests of the whole package, or at least because each state or group of states got enough of what it wanted.

In short, the case of the OWG shows that there are deliberative and democratic mechanisms available that could enable states in their actions and interactions and interactions to be more effective formative agents of justice. But what of the other main kind of agent with formal authority in global governance, international organizations?

International Organizations

So far in this chapter we have encountered international organizations (such as the UN in general, and the UNFCCC more specifically) mainly as arenas within which states interact. However, it is also possible to treat these organizations as agents (Caney 2013). Erskine (2004: 26) insists that the UN in particular can be analysed as a (potentially) moral agent on the grounds that it possesses 'an identity that is more than the sum of its constituent parts; a decision-making structure; an executive function; ... an identity over time; and a conception of itself as a unit'. To the degree international organizations develop autonomy in the way Erskine suggests, there is a risk that (just like states), when it comes to *formative* agency they will seek to define and advance justice in ways that veil and serve their own interest. Pingeot (2016) describes a 'strategic rapprochement' between the UN (in the form of the secretary general and secretariat) and transnational corporations in the context of the Development Agenda that was undertaken without any authorization from the UN's member states. This rapprochement meant highlighting partnerships with business of the sort that appear in Goal 17: 'revitalize the global partnership for sustainable development'. Such partnerships make sense to the self-interest of the UN as an organization because corporations and foundations can help fund UN activities when member states fail to pay their dues – which happens a lot – though Pingeot (2016: 197) believes that what the UN really wants in this context is for business to lobby governments (especially the United States) to pay up. Given that one main reason for rapprochement was 'to gain legitimacy and authority in a neoliberal world' (Pingeot 2016: 189), the danger here is that the UN will pursue business-friendly neoliberal conceptions of global justice to the detriment of alternatives that involve meeting the needs and interests of the poor more directly (rather than through indirect trickle down).

Sometimes an international organization can exercise autonomy in other directions. We have noted that the SDGs avoid any explicit mention of democracy – due in part to China's influence. However, the UNDP has different ideas. In a document setting out its key role in the implementation of the SDGs, it says: 'Our strategic plan focuses on key areas including poverty alleviation, democratic governance and peacebuilding'.[2] The UNDP can be seen as an important agent in the process, ranging from early scepticism toward the whole idea of the SDGs to eventually helping to drive the process. However, to the annoyance of their leaders, all UN agencies were inhibited from playing a large part in the negotiations on the SDGs given the secretary general's position that they should not be lobbying negotiators on behalf of their own mandates.

At any rate, to the degree an international organization does develop its own autonomy in ways that serve its own interest but constrict the kinds of global justice it can advance, the democratic remedies introduced in the earlier discussion of states become relevant: notably, an

---

[2] See www.undp.org/content/undp/en/home/sustainable-development-goals.html.

expansion of deliberative engagements, be it with states, other international organizations, civil society, or citizens.

In practice, the autonomy of international organizations can be limited because they are conditioned by the treaties that establish them. These treaties are negotiated by states, which means that international organizations will only be granted real power to the degree its exercise is expected to be consistent with the shared core material interests of the states whose support is needed to set organizations up and enable them to operate. (A state can withdraw from or try to undermine any international organization that develops autonomy in ways that do not serve the state's interests.) So the UN Security Council reinforces the core security interests of states (especially the powerful states that are its permanent members), while the IMF, World Bank, and WTO reinforce the core economic imperatives of states. The IMF and WTO pursue and enforce a neoliberal conception of justice that stresses economic growth through unregulated markets and secure private property rights. The World Bank has in the past pursued a similar conception of justice in (for example) structural adjustment programmes that forced austerity policies on governments in developing countries. Remarkably, the World Bank resisted getting involved in the implementation of the MDGs until five years after they were adopted – despite the MDGs being fully consistent with the World Bank's developmental and anti-poverty mission (Kamau et al. 2018: 122).

Their formative agency is problematic to the degree that international organizations stick to principles in a way that is unresponsive to the concomitant production of injustice. The IMF, World Bank, and WTO were long criticized for unbending adherence to the 'Washington Consensus'. The Washington Consensus, so named because it spanned the IMF, World Bank, and US Treasury, all headquartered in Washington, DC, involved a commitment to fiscal discipline, open markets, small government, deregulation, free trade, and foreign investment. Ignoring criticism and other versions of justice is itself a kind of formative agency. The criticisms often come from those who do not share a neoliberal view of justice and point to (for example) the suffering of the poor caused by the austerity conditions accompanying structural adjustment packages implemented by the World Bank, or the suppression of any concern with environmental damage in WTO decisions (Abouharb and Cingranelli 2007). But the criticism also comes from those who thought that (for example) structural adjustment packages impeded rather than promoted the economic growth that is the main justification of neoliberalism. Criticism from the point of view of non-neoliberal concerns implicitly targets the formative agency of international organizations, while criticism from the point of view of economic growth implicitly limits itself to the effectiveness of these organizations in meeting their own ostensible commitments (i.e. their performance as effectors of global justice, albeit justice of an impoverished neoliberal sort).

Redeeming the Formative Agency of International Organizations

How then might international organizations gain a more critical capacity that would make them less problematic agents of justice? This sort of capacity accompanies the deliberative aspects of democracy.

International organizations have some advantages here. International organizations (including the UN General Assembly and UN Security Council) often seek to approach consensus or unanimity among their members, even when a simple majority vote could produce a decision (Payton 2010). This is because in a world where compliance with decisions can be problematic, a decision will carry much more weight and be regarded as more legitimate if it has something close to unanimity backing it. What this means is that the organization's members have to try to take into account the interests of those with whom they have differences. One way to do that is through deliberative interaction in which all sides strive to understand the others' perspectives and craft positions sensitive to all perspectives. A requirement of consensus or unanimity can mean that all participant have to be persuaded, as they cannot be ignored if (for example) they are not in the majority. These considerations open the door to, though of course they do not guarantee, deliberative interactions. Other deliberatively less desirable dynamics are also possible, such as side-payments to buy votes, or a search for a lowest common denominator that all sides can accept. And if formalized (as in the UNFCCC), unanimity norms can enable recalcitrant parties (such as fossil fuel producing states) to paralyse collective action.

Currently lines of influence to, and accountability from, international organizations run mainly to states – often to the executive branches of states with economic or security mandates. Traditionally these are the areas of national government most insulated from democratic input. How might more direct input and accountability be sought, if not via states? Here, engagement with civil society can increase the range of concerns that international organizations must attend to. The extensive framework of consultation with civil society that took place in the formulation of the SDGs is indicative of the possibilities here, though that consultation fell short of holding the UN accountable for implementation of the SDGs (and civil society organizations have their own democratic problems, addressed in Chapter 5). Yet the glass here is half-full, as a comparison with the way that the IMF and WTO operate with much less engagement with civil society attests. Over time, norms of inclusion have increasingly come to pervade international organizations, as illustrated by the contrast between the processes that yielded the MDGs in 2000 and the SDGs in 2015. Engaging those included in deliberative fashion can help advance the legitimacy of both processes and outcomes (Higgott and Erman 2010), such that engagement does not have to be merely symbolic and inconsequential.

More extensive and meaningful engagement with civil society organizations (and indeed other intergovernmental bodies) can accompany the recent trend in international organizations toward orchestration as a mode of governance, which we discussed earlier in terms of how it changes the relationship between states and civil society organizations. In the context of climate change, orchestration is conducted by the UNFCCC – or rather some body within it, involving the secretariat, presidency, and UN secretary general – which enlists civil society to hold states accountable for their emissions reduction pledges, and to help induce ratcheting up of state commitments (Bäckstrand and Kuyper 2017). In the context of the SDGs, Bernstein (2017) argues that orchestration is the only real governance mode available to the UN's High-Level Political Forum on Sustainable Development (HLPF) established in 2013 and charged with overseeing implementation of the goals. (The HLPF was sidelined in favour of the OWG when it came to formulation of the goals and targets, though the OWG did take on board a HLPF report that suggested and specified ten goals.) The HLPF has no direct authority and few resources. As a result it has to orchestrate by recruiting intermediaries and using its powers of influence over other international organizations, and over civil society organizations, which in turn can try to persuade states to implement the goals effectively.

The deliberative worry that accompanies orchestration is that it puts civil society organizations in a subservient role, devoting their finite resources to helping implement the goals of others. As such, they are not in a good position to be independent critics of international organizations, states, and the overall structure, process, and outcomes of global governance. Orchestration may therefore diminish this crucial democratic role of civil society (Dryzek 2017b). However, there is another way of looking at the deliberative potential of orchestration, even though there are no signs this has yet been realized in global climate governance or the SDGs. Orchestration changes the balance of power between an international organization and civil society – because the international organization now needs civil society to achieve its aims. Historically, there has been a lot of inconsequential civil society activity surrounding global governance – any influence on the official climate change negotiations has often been hard to discern, even though civil society activists in their thousands attend conferences of the parties to the UNFCCC. Orchestration means that civil society organizations could demand to be taken more seriously. They are thus better placed to influence the positions taken by international organizations – which includes correcting any tendency of these organizations to pursue their own interests, to backslide on stated justice commitments, or to bend too easily to powerful states obstructing justice. For the SDGs, the HLPF is already charged (by resolution 67/290 of the UN General Assembly) with 'further enhancing the consultative role and participation of the major groups and other stakeholders'. Orchestration provides an opportunity for that role to become more meaningful in deliberative terms.

More confrontational action from global civil society can also play a part. Disruption and protest can sometimes play a deliberative role by inducing international organizations to reflect upon and change their principles and practices. According to the World Bank's former chief economist, anti-globalization protests beginning in 1999 had exactly this kind of effect on the operating principles of the World Bank as it re-thought its commitment to the Washington Consensus (Stiglitz 2002).

Finally, international organizations themselves can sometimes induce broader deliberative practice in the international system.

Milewicz and Goodin (2018) discuss the case of Universal Periodic Review of all countries established in 2006 and coordinated by the UN's Human Rights Council. This mechanism forces countries to justify their records and intentions to other states, to civil society, and to the UN, thus advancing human rights norms globally, with real consequences for national practices on human rights.

Conclusion

Though central to global governance, states and international organizations are structurally problematic but not irredeemable formative agents of justice. States have priorities and imperatives unrelated to justice that are rooted in security and economics, which can get exported to international organizations. When they do engage questions of justice, states can bend them in ways that serve their own material interest; this tendency too can be exported to international organizations. These problematic tendencies can, however, be corrected (though not eliminated) through deliberative and democratic engagements that induce critical and reflective capacities. We have set out the deliberative-democratic ways in which justice can become something more than a rationale for material interest or something that can be safely ignored, notably through the following:

- Deliberative forums in minilateral negotiations (as suggested by the OWG on the SDGs).
- Deeper engagements with civil society and citizens making it harder to manipulate the language of justice to serve material self-interest.
- The need to establish and maintain credibility in public justification meaning that principles get more effectively embodied as guides to state behaviour, such that state interests can be reformulated in deliberative fashion.
- Norms of consensus and unanimity in the decision making of international organizations inducing member state representatives to take into account the interests of others, and appeal to common interest justifications.
- Compliance with growing norms of inclusion in global governance, which can be sought in deliberative fashion, which in turn can enhance the legitimacy and so effectiveness of collective decisions.
- Critique accompanied by protest-inducing reflection on principles.

- The need for orchestration to implement agreements enhancing the likelihood of a meaningful deliberative engagement involving states, international organizations, and civil society.

The mechanisms here mostly depend on engagement with others – not just other states and international organizations, but also non-state actors of various kinds that we will meet in subsequent chapters. Each engagement may not look very consequential in isolation, but together they become more significant as components of larger deliberative systems involving different kinds of actors and agents. However, these other agents can themselves be problematic, as we will see in the next chapter on the rich, corporations, and foundations, for which somewhat different deliberative-democratic correctives prove appropriate.

4 | *Democratizing Money*
The Rich, Corporations, and Foundations

Money talks when it comes to global justice, no less than elsewhere. But what does money say? And does what money says have any legitimate role in determining the content of global justice? The persistence of injustice in a world dominated by the wealthy suggests immediately that they should not be relied upon to secure justice. That, however, does not preclude them playing a role in ameliorating injustice, especially if they were to do better than they have in the past.

In this chapter we will address and evaluate the parts played in global justice by those with money: specifically, the rich, corporations, and foundations. Corporations and foundations are a bit different from the rich in general because they have organizational purposes. Corporations then differ from foundations in that the purpose of corporations is to generate profits, while the purpose of foundations is ostensibly to do good for others, a purpose that can enter the domain of promoting justice. We will show how the problematic features of the rich and foundations can be ameliorated by embedding them in inclusive democratic deliberation that empowers poorer agents. Corporations are more difficult in that ideally their influence should simply be curbed in order to open spaces for meaningful democratic deliberation. But if that proves impossible, deliberative counterweights to corporate influence should be empowered as much as possible.

There are of course also plenty of questions that might be asked about the structural injustice of systems such as capitalism that enable concentrations of wealth. But we do not intend adding to this vast literature: our concern is with the agency of the rich, corporations, and foundations, not the structures that created and sustain them. We take the basic context of global capitalism as given, not because we believe it is just or defensible, but because we are analysing agents whose wealth depends on that system, so it would make little sense to analyse what they do, could do, and should or should not do with their wealth if that system were radically transformed. The deliberative prescriptions we propose, many of which involve empowering actors who can counter the power of money, for the most part do not challenge the basic structure of the global capitalist political economy, and as such are feasible within it. The only exception comes with our suggestion that the formative agency of corporations should be greatly diminished; but we have a feasible backup should that prove impossible.

The Rich

By the rich we mean not just the super-wealthy who are able to fund causes, but also those with enough surplus wealth to make significant donations across national boundaries. Accordingly, the rich can affect the content of global justice in two major ways. The first involves explicitly formative agency, when wealth is deployed to promote causes in public discourse and public affairs more generally. Here the rich (and it is often the super-rich) are acting as global justice entrepreneurs, to use the terminology we developed in Chapter 2. The second is in voluntarily giving some of their wealth to aid others. We will address these two in turn.

The Advocacy of the Rich

Should they conceptualize justice at all, many of the rich define it in ways that serve their material self-interest, be it in libertarian fashion or through appeal to trickle-down mechanisms for the spreading of wealth. The extreme cases of this tendency are well known. In the United States, the Koch brothers have been active in promoting neo-liberal and libertarian conceptions of justice that emphasize the primacy of untrammelled private property rights – by funding candidates for public office, university programmes and appointments, media campaigns, and think tanks. They have been particularly active in organizing and funding climate change denial, thus implicitly trying to erase any concern with climate justice, and how (for example) climate change might be affecting the poor and vulnerable (Dunlap and McCright 2011: 149). If justice serves self-interest, everything we said in the previous chapter in the context of state behaviour in international negotiations about the need for appeals to justice that serve material self-interest to be subject to democratic deliberation applies here too. As we showed in that chapter, expanding deliberative engagement can serve as a check on the veiling of material self-interest in the language of justice. The problem is that for the rich there are fewer incentives to enter such engagements. Unlike states, the rich do not need to generate legitimacy for their activities, or to be accountable to international organizations and civil society, or to establish credibility in negotiations. In this sense, the rich are much more problematic formative agents of justice than are states.

The rich may though also advance conceptions of justice that are not so obviously a cover for material self-interest, that can, for example, be liberal or social-democratic, even requiring higher tax rates for themselves. Billionaire George Soros has advanced ideas about transnational justice involving liberal rights and liberties and a strong civil society. His Open Society Foundation was active in lobbying for Goal 16 of the Sustainable Development Goals (SDGs) on 'effective, accountable and inclusive institutions' (Harris 2015). Long ago, Friedrich Engels used his wealth to advance (among other things) a radical conception of justice – 'from each according to his ability, to each according to his needs' – formulated by his friend Karl Marx.

Advocacy funded by the rich is problematic irrespective of its ideological content. In a world of multiple conceptions of justice, what should prevail in any given context is the conception (or compromise) that can be backed by the best reasons and considerations, not the one that is backed by the most money. And this is exactly what deliberative democracy promises, with the quality of different arguments and considerations being assessed by all those who will have to live with the consequences, not just by well-funded advocates. It is a corruption of politics when any rich minority gets to determine the content of global justice simply because it is rich.

The Giving of the Rich

Advocacy aside, it might seem that the rich are better placed to effect global justice than anyone else – if justice is conceptualized as something that money can buy through redistribution from rich to poor. If justice is conceptualized instead as a matter of recognition of the full standing and humanity of the disadvantaged and marginalized (see Chapter 1), justice cannot be bought by money – and so justice as recognition is likely to be downplayed if not erased by any emphasis on the effective agency of the rich.

At any rate, the rich by definition possess the wealth that could be redistributed to make the world a fairer place, and as such act as what in Chapter 2 we categorized as effectors or implementers of global justice. Here, as suggested earlier, we can define 'the rich' as those able to donate across national boundaries without adversely affecting their own ability to satisfy the basic needs of life. The category therefore includes anyone making a decent income by developed country standards (including ourselves).

The fact that they possess wealth does not have to mean that the rich always get to choose the kind of justice that this wealth will serve. The rich could instead be compelled to give up some of their wealth through taxation, which could then be redistributed to those in greater need. To a degree this already happens, as taxes in wealthy countries fund aid programmes to poorer countries, as well as a social safety net at home. It has long been recognized within wealthy countries that relying on charity is a poor substitute for transfers organized by a comprehensive welfare state. But there is nothing like the welfare state at the global level, such that charity inevitably looms larger.

If the rich do choose to give away some of their income and wealth in the form of charity (voluntary giving), they may simply be following what they think morality demands of them. This kind of charity does not necessarily come under the heading of justice, especially for moral philosophers who would insist on a distinction between (perfect) duties of justice and (imperfect) duties of charity (see Chapter 2). But charity becomes a question of justice to the extent it becomes important in ameliorating injustice (or, should it go wrong, making injustice worse). The choices made by the rich in deciding where to allocate their giving can affect the weight of different conceptions of justice, and so help give shape to what justice means in the world. It makes a difference on this dimension whether the rich choose to donate to famine relief, or instead to development projects that develop the capabilities of their recipients. It makes a bigger difference still if governments in recipient states look at the amount of voluntary giving and decide that it reduces governmental obligation to act. The consequence may also be that such governments do not have to think about reforming their countries' political-economic systems, and face less pressure from their citizens to alleviate misery, or guarantee rights to the satisfaction of basic needs.

Charity can undermine the impetus for structural reform. Voluntary giving can involve the privatization of global justice. To the extent their giving affects the weight of different conceptions of justice that prevails in the world at large or in more local contexts, the rich become formative agents.

The largesse of the rich is emphasized by some of the more prominent philosophical advocates of global redistribution, notably Thomas Pogge and Peter Singer. Both argue that that the rich should voluntarily give more of their income and wealth to the poor. To Singer (2009), it is unconscionable that people anywhere in the world should be allowed to suffer and die when their suffering and death could be prevented by donations from wealthy individuals. To Pogge (2002), distributive justice applies irrespective of national boundaries, and justice demands that those most culpable for the production of injustice (especially wealthy people) should bear the greatest responsibility for doing something about it. We will have more to say about public intellectuals such as Pogge and Singer in Chapter 5. Here, our concern is with the relatively wealthy individuals that Pogge and Singer target with their arguments.

We now take a closer look at the most explicit attempt to render such giving a powerful instrument of global justice: the idea of effective altruism.

Effective Altruism

Some persuasive appeals to the consciences of the rich have been made under the banner of effective altruism, associated with Singer (2015; see also MacAskill 2015) and the inspiration for a political movement associated with the meta-charity GiveWell. Effective altruism is unremittingly rational and evidence-based in calculating the most good that can be done for a given donation. For example, if you have $1,000, the idea is to identify the very best use for this money – be it for the distribution of mosquito nets impregnated with insecticide to protect against malaria or a programme to eradicate schistosomiasis. The metric on which benefit is assessed can be a matter of individual judgement. It might be lives saved; or lives saved weighted by life expectancy (so children's lives matter more than old people's); or basic needs (beyond mere survival); it could even be sensitive to the well-being of animals, or future generations. GiveWell provides information that enables comparison of different programmes in terms of how much it costs to save one life (as well as other metrics).

At its most ambitious, the movement is not just about how one allocates donations to charity, but how one lives. Careers can be chosen on the basis of how much justice they will produce: is it better to try to become a professor of public ethics, or to train as a doctor and work for Médecins sans Frontières, or to run for political office so as to be able to increase aid budgets? Effective altruism can also be about *becoming* rich to be able to give more. So an effective altruist might choose a career in banking or financial trading in order to make a very high income that can be donated. As Deng Xiaoping is once supposed to have said in a slightly different context, 'to get rich is glorious'.

So what could possibly be problematic about such a rational, evidence-based, ethical approach?

To begin, effective altruists are formative agents who participate in deciding what justice means. That decision is partial. First and foremost, justice for effective altruists means redistributing resources. This proceeds in a context where it is unclear that a transfer of resources from global rich to global poor is a better instrument for promoting the long-term well-being of the poor than (for example) political reforms empowering the poor, or structural changes enabling the poor to compete more effectively in the global political economy (Kuper 2002), or efforts to increase the capabilities of the poor (Sen 2009). For effective altruists, redistribution is guided by a cosmopolitan ethic that treats all lives all over the world as of equal value. This ethic is disputed by more nationalistic theorists of justice, who might, for example, see value in the creation of a national egalitarian society, with a welfare state restricted to its own citizens and residents of the sort that extreme cosmopolitan moralists would have to rule out.

A decision then needs to be made about the metric upon which effectiveness is assessed, and calculations performed to show where money is most efficiently spent (the calculations can be done by experts). Yet whatever the metric, it is the rich who choose it. To put it crudely, an emphasis on redistribution can mean the poor are implicitly seen as holding begging bowls: the question is only, 'which begging bowl is it most efficient to fill?' Effective altruism concentrates agency in the hands of the rich, and denies it to the poor. This is an undemocratic political hierarchy.

For effective altruists, the content of justice is not something to be decided through collective political means, democratic or otherwise. This content is not a matter for formulation by a public authority that then (for example) levies taxes and targets expenditures, or secures a universal basic income, or legislates minimum wages and working standards. The movement prioritizes voluntaristic individual action (such as charity) over the construction and application of collective, accountable public authority, for example in deciding how money should be raised and where and on what it should be spent. Public authority can of course itself be problematic, as we argued at length in the previous chapter on states and international organizations. Our point is simply that effective altruism means it is this formative agency of the rich that is decisive in determining the content of justice – not the agency of the state, or of international organizations, or any democratic system.

The Political Problem with the Agency of the Rich

Contemplation of effective altruism drives home the point that ethical prescription can also generate or reinforce political relationships, and the desirability of those relationships cannot be read off from the desirability of the ethic. The hierarchical relationship reproduced by effective altruism is one in which the rich are active and decisive, while the poor are passive recipients of the actions of the rich. The rich are accountable to nobody and nothing but their own calculations.

The really problematic aspect of emphasizing the agency of the rich – in effective altruism and elsewhere – lies in any distinction between the main agents of justice as the relatively wealthy, and the recipients of justice as the relatively poor. Critics of the approach to global justice taken by advocates of global redistribution such as Pogge (2002) and Singer (2009) point out that ignoring the agency of the poor may have detrimental consequences such as their continued dependence on the largesse of wealthy donors.

Any approach to global justice that involves dependence on the continuing goodwill of wealthy donors violates the key principles of two leading approaches to justice. The first treats justice as a matter of recognition, of validation of the standing and identity of historically oppressed individuals and groups (see e.g. Honneth 2004). Monetary transfer cannot substitute for recognition – and may undermine it, if recipients are constructed merely as recipients of giving. The second is that advanced by republican thinkers such as Pettit (1997) who insist that freedom is not primarily a matter of individual liberties being protected against other people and against potentially oppressive governments. Instead, real freedom is found in non-domination: in not being subject to the discretionary actions of others. In this light, dependency of the poor on the discretion of the rich (to decide, for example, who is deserving and who is not) is a violation of their freedom, because unjust conditions of domination persist – and would continue to persist, even if the rich fully funded the needs of the poor. So even should the rich decide to act upon the pleas of Singer, Pogge, and effective altruists, their agency would still remain problematic. Republican political theorists would point out that so long as the poor depend upon the largesse of the rich, then unjust domination remains. To use the language of Kuper (2002: 116), *the poor are rendered 'moral patients'*. There is no problem in the rich being under an obligation to promote justice by redistributing a portion of their wealth, but they have no moral right to decide what constitutes justice merely by virtue of their wealth.

If this criticism is taken seriously, justice requires the extension of agency beyond the rich toward the poor – especially when it comes to formative agency, whose conclusions about what justice should mean should then determine what the rich do with the money they are willing to allocate in the interests of (redistributive) justice. Rich and poor would then be joined across national boundaries in meaningful deliberative and democratic communication; democracy would be advanced, and plutocracy would be curtailed.

Would such deliberative democratization mean that the rich decide to give less, because they could no longer determine how their donations are allocated? We think not, because such democratization ought to make the rich more confident that their donations really do make the world a more just place, which in the end is a motivation that all altruists, effective or otherwise, surely do share.

Democratizing effective altruism and other approaches to global justice that currently rely on the agency of the rich along these lines is no easy task. There are currently all kinds of barriers to the effective participation of the poor in global processes. We will detail these barriers – and show how they can be overcome – in Chapter 6. Here, though, we need to say a bit more about how the formative agency of the poor could be exercised in relation to the charitable giving of the rich by democratizing altruism. That agency should not be directed in relation to how much the rich give, but rather toward the destination of the funds once the rich have decided to give to the poor. Just as it is possible to rate charities and their programmes according to how well they perform according to the calculus of effective altruism, so it would also be possible to rate these same charities and programmes according to the degree of deliberative participation on the part of the poor they embody, with the idea that this information could inform the donation choices of wealthy individuals. There are a number of ways in which the deliberative participation of the poor might be organized, including tribunals in which the poor could ask charitable organizations to appear to justify their choices, the establishment of relationships between such organizations and poor-led social movements (such as Slum Dwellers International), and deliberative assemblies with targeted recruitment of the poor affected by a particular set of programmes or the activities of a particular charity. We will have more to say about such possibilities in Chapter 6.

Corporations

Like the rich, corporations possess wealth – but they also possess organization and the power that goes with it. A flourishing academic field of business ethics suggest this power can be exercised ethically, though whether business pays much attention is another question. The morality of business has generally been thought of as a matter of corporate social responsibility, rather than justice (Hsieh 2011). In this light, corporations have a responsibility to treat their employees well, respect human rights, attend to working conditions and environmental impacts in their supply chains, and so forth. But justice comes into play in a big way when corporations exercise governmental or public functions, either on their own (Sinclair 1994) or in partnership with national and sub-national governments, international organizations, and non-governmental organizations (NGOs) (Scherer and Palazzo 2011). This exercise has a long history (think of the British East India Company, which effectively governed India). More recently, this role has increased with globalization, under which control over political-economic systems increasingly eludes sovereign states (and where many corporations themselves are complicit in subverting and corrupting the governments of the countries where they operate; see Montero 2018). Justice enters in a still bigger way when corporations get involved in processes that are all about defining justice – we will look at the formative corporate role in the SDGs and climate justice in this light.

The Public Role of Business

Lindblom (1977: 171) insisted long ago that we recognize corporations discharge public functions, beginning with deciding 'a nation's industrial technology, the pattern of work organization, location of industry, market structure, resource allocation, and, of course, executive compensation and status'. More recently, Wettstein (2009) has argued that standards of justice apply to the operations of corporations to the extent they perform governmental or quasi-governmental functions. This happens when (for example) privatization means that corporations provide services (such as health or social welfare) and infrastructure, or regulate themselves in the absence of governmental regulation (as called for in the United Nations Global Compact, to which thousands of corporations subscribe[1]). This kind of self-regulation can be accompanied by voluntary accountability mechanisms, such as the Global Reporting Initiative on sustainability and human rights and Social Accountability International's auditing of labour standards. O'Neill (2001a: 192) argues that especially in the presence of weak and failed states, corporations might usefully take on what she calls primary agency (acting as what we would call effectors of justice), meaning they become the main agents upon whom the obligation to promote justice rests. This in turn requires that they be 'responsible corporations' whose motives cannot be reduced to profit maximization; though as we have just indicated, justice requires more than corporate social responsibility.

For Wettstein (2009), agency here does not just mean that corporations should respect human rights in their operations – that would be uncontroversial as a matter of moral principle (though unfortunately not as a matter of corporate practice), and can apply to just about any actor. Wettstein (2009) argues further that corporations have a duty actively to promote human rights. This task becomes especially

---

[1] See www.unglobalcompact.org.au/about/un-global-compact.

important when they are operating in countries whose governments routinely violate those rights. In practice this might mean promoting rather than just applying standards for working conditions, environmental protection, even free expression, in places where governments would happily see exploited workers, a polluted environment, and jailed critics. Abiding by standards is an aspect of corporate social responsibility; promoting such standards is more a matter of justice.

This idea that corporations should promote justice in this manner draws on Iris Young's (2006) social connection argument about responsibility for justice (Scherer and Palazzo 2011: 913). For Young, all actors enmeshed in and benefitting from a social structure that yields injustice have a responsibility to rectify that injustice. This recognition imposes a heavy burden on corporations (as well as wealthy individuals), not just to examine their supply chains, but also to think about the shape of the capitalist political economy of which they are a part.

These kinds of discussions of the justice responsibilities of corporations often have in mind the operations of multinational corporations in developing countries with weak or corrupt states. But the role of corporations in transnational and global governance comes into sharper focus once we recognize their central role in governance networks that now flourish alongside globalization. These networks join multiple actors that produce collective outcomes without subordination to a government or international organization. They often operate across national boundaries. For example, the New Alliance for Food Security and Nutrition was established in 2012, involving the G8 group of large economies, 10 African countries, more than 50 multinational corporations and 100 African companies, to develop and fund agriculture (McKeon 2014). On some accounts, ours is an age in which governance is displacing government – and networks have a lot to do with this (Peters and Pierre 1998).

In climate change, networked governance is often praised and advocated as an alternative to the failed multilateralism of the UN Framework Convention on Climate Change (UNFCCC) negotiations (the 2015 Paris Agreement notwithstanding). Hoffmann (2011) celebrates what he calls a system of experimental governance, many of whose market-oriented initiatives involve corporations, be it in the Climate Wise consortium of insurance companies, or the Investor Network on Climate Risk. Sometimes corporations form partnerships with national and subnational governments, for example in the Climate Technology Initiative's Private Financing Advisory Network that channels investments in low-carbon technology as well as in adaptation in developing countries. Sometimes the network involves only the private sector, for example Verified Carbon Standard, which regulates and certifies voluntary international markets in offsets (Stevenson and Dryzek 2014: 86–119).

The 2015 Paris Agreement signalled among other things a reconciliation of the top-down multilateralism of the UNFCCC and bottom-up experimental (Hoffmann 2011) or polycentric (Ostrom 2009) governance. Bäckstrand et al. (2017) call this emerging new system 'hybrid multilateralism'. It puts corporations more firmly than ever at the centre of global climate governance, with clear consequences for climate justice, as this new pattern of governance will help determine where the benefits and burdens of emission reduction will fall (e.g. if an offset scheme means displacing peasants in order to plant fast-growing trees).

In sum, corporations are increasingly enlisted to perform governmental functions. Like it or not, they are agents of justice. Mostly this role will mean either implementing or obstructing specific versions of justice, involving, for example, human rights, labour standards, or income security.

But are corporations reliable agents of justice here? The record when it comes to corporate social responsibility – let alone any more demanding corporate justice responsibility – is mixed. Corporations are hard-wired for the pursuit of profit.[2] Indeed, Milton Friedman (1970) famously insisted that their only social responsibility is to increase profit – and if they are to do anything else, it has to be forced upon them by government. In this light, if they have a choice, corporations will support sustainable development, exercise social responsibility, promote human rights, and adopt ethical codes of conduct only to the extent such behaviour is instrumental to profit, possibly because it is good for the corporation's image among potential customers, heads off boycotts, or improves their image among politicians who

---

[2] The 'varieties of capitalism' literature (Hall and Soskice 2001) might suggest this hard-wiring is less absolute when corporations operate in the coordinated market economies of countries in Northern Europe. However, our concern is with corporations in the global system, which never operates as a coordinated market economy.

will make decisions that affect the company. It is not unknown for corporations to highlight their ethical and socially responsible actions in public relations offensives while at the same time polluting, developing fossil fuels in marginal areas, or exploiting their workers. In 2000 BP positioned itself as an energy company that was moving 'beyond petroleum', while continuing to plan for more oil drilling, and eventually showing that fossil fuels really did represent its future (Landman 2010). Seemingly socially responsible corporations still shift manufacturing to where labour and environmental standards are low or non-existent, or pay their own workers less than a living wage.

Any involvement of large corporations in governance means that the causes of, and so remedies for, injustice can only be addressed in limited ways that benefit corporations themselves. This benefit comes either by maintaining the political-economic order in which corporations flourish, or in generating contracts, tax breaks, and positive publicity. Fisher (2011) analyses the role of companies such as Walmart and Target in funding food banks in the United States. Their involvement means that the structural causes of food insecurity – such as the low wages paid by these same companies to their own workers – go unaddressed. The idea that food security could be a human right essential to social justice, as opposed to something to be secured by the market and charity, is also undermined. The anti-hunger organizations that might otherwise raise these kinds of questions do not do so because they fear losing corporate support.

So long as corporations are accountable to shareholders rather than citizens they are unreliable agents of justice who will ensure that if any conception of justice is pursued at all, it will only be done in ways that do not hurt their financial interests. The resultant democratic task here can be framed as the need to counter the shift in authorization and accountability from citizens to shareholders that the privatization of public authority connotes. How then might corporate participation in governance be re-embedded in a system of democratic control? Limited measures might involve making corporations more accountable to publics, governments, and international organizations for their actions, especially when it comes to how they affect human rights. Kobrin (2009) suggests this can done through voluntary agreements, subjection to international law, codes of conduct, or (Kobrin's favourite) codes formulated in public/private partnership. But accountability of this sort means only monitoring the operations of corporations: it is not an effective response to corporate exercise of *formative* agency, when corporations get to define what justice means. To see how this operates, we look at the formative role of business in the process that yielded the SDGs.

The Corporate Role in the SDGs

Business played a substantial role in the formation of the SDGs, early on in membership of the High-Level Panel on the Post-2015 Development Agenda that reported to the UN in 2013, and in the form of the Global Compact (organized under UN auspices) that was established well before the SDGs, describing itself as 'the world's largest corporate sustainability initiative'.[3] Corporate members of the Global Compact commit to principles concerning human rights, the environment, and opposition to corruption, and to an annual report on their progress in these terms. The Compact does not see itself as a lobby for the interests of business, and seeks to work with non-corporate groups in civil society. The Compact is also a network with many national branches that in some cases (such as Australia) were arguably more active than the national government in following up on the SDGs, and inducing corporations to implement them. Pingeot (2016: 190) points out that the UN secretary general and secretariat were pro-active in encouraging corporate participation in the SDG process. Pingeot (2014: 26) also notes the more informal influence of business on policy makers in national governments involved in the process. The mining industry proved especially prominent (Pingeot 2014: 26); obviously if sustainability is defined in a way that makes mining problematic this industry has a lot to lose. The World Business Council for Sustainable Development (WBCSD) was prominent in the Business and Industry Major Group recognized by the UN, which was active in the meetings of the key Open Working Group (OWG) described in Chapter 3. The WBCSD also links itself to implementation of the goals.[4]

Large corporations supported the idea that economic growth is the main driver of development, which infuses the SDGs, implicitly advancing a neoliberal conception of justice. In addition, the SDGs see technology provided by the private sector as essential for the pursuit

[3] See www.unglobalcompact.org.au/about/un-global-compact.
[4] See www.wbcsd.org/Programs/People/Sustainable-Development-Goals.

of sustainability (Pingeot 2016: 191). The private sector is also called upon as a major source of finance for development. Voluntary codes of conduct rather than legal regulation are stressed (Scheyvens, Banks, and Hughes 2016: 373). For example, Target 12.6 is 'encourage companies, especially large and transnational companies, to adopt sustainable practices and to integrate sustainability information into their reporting cycle'.

Goal 17 of the SDGs is to 'strengthen the means of implementation and revitalize the global partnership for sustainable development'. This goal envisages a future in which the UN works in partnership with corporations (Gelbspan 2017) in implementing the SDGs, thus reinforcing the role of business in governance networks that we discussed in the previous section. Such partnerships have a history that dates back at least as far as the 2002 Johannesburg World Summit on Sustainable Development – Goal 17 envisages a major expansion.

The SDGs, and especially Goal 17, validate the idea that businesses can be benign forces for good, as opposed to profit seekers that need regulating in order to avoid harmful social and environmental effects (Spangenberg 2017: 316). At the same time, the SDGs do not address the possibility that the structure of the global capitalist economy could itself be a cause of the problems that the SDGs are designed to address. The title of the 2030 Agenda for Sustainable Development in which the SDGs are presented is of course *Transforming Our World*. Large corporations are being enlisted in what is ostensibly a major effort to remodel the same global order in which they have done so well in the past, so presumably have little incentive to change in fundamental ways (Adams and Luchsinger 2015).

Corporations in Perspective

We have already highlighted a pervasive tendency for actors to conceptualize justice in ways that veil and serve their material self-interest. Given they are hard-wired to pursue material self-interest in the form of profit, corporations are perhaps the kind of actor most susceptible to this tendency. Think for example of the enormous resources they can and do bring to bear in financing campaigns against a tax or regulation that would hurt their interests – and trying to convince publics and politicians that this is a matter of fairness, or necessary to maintain market conditions in which business can flourish and serve the public interest in economic growth and employment. It is no surprise that corporations are often keen on neoliberal or libertarian conceptions of justice that validate their own need for profitability.

Corporations could be reliable formative agents of justice only to the degree they can act ethically without that action being instrumental to their financial interest; in other words, to the degree they cease to be corporations. In this light, corporations have no legitimate role in shaping alone what global justice should mean. In an ideal world, justice requires that corporations should yield to authority that is constituted on a more inclusive and deliberative basis – to democratic authority. As Lindblom (1977: 356) concludes his extensive contemplation of corporations and democracy, 'The large private corporation fits oddly into democratic theory and vision. Indeed, it does not fit.'

In our flawed world, there is no way to stop firms trying to interpret and define justice in ways that serve their material interest, and advancing this definition at every available opportunity. Yet it is possible to at least expose and criticize this activity, and in so doing ensure that corporate formative agency is not decisive in determining what kind of justice (or injustice) shall be collectively pursued. This agency can also be restricted by a refusal simply to transfer public authority to corporations. The practical – if monumental – democratic task is to curb corporate formative agency. This is a task for democracy in general, rather than deliberative democracy in particular.

The specifically deliberative remedies enter only to the degree corporate formative agency (of the kind we see exercised in the case of the SDGs) is accepted as inevitable. Then at least we can insist that the formative activity of corporations should be forced to operate under deliberative conditions that maximize the possibility of scrutiny of corporate claims about the content of justice. Such scrutiny might take place in deliberative forums or in the more informal processes of the larger public sphere. Given the resources that corporations can bring to bear, it is vital that other agents – experts, public intellectuals, critical journalists, advocacy groups, citizens, and the poor – be empowered to take on this deliberative task. We explore ways in which this might happen in Chapters 5 and 6.

The monumental democratizing task of curbing corporate formative agency and the deliberative equalizing task that comes into play when corporate formative agency cannot be curtailed are both hindered by the structure of the capitalist political economy that corporations help constitute. The first priority of contemporary states is the economic one of securing investor confidence in order to secure continued economic growth. This imperative constricts the scope of democracy within states, meaning that it is important to cultivate democracy apart from, against, and across states (Dryzek 1996). One glimmer of light here is that the system of global governance can be less constrained in these terms than the state (even though some international organizations such as the World Trade Organization (WTO) and International Monetary Fund (IMF) reinforce the economic imperative).

Foundations

Foundations are like the rich in that they can choose to give away wealth to serve causes but like corporations in that they are highly organized. They can mobilize resources in a concentrated way that is not necessarily available to the rich in general. And unlike corporations, they are not hard-wired to pursue profit – their core purpose is to give money away, not make it – and so they ought to have more discretion in how they can allocate resources. Our discussion here will emphasize large foundations that operate globally and look for social problems to solve. We will conclude that foundations need to be embedded in inclusive deliberative relationships with those who are the targets of their programmes.

The Public Role of Foundations

Foundations such as Rockefeller, Ford, and the UN Foundation (founded by CNN mogul Ted Turner) in some respects have a larger public and governmental role than corporations. They are active in anti-poverty programmes, education, health, agriculture, human rights, the promotion of good governance, environmental policy, and adaptation to climate change. Large foundations can take on essentially governmental roles in programme design and delivery, but with none of the accountability to which governments can (sometimes) be subject. Indeed, foundations are even less accountable than corporations, because they have no customers who might stop purchasing their products if they do not like what the organization is doing (Reich 2013).

Foundations establish partnerships with international organizations and states, and the massive funds some of them can deploy gives them policy-making influence and power. The resources available to them have grown along with global inequality and the concentration of wealth in the hands of the mega-rich (Martens and Seitz 2015). The biggest such operation is now the Bill and Melinda Gates Foundation, which has assets of over \$40 billion and gives away up to \$4 billion a year in grants. Active primarily in the areas of health and agriculture, the Gates Foundation spends more on global health programmes than any country, and covers more than 10 per cent of the budget of the World Health Organization. The Gates Foundation is also a dominant player in funding health research, especially on tropical diseases such as malaria.

The Gates Foundation chooses to spend money on some things, but not on others. In agriculture, it funds programmes involving genetically modified organisms and high use of chemicals; it has no interest in agroecology and food sovereignty that would involve local control and the deployment of local knowledge as opposed to integration into a global corporate system (Curtis 2016: 6). In health, it promotes vaccination; but downplays sanitation, clean water, and public health (Curtis 2016: 14). It funds programmes largely administered by NGOs, but does not help build infrastructure and the health policy capacity of governments in developing countries, preferring a privatized approach (Curtis 2016: 14). It does exhort governments in both developed and developing countries to do better. The Rockefeller Foundation has been pushing similar priorities in the areas of agriculture and health for much longer than Gates. Along with the Ford Foundation, Rockefeller led the original 'green revolution' in the 1950s and 1960s that deployed technology and chemicals to increase crop yields in developing countries.

The Gates Foundation promotes public–private partnerships (see our earlier discussion of corporations). It works closely with big pharmaceutical companies and opposes efforts to make their drugs more cheaply available in developing countries. It works with Monsanto on genetically modified foods and with Cargill to promote more productive soya monocropping (Curtis 2016: 20).

Beyond the programmes that it funds, the size and scope of the Gates Foundation's activities buy it a place in global policy making, in the UN and elsewhere. The Gates Foundation's media programmes help ensure that what it does gets favourable coverage (Curtis 2016: 15). When there was global move for a moratorium on controversial gene drive technology that it favours, the Gates Foundation paid a public relations company to recruit pro-gene drive scientists to participate in a UN-organized expert forum on the issue.[5]

The Gates Foundation has been active in the process that yielded the SDGs. However, leaders of the foundation (including Bill Gates himself) have criticized the large number of goals and targets, the lack of priority across them, and their hazy aspirations, advocating instead more concrete and achievable targets (Martens and Seitz 2015: 18). The UN Foundation and Rockefeller are less equivocal in their support for the SDGs. Rockefeller led the Post-2015 Partnership for Philanthropy, established in 2014 to strengthen the role of foundations in the Development Agenda.[6] The website www.sdgfunders.org tracks foundation contributions to each of the seventeen SDGs – identifying a total of $49 billion in 2016 (though most of this funding was already happening without reference to the goals).

The Gates Foundation takes sides on controversial issues of global justice and economic globalization. Its approach to development validates the role of multinational corporations in health and agriculture, high-technology solutions, and neoliberal economics. It has little interest in structural change in the global political economy. The Gates Foundation helps determine that global justice will be ordered according to a specific set of priorities that its executives decide – which are not necessarily the priorities of people, especially poor people, in the developing countries where it operates. It is a weighty formative agent of justice in global affairs.

In taking and advancing these positions, the Gates Foundation is not formally accountable to anyone or anything except the US legal system under which it is established. Because it is seen as a force for good, it evades much of the scrutiny that attends the operations of multinational corporations. Criticism is further muted to the degree organizations on the ground in developing countries do not want to alienate a potential funding source.

The core problem with foundations lies in their large and growing power to establish and reinforce conceptions of global justice that they decide for themselves, which would not necessarily stand up to either analytical or democratic scrutiny. As James Kwak puts it in

[5] See http://genedrivefiles.synbiowatch.org/2017/12/01/gates_foundation_pr.
[6] See www.issuelab.org/resources/22480/22480.pdf.

commenting on Facebook founder Mark Zuckerberg's Chan Zuckerberg Initiative (established legally as a limited liability company rather than a foundation), the promise is effectively 'I pledge to keep all of my wealth and use a lot of it to make the world a better place, provided I get to define "a lot" and "better"'.[7] Foundations play a heavy role in producing and reinforcing political order, not only justice. In the case of the Gates Foundation, this political order is privatized and hierarchical. In treating poor people in developing countries as the recipients of aid and technology, it erodes republican freedom in the way we analysed earlier in our discussion of the rich – but now in highly organized and vertically integrated fashion, stretching from the global headquarters in Seattle to villages in Africa. This hierarchy is illustrated by the way the Gates Foundation in 2019 trialled genetically edited mosquitos (with a gene drive to eradicate the species that carries malaria) in Burkina Faso without adequate consultation with the local population, leading to charges of neocolonial practice (African Centre for Biodiversity 2019).

Democratizing Foundations

The global activities of foundations undoubtedly save lives and promote welfare, and they can advance justice in terms that benefit the poor and marginalized directly (rather than mask their concerns by aggregating them into states, which is what international justice as practised in global climate governance and elsewhere does). But that is not sufficient reason to let them define what global justice means, and how it should be pursued. Deliberative democratic scrutiny would force foundations to defend what they do in light of competing conceptions of justice – not just the one they have chosen – so that they do not inadvertently produce injustice along lines we have indicated.

Democratic participation by the poor themselves (along with other stakeholders) in the implementation of programmes on the ground has been the staple of a 'participatory development' approach for some decades now (endorsed by the World Bank, among others), but that is not our concern here. When it comes to how principles of justice get formulated globally, and embodied in programmes, it is important to

[7] See https://medium.com/bull-market/mark-zuckerberg-s-45-billion-loophole-7dcff7b811b3.

involve the poor themselves in the design of programmes and contemplation of the principles that underlie them. In addition, foundations ought to be responsive to critical scrutiny from old and new media and civil society. To a certain extent the scrutiny already occurs, for example in the Global Justice Now report on the Gates Foundation that we have cited (Curtis 2016) – to which the Gates Foundation made only a dismissive response. Foundations are not in a good position to engage with their critics because they must not only do good, but be seen to be doing good. The people who fund, run, and work for foundations believe strongly that what they are doing is right and just, and that belief in itself can make them reluctant to engage critics. But engagements with those at the receiving end of programmes as well as critics would yield not just democratic but also epistemic benefits in ensuring that the full range of relevant kinds of knowledge and ethics are brought to bear. Realization of these epistemic benefits requires not just participation, but also deliberation, in order to ensure that the different bits of knowledge held by different sorts of agents, poor and wealthy alike, can be integrated productively and creatively (Landemore 2012). The relevant knowledge might be in the hands of poor-led social movements (such as Slum Dwellers International and La Via Campesina), and communities who are the target of foundation programmes – not just in the hands of foundation leaders and the experts they employ. And if the epistemic argument holds, enlightened foundations ought to recognize these epistemic benefits and so welcome the kind of inclusive deliberation we have proposed.

Conclusion

The medium of money is of course essential when it comes to achieving global justice; though there are some kinds of justice (such as recognition) that money cannot buy. That does not mean that those in possession of the most money – be they the rich, corporations, or foundations – should have a decisive formative say in the kind of global justice that should be served. However, the formative agency of those with money can be redeemed by:

- subjecting the advocacy of the rich on behalf of any conceptions of justice to inclusive deliberative scrutiny;
- crafting deliberative relationships encompassing rich and poor;

- bringing rich donors and the charities they support into deliberative accountability relationships with the poor who are the object of their concern;
- rating charities and their programmes according to how well they embody the deliberative participation of the poor;
- establishing tribunals before which donors could justify their choices to the poor;
- creating deliberative assemblies of the poor to examine the priorities of charities and foundations;
- curbing the *formative* agency of corporations; and
- empowering deliberative counterweights if corporate formative agency cannot be curbed.

In the end, democracy, not money, should talk.

5 | Democratizing the Power of Words
Experts, Public Intellectuals, Advocacy Groups, and the Media

Words matter, in global governance no less than elsewhere, for governance is transacted through the medium of language. Even the exercise of power generally needs to be justified to those subject to it in terms of reasons; and that need opens the possibility for power to be challenged (Forst 2015). In this chapter we examine the agents whose ability to influence the content of global justice depends mainly on the content of the words they can muster, be it in contemplating and specifying basic principles of justice (pure formative agency) or advocating principles and actions that flow from them (global justice entrepreneurship). Experts and public intellectuals (there is some overlap between the two categories) rely pretty much exclusively on words (and numbers) to exercise influence, though words without reputation or credibility and performance are not enough. Advocacy groups can sometimes mobilize material resources as well as words, for example in promising support in an election campaign in return for support for their position, or in organizing boycotts of a misbehaving corporation. They can sometimes receive formal recognition from international organizations such as the United Nations (UN) (especially in the form of the Major Groups). But in international politics, it is the arguments and rhetoric they can muster that matter most.

We will also examine the role of the media. Unlike experts, public intellectuals, and advocacy groups, the media is not a category of agents. However, media figures (be they journalists, bloggers, or trolls) are agents. And the media channels, mediates, amplifies, interprets, and softens the communicative activity of many kinds of agents. The role of social media in changing the terms of political communication is now well recognized. But the traditional media of print, television, and radio is still with us, and so are its standards and biases for what counts as newsworthy.

We will examine experts, public intellectuals, advocacy groups, and the media and their discursive activity that is consequential in determining the contours of global justice. We conclude that their exercise of formative agency is redeemable to the extent it proceeds in deliberative and democratic fashion, both in itself and in relation to other actors and processes. This democratization can begin with deliberation across the disagreements of experts, public intellectuals, and advocacy groups. But it cannot end there, for such deliberation must involve broader publics, for the sake of effective definition of what justice should involve, not just democratic legitimacy. In the case of advocacy groups, deliberative engagement with constituents is crucial to redeem representation claims. Good deliberation requires reflection, not just expression, which is why we will stress the need for reflective spaces and venues, inside the media, and beyond.

Experts

The influence and authority of experts rests on their deployment of some body of knowledge established in a professional community (be it science, economics, social science, engineering, ethics, or policy analysis). The role of experts in the policy process generally involves direct advisory links to formal authority that do not have to be mediated by public opinion. There is, however, some overlap between experts and public intellectuals when an expert increases his/her public profile.

Democracy and expertise have long been seen in tension (this goes back at least to Plato; see Popper 1966). Especially in the context of complex problems, there are persistent worries that democracy may be overwhelmed by technocracy or governance by experts (Fischer 1990), though governance by those with the most knowledge has its advocates (Brennan 2016).

Experts in the Sustainable Development Goals and Climate Justice

On a stylized account, the Millennium Development Goals (MDGs) were formulated by a small group of UN experts (Ford 2015), then adopted by the UN as a whole. If so, the MDGs are on the face of it a good example of technocracy, with experts as the key pure formative agents as well as entrepreneurs (though real technocracy would involve the crafting and implementation of policy actions, not just goals).

Defenders of technocracy could say that there was nothing much wrong with this. The MDGs provided metrics for assessing progress that were widely considered to be useful guides, which is why when they expired, replacement global goals were widely seen as necessary, eventually yielding the Sustainable Development Goals (SDGs).

In reality, the MDGs were the final product of a process that involved more private and public actors than the stylized account suggests (Hulme 2007). At the same time, there was widespread dissatisfaction with the political legitimacy of the relatively narrow way the MDGs had been formulated, which largely explains the move to a more inclusive process for the SDGs. However, experts took their place in this new process – though now in multiple locations and phases. Experts were important in helping to set the initial agenda for the SDGs and think tanks (such as the International Institute for Environment and Development) got in early. The prominent Sustainable Development Solutions Network (SDSN) is another good example. The SDSN is composed of scientists, social scientists, statisticians, and technological experts (along with a few politicians and representatives from business and non-governmental organizations (NGOs)). Many of its members are high-profile in their disciplines. It was founded in 2012, directed by Jeffrey Sachs, and reports to the UN secretary general. In 2013 the SDSN produced *An Action Agenda for Sustainable Development* specifying ten 'priorities' that bear a clear family resemblance to both the MDGs and SDGs.[1] The simplicity of these priorities echoes the MDGs, but their substantive content moves in the direction of the broader SDGs. So the ten priorities could be seen as an intermediate step between the MDGs and SDGs. The SDSN was very assertive and entrepreneurial (Kamau et al. 2018: 126–7), and it is much easier to trace its influence than it is to figure out the influence of all the public consultation exercises conducted on the SDGs that we will cover in Chapter 6. The year 2013 also saw the establishment of the Intergovernmental Committee of Experts on Sustainable Development Financing. Despite its name, its proceedings were not confined to experts, as it also organized consultations with civil society and business.[2] This committee issued reports on financing, though the

[1] See http://unsdsn.org/resources/publications/an-action-agenda-for-sustainable-development.

[2] See https://sustainabledevelopment.un.org/intergovernmental/financecommittee.

SDGs themselves were silent on who should finance their pursuit. The other relevant body of experts is the Scientific and Technological Community Group that is one of the Major Groups recognized by the UN; on the SDGs, they were (on interview evidence) more internally deliberative than the NGO Major Group.

What the SDGs lack is a high-profile scientific assessment body like the Intergovernmental Panel on Climate Change (IPCC) or Intergovernmental Science-Policy Platform on Biodiversity and Ecosystem Services (IPBES). The IPCC traditionally focused on assessing and summarizing the findings of climate science (though as its 'intergovernmental' title suggests, its findings are edited by representatives of governments, in the production of the summaries that are its most readable outputs). Climate justice was initially not on its agenda. However, this changed with the addition of ethical analysis in its Fifth Assessment Report (in Working Group III's contribution on 'Social, Economic, and Ethical Concepts and Methods'), published in 2014, which as a result contains material on justice. Several philosophers (including John Broome and Simon Caney) participated.[3] The ethical analysis does not reach any prescriptions. That would be overstepping the mark of what the IPCC is supposed to do in deploying any kind of knowledge, including natural science and social science. But the analysis does try to synthesize the relevant literature, uncover implicit ethical implications in technical decision making, clarify the ethical issues at stake, and in general promote the idea that climate justice should be on the agenda (Pickering 2018). In that sense it did strive toward some fairly pure formative agency. The SDGs also lack a consensual 'epistemic community' of the sort that can sometimes be seen on global issues – including climate change (though such a community did exist on specific goals and was notably instrumental in getting Goal 14 on oceans adopted). Such a community combines experts (usually scientists) and activists, and has been instrumental in (for example) global action on ozone layer depletion (Haas 1992).

The Limitations of Expertise

The conventional approach to the role of experts in policy making would be that they simply give advice to be acted upon by decision

---

[3] See www.ipcc.ch/assessment-report/ar5.

makers and keep their distance from the political fray. But that model fails in several circumstances:

1. When expertise itself becomes politicized.
2. When lay as well as expert knowledge is pertinent.
3. When expert advice contains unacknowledged political implications.
4. When experts cannot resolve their disagreements with one another, especially when they come from different backgrounds.
5. When technical expert advice is resisted because it seems to contradict the common sense established in dominant discourses.

All these conditions arise in climate justice. On the first condition, climate science is highly politicized. Politically motivated attacks try to undermine the credibility of scientists and their findings (Dunlap and McCright 2011), leading in some cases to policy paralysis as fights over the science preclude even getting to questions about justice. For the second, lay knowledge is clearly relevant when it comes to local adaptations to climate change, for example in trying to ascertain the consequences for poor farmers of any change of crop composition in response to changing rainfall and temperature patterns. For the third, geoengineering may look promising in cost–benefit technical terms (Lomborg 2010), but has dramatic political consequences, requiring centralized and permanent global governance on a scale unprecedented in human history, with consequences for human rights globally. For the fourth, ethicists and economists disagree about the appropriate discount rate to apply when it comes to climate change. The Stern Review in the United Kingdom famously used a low discount rate of 0.1 per cent in the interests of intergenerational justice, so that future generations were not disadvantaged by an emphasis on what happens in the near future (Stern 2007). Economists such as Nordhaus (2007) were horrified, because it contradicted the idea that discount rates should reflect the market return on investments, and so be around 3 per cent. The difference between 0.1 per cent and 3 per cent has massive consequences for global action (and reflects a dispute between two conceptions of justice). For the fifth, ethical arguments such as that justice requires a special concern for the vulnerable wherever they live and that obligations depend on income level, not country of residence, have a hard time gaining traction against a dominant discourse that sees justice in international as opposed to global terms. In this distinction, established by Brown

(2006), international justice treats nation states as the units of concern and obligation.

In the case of the SDGs, expertise is not as heavily politicized as in the case of climate change, and so the first condition does not apply, but the other four do. For the second condition, lay knowledge is pertinent, for example, when it comes to exposure to health risks and hazards – Target 3.9 is: 'By 2030, substantially reduce the number of deaths and illnesses from hazardous chemicals and air, water, and soil pollution and contamination'. Experts such as epidemiologists often have a hard time confirming claims of health damage made by those exposed to pollution (Brown 1992). Such exposure is of course greatest among the poor and vulnerable. For the third condition, unacknowledged political implications of expert advice, the field of development in general is riven with technocratic interventions that change the distribution of power. For example, the introduction of genetically modified crops may increase yields, but at the same time create a relationship of dependence on multinational biotechnology companies that undermines local community control, and diminishes the agency of individual farmers (Lapegna 2016). For the fourth condition, relevant to Goal 8 on economic growth, economists generally reject the kinds of ecological limits to aggregate human economic activity that ecologists find so important. For the fifth condition, relevant to Goal 10 on reducing inequality, expert findings about the corrosive social effects of material inequality on everyone, not just on those worse off (Wilkinson and Pickett 2009) are resisted by policy makers and politicians who have thoroughly assimilated neoliberal ideology, for whom such inequality provides appropriate incentives to make the economic system grow.

Expertise and Politics

Under any of the five circumstances we have listed it is necessary to involve experts in political dialogue. In this dialogue, expert knowledge itself (be it climate science, ethics, epidemiology, or economics) need not be the target of reformulation. However, the degree to which the knowledge in question should guide public decisions is a legitimate matter for public deliberation. Deliberative processes should not be seen simply as ways of checking expert knowledge. They can also enable expert knowledge to be utilized more effectively, for example in providing information about public perceptions of risks, in integrating expert and lay knowledge, and indicating what sorts of expert communications are likely to find public acceptance.

It is not hard to find the interface between experts and politics working poorly. Ethicist John Broome's (2014) reflections on his experience as a member of the IPCC in producing its Fifth Assessment Report contain a lament about what happened in the move from the full report of his Working Group to the summary. The full report, produced by the experts alone, is long at 2,000 pages and read by few. The 'Summary for Policymakers' is much shorter at 30 pages, and more likely to be noticed and read. It is in producing the summary that representatives of governments (107 sent delegates) enter the picture. They edit the text in a tortuous process requiring consensus on every sentence that leaves little of the original language unscathed. Government representatives here were largely protecting the interests of their own states, interpreting justice in self-serving ways (along the lines discussed in Chapter 3). So, on Broome's account, a group of countries (led by Saudi Arabia) wanted to delete any mention of how emissions growth differed by the income group to which a country belonged, because it made these countries look bad.

The IPCC and UN Framework Convention on Climate Change (UNFCCC) exist at some distance from each other, though UNFCCC negotiators can, if they wish, read IPCC reports. A somewhat closer relationship between experts and representatives of states can be seen in the process that yielded the SDGs. The key Open Working Group (OWG; discussed in Chapter 3) in its early 'stocktaking' phase heard from and could question eighty-seven experts of many nationalities drawn from universities, UN agencies, other international organizations, and research centres (see Kamau et al. 2018: 269–74 for a list). Their expertise covered areas such as development, economics, agriculture, energy research, water policy, health care, finance, governance, urban studies, and forestry (but not ethics). These presentations helped set the agenda for the OWG. There were also many interactions with the experts organized into the SDSN, including meetings with the co-chairs of the OWG and with individual delegates. The SDSN produced a number of reports for the OWG. The picture is one of sustained interaction between experts and negotiators; and as we saw in Chapter 3, the OWG did have some deliberative features, which extended to its interactions with experts.

Democratizing Expertise

Missing in the engagement between experts and the state representatives on the OWG were the voices of publics, and especially of the most vulnerable (some advocacy groups were involved in the OWG proceedings, but they do not constitute publics). As argued earlier in the chapter, it is necessary to hear from publics because of the relevance of lay as well as expert knowledge when it comes to many of the issues that the SDGs address. It is necessary to hear from the most vulnerable, particularly when well-intentioned technocratic interventions can end up changing power structures to further disadvantage poor and marginal communities. Consultations with publics did take place in the SDG process; but the tracks involving experts and publics were largely separate, and in the end it seems the track involving experts fed more strongly into key policy-making moments (interview evidence). For the sake of producing better policy outcomes – as well as political legitimacy – more effective integration of experts, citizens, and representatives in deliberative and democratic relationships is necessary.

Such integration can draw on a long tradition in deliberative policy analysis (Fischer and Boossabong 2018). Conventional policy analysis is an expert activity that seeks to identify effective means to clarified ends. Deliberative policy analysis broadens participation to affected and interested publics, extends its scope to questions of value and meaning (e.g. the meaning of poverty), and seeks interaction in deliberative terms in order to produce outcomes that have democratic legitimacy while still being effective solutions. Its currency is not the means–ends calculation of conventional policy analysis but rather arguments for and against policies, principles, and practices. Experts still have a place, both as suppliers of substantive arguments about the issue at hand and as people who are in a position to contemplate what good process would look like (exactly what we ourselves are doing here). Given that it admits questions of value and meaning, deliberative policy analysis is clearly much more conducive to the democratic exercise of formative agency than is conventional policy analysis.

One possible process along these lines would involve constituting mini-publics composed of lay citizens to meet in conjunction with expert gatherings such as the IPCC or SDSN. Vast experience around the world with such bodies shows that with enough time and resources they are perfectly capable of coming to grips with complex policy issues, including those that are scientifically or technologically complex such as climate change, health, and genetic technologies (Grönlund, Bächtiger, and Setälä 2014). This kind of connection could then form the basis for outreach to broader publics. We will have much more to say on the involvement of lay citizens and publics in Chapters 6 and 8.

Public Intellectuals

Public intellectuals are thinkers, sometimes academics, who also play a public role and try to reach non-academic audiences. They want their exhortations to be adopted by broad publics, not just by policy makers that experts may seek to influence. Public intellectuals can be experts, but they can also be generalists, and a few serious journalists would also fall into this category. Fuller (2006: 149) suggests that 'the public intellectual is a professional crisis-monger', though the intent in invoking crisis is normally to advance some moral or political agenda. Public intellectuals do of course lack formal authority. Their influence depends not just on the substantive content of what they say, but crucially on how they perform in the dramaturgical sense (Hajer 2009). Credentials, eloquence, personality, and notoriety can all help determine influence, not just pure expertise. This has long been recognized by students of rhetoric, who since Aristotle have stressed the importance of *ethos* – exhibition of the virtuous character of the speaker.

Public intellectuals can exercise what we described in Chapter 2 as pure formative agency (contemplating and establishing principles). More significant is their activity as discourse entrepreneurs who can advance the standing of a particular discourse. In the context of our discussion, this means they can also play an ambitious role as global justice entrepreneurs (see Chapter 2) promoting a certain conception or principle of global justice. In previous chapters we encountered the various discourses of neoliberalism, sustainable development, and human development. Further examples of discourses relevant to global justice include economic nationalism, human rights, anti-globalization, and various religious discourses. A discourse is a shared way of making sense of the world, constructing meanings, establishing common sense, and delineating what kind of knowledge is legitimate. Any discourse depends on assumptions, judgements and contentions that provide terms for communication. Gro Harlem Brundtland and her team established sustainable development on the global stage in the 1980s

(World Commission on Environment and Development 1987). Human development discourse (which underpinned the MDGs) is associated with thinkers such as Amartya Sen (1999) and Martha Nussbaum (2011).

Neoliberalism, the dominant global discourse in economic affairs that now conditions any attempt to pursue global justice, can be traced to the efforts of public intellectuals from the discipline of economics. During her time as prime minister of the United Kingdom, Margaret Thatcher enthusiastically endorsed and pursued the ideas of F. A. von Hayek; former US president Ronald Reagan followed suit, and this conjunction eventually helped consolidate a neoliberal world economic order. The 'Washington Consensus' that spanned the International Monetary Fund (IMF), World Bank, and US Department of the Treasury was central to this order. Milton Friedman was (like Hayek) not only another Nobel Prize-winning economist, but also a publicist, writing popular books and producing a television series (*Free to Choose*). Nobel Laureates in economics can also be found advocating against neoliberalism – think of Joseph Stiglitz, former chief economist at the World Bank, whose profile increased when he turned to public advocacy on behalf of a more social democratic and redistributive approach to global justice (Stiglitz 2006).

Redistributive approaches to global justice can also be grounded in moral philosophy. Philosophers who make a living by thinking, writing, and teaching about justice are not formative agents unless they play a public intellectual role. Among the two most prominent philosophers here are Peter Singer and Thomas Pogge – already encountered in Chapter 4, in the context of their exhortations on behalf of monetary transfers from the rich to the global poor.

Public Intellectuals and the SDGs

The MDGs were, as we have already noted, grounded in a discourse of human development, which can in turn be linked to economist and philosopher Amartya Sen's (1999) approach to global justice, stressing individual human capabilities rather than aggregated income measures. Hulme (2007) argues that the MDGs combine discourses of human development and results-based management. When it comes to the SDGs, their very title suggests they are heirs to the discourse of sustainable development.

Public intellectuals were active on the SDGs, though more in the role of commenting on developments, rather than initiating them. Specific interventions included criticism of the reliance of the SDGs on endless and so ecologically unsustainable conventional economic growth and their failure to address seriously the question of inequality (see, for example, the 2016 'Open Letter to the United Nations' signed by Noam Chomsky, Thomas Pogge, Naomi Klein, and others[4]). Joseph Stiglitz (along with Michael Doyle) did propose a goal to 'eliminate extreme inequality at the national level in every country' along with associated targets and the establishment of oversight commissions in every country to monitor progress (Doyle and Stiglitz 2014), but that was not adopted. Instead, the milder aim to 'reduce inequality within and among countries' was adopted as Goal 10, with the even milder associated Target 10.1: 'By 2030, progressively achieve and sustain income growth of the bottom 40 per cent of the population at a rate higher than the national average'.

Economist Jeffrey Sachs has been one of the more prominent public intellectuals on issues of development, poverty, and the environment in recent decades. He has been a special advisor to the UN secretary general on both the MDGs and SDGs; his idea that the goals need to apply to all countries and embody economic, environmental, and social inclusion, and good governance, is consistent with the way the SDGs were eventually specified. On process, in 2012 he suggested that there should be two core principles for the SDGs: 'active worldwide public participation, political focus, and quantitative measurement; and lessons from the MDGs' (Sachs 2012: 2206). He also reflects the discourse of results-based management in speaking of the need for targets, timetables, and a road map to guide actions (Tyson 2015).

A more sceptical economic take on the SDGs has been developed by the Copenhagen Consensus Centre think tank, headed by the prominent public intellectual Bjørn Lomborg. The Copenhagen Consensus Centre conclusion is that most of the 169 targets under the SDGs are not cost effective and should be rejected, and that instead the world should focus on just 19 of them.[5] Their analysis shows that focusing on these 19 targets would yield an expected net benefit of $10 trillion, as

---

[4] See www.huffingtonpost.com/alnoor-ladha/an-open-letter-to-the-uni_2_b_8197178.html.
[5] See www.copenhagenconsensus.com/sites/default/files/expert_outcome_one_pages_combined.pdf.

opposed to the $2 trillion that is achieved by pursuing all 169 targets simultaneously. These 19 include:

- lowering child malnutrition by 40 per cent (Target 2.2 says, however, 'By 2030, end all forms of malnutrition');
- 'phasing out inefficient fossil fuel subsidies' (the language is again a bit different, Target 12.c actually says, 'Rationalize inefficient fossil fuel subsidies that encourage wasteful consumption by market distortion' followed by some qualifiers);
- 'reduce trade restrictions' (again, Target 17.10 is actually 'promote a universal, rules-based, open, non-discriminatory and equitable trading system' while Target 17.12 refers to 'duty-free and quota-free market access ... for all least developed countries').

The Copenhagen Consensus Centre methodology is cost–benefit analysis, which converts all the costs and benefits of a measure (including lives saved) into money; an example of the kind of conventional policy analysis we mentioned earlier. Cost–benefit analysis was invented by economists to evaluate specific projects (such as building a dam); the Copenhagen Consensus Centre has no hesitation in applying it to planetary scale programmes.

On the face of it, this sort of analysis shows exactly how the SDGs should be designed to best advance global justice. The analysis itself is silent on who pays for the programmes that are needed – but then so are the SDGs themselves. However, cost–benefit analysis is controversial and rejected by many ethicists because in converting everything into the metric of money, its valuations are based on market prices. This includes the value of a life, which can be measured in many ways, including net present value of future earnings. Converting future benefits to present value is also controversial because in deploying a discount rate based roughly on the rate of return on all investments in the economy, it severely downweights anything that happens to future generations, be it for better or for worse (see our earlier discussion of the controversy surrounding the Stern Report on climate change).

Public Intellectuals and Climate Justice

Public intellectuals have also played a part on climate justice, though their role is minor compared to scientists on climate change in general. Lomborg (2007) argued that it would be much better to spend money on combating malaria than on controlling greenhouse gas emissions – thus folding climate justice into global justice more generally, and finding there is no reason to pursue climate justice. This is an odd argument: there is no reason why the world could not both combat malaria and do something about climate change. In addition, his conclusion once again depends on highly controversial cost–benefit analysis.

The more philosophical (as opposed to economic) discourse of climate justice often endorses much stronger action to curb greenhouse gas emissions. Prominent Australian public intellectual Clive Hamilton (2014) believes that 'the ethical winds blow strongly in one direction'. For Hamilton, there is little reasonable disagreement about the essence of climate justice (of the sort set out in Chapter 1). Instead, the problem is only 'moral subversion' by liars, deniers, and people shirking their responsibility (see also Gardiner 2011).

Resolving the Disagreements of Public Intellectuals

Hamilton's assertions notwithstanding, moral disagreement is rife among public intellectuals who bring different frames of reference to bear. There is an enormous difference between the worldview of Milton Friedman, for whom corporations should be free to generate the public good in markets (so long as they are not allowed to collude with government), and that of Noam Chomsky, for whom corporations are inherently oppressive and necessarily connected to unjust government. For the SDGs, we see that some public intellectuals such as Jeffrey Sachs are broadly supportive of the process and content, others such as Noam Chomsky, Thomas Pogge, and Naomi Klein are very critical.

How should the disagreements of public intellectuals be processed? Very rarely, a political leader might be in a position to adopt one idea about justice, impose it on government, and dispense with all other ideas. Former British prime minister Margaret Thatcher once famously took a copy of Hayek's *Constitution of Liberty* and slammed it on a table to interrupt a meeting at her party's research department, saying, 'This is what we believe!'

For all their differences, Clive Hamilton on climate ethics, Margaret Thatcher on neoliberalism, and perhaps some of the more uncompromising philosophical proponents of global redistribution such as

Singer do not accept the political reality of reasonable disagreement. But once we accept the plausibility of different conceptions of justice (such as the multiple conceptions of climate justice set out in Chapter 1), some way is needed to sort out their relative merits. Any attempt to do so in the abstract would only continue the disagreements of academic moral and political philosophy. The alternative is to proceed in particular policy contexts, with a view to deciding only what should be done in that context. Now, such a process might involve only public intellectuals; MacIntyre (1984, pp. 500–1) notes that moral philosophers who disagree on ethical fundamentals can nevertheless often agree on particular policy prescriptions. In this light, it is no surprise that Thomas Pogge (2002), who emphasizes basic human rights, and Peter Singer (2009, 2015), a utilitarian for whom the basis of morality involves best satisfying interests, can and do support each other's conclusions (and even arguments) about measures to promote global redistributive justice.

Why the Resolution Must Be Democratic

Does this mean that we can rely on public intellectuals themselves to deliberate with each other on practical questions (as opposed to first principles), and eventually reach a resolution? Such convergence will not happen when, for example, a neoliberal inspired by Hayek or Friedman encounters a radical critic of capitalism such as Naomi Klein or Noam Chomsky. But there is also something inherently wrong about leaving public intellectuals to decide among themselves what should be done. This follows from the very idea of going public that being a *public* intellectual entails. For in seeking to persuade, the public intellectual must appeal to that public's considered judgement, and thus also respect the public's capacity to question and assess arguments. If the public is hearing from different public intellectuals that also means respecting its capacity to adjudicate across this difference.

This deliberative and democratic approach to the processing of multiple and competing reasonable arguments made by public intellectuals is consistent with the conclusions of several theorists who have contemplated plural justice claims, such as Sen (2009). Similarly, Fraser (2009) seeks democratic adjudication of competing ways of framing justice (such as national versus international versus cosmopolitan). Valentini (2013) believes that under 'deep reasonable disagreement' about what justice requires, democracy in the form of the need for mutual justification across different positions (the essence of deliberation) becomes intrinsic to justice.

The process that yielded the SDGs was interactive but fell short in these terms because competing justice arguments associated with public intellectuals were not adequately processed in public deliberation. Some radical challenges – notably those that questioned the viability of conventional economic growth in light of ecological constraints, or sought recognition of planetary boundaries that cannot be transgressed, or sought a massive reduction in inequality both within and across countries – were sidelined in the pursuit of an international agreement (Hajer et al. 2015; Carant 2017). It is not that these positions were processed in public deliberation and found wanting by all concerned; rather they simply failed to find enough advocates with enough political weight at key moments in the process.

The SDG process did a much better job of accommodating concerns that could be expressed within the dominant discourses of de-radicalized sustainable development, human development, and neoliberalism. Different views could be accommodated either in the same goal or in different goals. So Goal 10 validates both the neoliberal commitment to perpetual economic growth and a weak sustainability commitment to making that growth 'inclusive and sustainable' (while avoiding the radical questioning of whether growth can possibly be ecologically sustainable). Human development appears in many places in the goals and targets, in references to health, education, employment, and so forth.

We should not look at the dismissal of radical challenges in the SDG process and conclude that public deliberation is incapable of processing deep moral disagreement, which is by definition when partisans reject the legitimacy of others' values. Deep disagreement is exactly when public deliberation is most needed, whether or not it involves public intellectuals. Deliberation is still possible and productive under such circumstances. In a seemingly different context, Gutmann and Thompson (1996) examine the possibility of effective deliberation across different sides on the divisive issue of abortion in the United States. They show how some of the values of each side can be reconciled in a search for deliberative agreement on concrete actions such as financial aid for single parents and better education for teenage girls (note that these two proposals have a form similar to the SDGs). Even neoliberals are not committed to endless economic growth because of its intrinsic value, but rather because they think it is instrumental to human well-being. Proponents of planetary boundaries similarly care about human well-being, though they might interpret it in different terms to neoliberals. The generation of a normative meta-consensus in which people from different sides come to recognize the legitimacy of the values of others – even if they do not share those values – can be hard work and may require the reflective reformulation of values on all sides, but it is the central task of deliberation under conditions of deep moral disagreement (Dryzek 2010: 102–5). And as we have stressed, that deliberation must involve broader publics.

Public intellectuals themselves can help create deliberative practice by performing as if their arguments themselves need deliberating, rather than merely accepting. Here, it is instructive to contrast Peter Singer and Amartya Sen. When Singer speaks or writes on the imperative of charitable giving (see e.g. Singer 2009), his intent is to convince listeners or readers of the rightness of his arguments, and change their behaviour accordingly. When Sen presents his account of human capabilities that he thinks should be secured as the essence of justice, he recognizes they can and should be open to disagreement and deliberative reformulation in local contexts (see e.g. Sen 2009).

Advocacy Groups

Advocacy groups loom large in world politics. UN Secretary General Kofi Anan once described NGOs (with slight exaggeration) as 'the new superpower'. Together, such activists and advocates constitute what is often called 'global civil society'. Many advocacy groups exist to promote particular values, such as environmental conservation, human rights, the elimination of poverty, freedom of political expression, and so forth. These values often have a lot to do with the various dimensions of global justice, so in this sense advocacy groups can be quintessential global justice entrepreneurs. Ypi (2012) celebrates what she calls the 'avant-garde' agency of activists committed to cosmopolitan justice ideals.

Sometimes advocacy groups claim to represent a category of people (though for some discourses, such as ecocentrism, or transparency, or peace, there is no category of people). Oxfam claims to represent the global poor. Celebrity activists such as Bono have also self-appointed as representatives of the poor – in Bono's case, the poor of Africa (Saward 2009: 1). Bono has been criticized for depicting the African poor as claimants on the conscience and charity of the rich, but with no agency of their own. Such agency for the poor is not recognized in the world dominated by global elites (such as the G8 or G20 groups of large economies) targeted by celebrity activists who implicitly claim for themselves a formative role in determining what justice should mean, and for global elites the role of implementing agents of justice. The campaign by activists from developing countries 'Not About Us Without Us' was launched as a corrective to the celebrity-studded 'Make Poverty History' campaign (Brassett and Smith 2010: 426). (At a 2013 G8 meeting Bono was pursued by protestors with placards declaring 'Make Bono History'.) Such controversy suggests that 'bearing witness' and 'a concern for social justice' (to use the words of Deveaux 2015) are not in themselves sufficient warrant for formative agency in the absence of any check on how such agency is claimed and exercised. If the critics are right, advocacy groups may even obstruct justice by keeping the poor in their place, and benefitting from their being in this position. They may indeed help constitute and empower a global activist elite, mostly coming from wealthy countries, rather than providing a true check on the powerful (Heins 2005). A separate but very important problem from that of the moral standing of representative claims made by NGOs is the way in which NGOs can misuse their quasi-governmental powers (Rubenstein 2014, 2015). Seeing the relationship between NGOs and the poor through the power lens is equally, if not more, important than seeing it through the representative lens (Rubenstein 2014, 2015).

Critics of global civil society often seem to compare its current reality with a pure egalitarian democracy. If instead we compare civil society with what currently dominates global governance – large corporations, hegemonic states and superpowers, neoliberal international organizations, low-visibility financial networks – then civil society starts to look much better in a democratic light. Moreover, members of global civil society can be aware of some of their problems and try to correct them. The Beyond 2015 coalition of 1,500 advocacy groups established in 2010 to push for successors to the MDGs had as one of its aims the correction of imbalances in the power of NGOs based in the Global North and South.[6]

It is possible to think a bit more deeply about how the representative claims (Saward 2010) of advocacy groups might be redeemed. The *Economist* famously asked in 2000, 'Who elected Oxfam?' The answer of course is that nobody did. If we think of representation in conventional terms as involving authorization of a representative by some constituency combined with accountability of the representative to the constituency, such bonds are normally lacking for advocacy groups, though some groups do cultivate accountability to their own members (e.g. the UN-recognized Women's Major Group active on the SDGs; see Gabizon 2016). However, it is still possible to think of the democratization of the relationship between advocates and constituencies, if in creative ways. The claims of non-elected and self-appointed representatives can be redeemed. For Montanaro (2018), the key is that the advocacy organization should be committed to empowering the constituency it claims to represent, rather than substituting for the constituency by cultivating only donors and advocacy group members. For Saward (2009), the key questions to ask concern the degree of connectedness of the representative with other actors within a political system, the extent to which there exists a constituency that could corroborate a representation claim, the independence of the representative from strategic benefit within the system, and their freedom from structural imperatives constraining action associated with (potentially repressive) states. In addition, advocacy groups can endeavour to offer what Mansbridge (2009: 384) calls 'narrative accountability', which means simply giving an account of what they do. In the world of advocacy groups, narrative accountability is common. 'Deliberative accountability' in Mansbridge's terms is much rarer and involves an exchange between advocates and claimed constituencies. But there is no reason why, for example, an anti-poverty group could not convene gatherings of poor people in order to explain its activities and seek opinion on them.[7]

While they promote values, and sometimes claim to represent categories of people, another way to think of the representative claims of

---

[6] See www.helpage.org/what-we-do/post2015-process/post2015-coalitions/ #Beyond2015.

[7] In Chapter 6 we will discuss the Ground-Level Panels organized by the Participate initiative that could be adapted to do this.

civil society is in terms of discourses. Amnesty International represents a discourse of political rights, Save the Children represents an anti-poverty discourse, Transparency International a discourse of commercial and governmental integrity, and Greenpeace an ecocentric discourse. In this light, global civil society can be interpreted as a pattern of discursive representation (Dryzek 2012). Democratization of this pattern necessitates dispersed and competent control over the engagement of different discourses on the part of formative agents. This in turn requires activists and advocacy organizations to be open to critical engagement with interlocutors, especially those who subscribe to different discourses. What often happens instead can be very different, if it involves the formation of enclaves in which like-minded partisans communicate mainly with each other. This is especially evident when it comes to climate change, where radicals engage mainly with other radicals, and more moderate sustainability advocates engage mainly with other moderates (Stevenson and Dryzek 2014: 41–58). Enclaves may have a place when it comes to the building of confidence and sharpening of arguments on the part of historically disadvantaged groups, but at some point they have to yield to engagement. The Major Groups recognized by the UN since 1992 and given privileged access to UN processes sometimes seem like an over-privileged enclave, despite the range of concerns they embody.

Advocacy Groups and the SDGs

Advocacy groups were ubiquitous in many of the processes that combined to yield the SDGs, and their concerns are reflected in the content of the goals. Their participation was sought and encouraged by the UN Secretary-General and others in the UN system as being central to the open and participatory way in which the SDGs were to be formulated (see e.g. UNDG 2013b). This participation was welcomed by some states more than others; generally, the more democratic the state, the more it accepts NGO participation in global processes. Some groups were more enthusiastic than others about taking up the challenge; large aid organizations (such as Oxfam) were not initially keen, while some small New York-based NGOs stepped into the gap (interview evidence). Advocacy groups were there in the beginning, in the various consultations, preparatory conferences, and high-level events. They played an important role in the thematic consultations on eleven subject areas covering the range of the goals. They were there at the end, with the Major Groups (and others) in the room when the OWG was finalizing the content of the goals (Kamau et al. 2018). Several alliances of advocacy organizations were organized: the Beyond 2015 Coalition of more than 1,500 groups, which we have already mentioned; the Financing for Development civil society coalition that emerged from the same meeting as the Addis Ababa Action Agenda in 2014; the Global Call to Action Against Poverty; the Green Economy Coalition; and the International Forum of National NGO Platforms that indirectly represented more than 22,000 NGOs from 64 countries.

But did all this activity contribute to the democratization of global justice? The role of advocacy groups is not necessarily deliberative. Some groups simply reiterate fixed and known positions at every opportunity and are preoccupied with strategizing and building alliances to get their position accepted, so interacting groups do not necessarily deliberate much. Success for a group would then come in getting its proposed goal or target(s) accepted, not in terms of the coherence of the goals and targets as a whole. The sheer quantity of activity does not necessarily augur well. Indeed, if that activity becomes a cacophony, it is easy for people in key decision-making positions (e.g. the OWG) to tune out. Alternatively, a small number of advocacy organizations may get privileged, and the rest (especially more radical groups) ignored. While often in global governance it is NGOs from wealthy countries that have a more effective voice, in the case of the SDGs that seems not to have been the case (interview evidence).

Arguably the formal UN recognition of nine Major Groups constructs a privileged set that is not comprehensive. One of the nine is NGOs, which is a catch-all category for those not in the other eight groups (women, children and youth, indigenous peoples, local authorities, workers and trade unions, business and industry, scientific and technological community, farmers; our interviewees disagreed about which groups were most and least effective). Lang (2012) argues that advocacy organizations can suffer from 'NGOization', by which she means the cultivation of an insider status with the officials of international organizations, professionalization, and bureaucratization, meaning they can become detached from any constituents they claim to represent. However, it could be countered that it is this professionalization that induces negotiators and officials to pay attention to what an NGO representative has to say. The Major Groups fit this profile. Sénit (2017: 118) concludes that it was in the more exclusive and informal spaces around the SDGs where interpersonal connections are cultivated that civil society advocates had the most impact, which is bad news from the perspective of democratization. Even the formal daily meetings that Major Group representatives held with OWG members were largely inconsequential on her account (Sénit 2017: 115).

Goal 10, 'Reduce inequality within and among countries', is crucial to the redistributive aspect of global justice. But as Sénit (2017: 112) points out, concerned advocacy groups organized into Beyond 2015, the Initiative for Equality, and Global Call to Action Against Poverty had to fight hard to get it included in the first place, then fight against attempts by states to dilute it or merge it with other goals. Eventually these groups failed to stop the weak way in which the targets associated with Goal 10 were specified. Overall, Sénit considers civil society influence on the content of the goals to have been moderate. However, this moderate influence could be seen as a glass half-full rather than half-empty; at least Goal 10 on reducing inequality was retained. It is easier to discern the influence of advocacy groups than it is of the publics that the various organized consultations were designed to reach (see Chapter 6).

Discursive representation worked incompletely in the SDGs. Carant (2017) demonstrates that radical discourses were not reflected in the content of the goals. Sénit (2017: 149) codes discourses by their degree of radicalism in relation to sustainability rather than justice, but finds that the texts of negotiation rarely reveal any reference to conceptions of sustainability that involve radical challenge to the status quo; mainstream and moderate discourses dominate. Again the glass could be seen as half-full: at least neoliberalism did not completely dominate, in the way it dominates global financial and economic governance (though the content of the goals shows that neoliberalism is not confronted, let alone rejected, and at key points is implicitly embedded in the SDGs, as we pointed out in Chapter 1). On the slightly more positive side, Sénit (2017: 139) notes substantial engagement across different discourses – but mostly within the moderate category. It is not as though radical discourses failed to survive deliberative contestation with moderate discourses, but rather that radical discourses failed to receive a fair hearing.

These deficiencies in the pattern of activity of advocacy groups notwithstanding, their presence did mean that a range of concerns got represented in the SDGs that would otherwise have been absent. It is important not to load too many deliberative and democratic expectations on global civil society, which is not the sole key to the democratization of global governance.

Advocacy Groups and Climate Justice

The global politics of climate change features if anything an abundance of advocacy groups greater than that observed for the SDGs. In Chapter 3 we noted the turn to orchestration as a mode of climate governance. Orchestration enlists advocacy groups in the service of the leadership of international organizations (notably the UN) to pressure governments to meet their emissions reduction commitments and so serve global goals. The fact they become key actors in policy implementation could increase the influence of these groups. At the same time, the focus of orchestration on existing national emissions reduction commitments could conceivably distract advocacy organizations from more explicit questions of climate justice and its meaning, which might involve the fairness and adequacy of national emissions targets, their trajectory over time, and the pattern of reductions across nations.

Activists are present in their thousands at every Conference of the Parties (COP) of the UNFCCC; though their influence on the negotiations can be hard to discern, and unlike the case of the SDGs, there are no formal channels to register their opinions on the key issues under negotiation. Often they create parallel gatherings, such as the Klimaforum09 at the 2009 COP in Copenhagen. Sometimes advocacy groups have international summits of their own, such as the World People's Conference on Climate Change and the Rights of Mother Earth hosted by the Bolivian government in Cochabamba in 2010, which as its name suggests was radical and ecocentric (Stevenson and Dryzek 2014: 51–4). Not all activists are explicitly concerned with climate *justice*, but many are. The International Climate Justice Network, Climate Justice Action, and Climate Justice Now! are among international coalitions of advocacy groups that have come and in some cases gone over the past two decades.

The very idea of *environmental* justice was originally the creation of community groups in the United States, who drove home the fact that many of the worst environmental hazards (polluting industry, toxic waste dumps, incinerators) were located such that most of the health damage was done to ethnic minorities and people on a low income (Schlosberg 1999). These groups eventually formed the core of a national movement, meaning environmental justice was a paradigm case of advocacy groups acting as formative agents of justice. The history of climate justice is a bit different in that, at least on the global stage, it is states that determined its original form with the 'common but differentiated responsibilities' principle adopted by an assembly of states at Rio in 1992 (see Chapter 1). With time, vulnerable states such as Tuvalu began to work closely with transnational activists to highlight the distributional inequity of the risks to life, health, and livelihood that climate change generates.

Eventually climate justice became a rallying cry for more radical climate activists, which means the discourse of climate justice shaded into climate radicalism. Climate Justice Now! was formed in 2007 as a more radical counterpart to the umbrella Climate Action Network that had long been prominent at the COPs. This identification of justice with radicalism was itself an important exercise of formative agency, for it implicitly defined 'justice' as necessitating radical action to control greenhouse gas emissions. As we pointed out in Chapter 1, the domain of justice is actually much broader than that, and justice arguments can even be made for not prioritizing emissions reductions over distributional equity or basic human needs.

Various advocacy groups pursue partial and different perspectives on the meaning of climate justice. The Global Justice Ecology Project emphasizes the need for mitigation through reforestation to involve the sustainable practices of indigenous peoples and peasants, not biofuels or offsets to finance fast-growing plantations.[8] The environmental organization 350.org has an eye on the condition of the Earth system as a whole. GenderCC links climate justice and gender justice. Oxfam's approach to climate change involves development that meets human needs while controlling emissions. Each view may only tell a part of the climate justice story. At gatherings of climate justice advocates (such as the Cochabamba Summit), all present can agree on the need for the wealthy countries and corporations to curb their emissions, and for the needs of the most vulnerable to be paramount in deciding where the

---

[8] See https://globaljusticeecology.org.

burden of mitigation should lie. However, looking beyond rhetorical solidarity, there are potential disagreements. For example, what burden should be placed on rich consumers in poor countries? To what degree should the poor and vulnerable be allowed to increase greenhouse gas emissions for the sake of lifting them out of poverty? How should the interests of present and future generations be balanced?

We have argued throughout that the existence of reasonable plural justice claims requires public deliberation for their resolution. Deliberation here should not just be in enclaves of like-minded activists such as the Cochabamba Summit, but across different sorts of advocacy groups. In global climate governance in general, and on climate justice in particular, there is a divide between moderate gatherings dominated by mainstream sustainability discourses and radical gatherings dominated by green radicalism (Stevenson and Dryzek 2014: 54–8). This divide is replicated in online communication. Mainstream sustainability seeks a reformed, more equitable capitalist political economy that makes good use of technology. Radical discourse rejects this system. A healthy deliberative democracy requires engagement across different discourses. This does not mean that moderates and radicals have to compromise. What is does mean is that the outcome of the engagement represents the best available reasons, which could be radical, or mainstream, or something entirely different. Diehard advocates of whatever persuasion may not be the best deliberators, which is why, just as for public intellectuals, broader publics need to be engaged in the deliberative processing of competing claims. One way of redeeming this requirement is to think in terms of the place of advocacy groups and publics in deliberative systems, which we will do in Chapter 8.

We conclude that the representative claims of advocacy organizations and activists, and so their formative agency on matters of global justice, can only be redeemed to the extent of their vertical and horizontal democratic engagements. Vertical democratization comes in the form of their accountability to, and cultivation of the agency of, the constituents on whose behalf they claim to speak. Horizontal democratization comes in the form of deliberative engagement with other advocates and activists and broader publics. To complete the democratization story, accountable advocacy groups then need to make an important difference when it comes to collective decisions (we will focus on this when we look at deliberative systems in Chapter 8).

The Media

The influence of different discourses relevant to global justice depends heavily on what happens in the media. In keeping with our focus on agency, our concern here is with the formative role of those who operate within the media: journalists, the owners of media corporations, and all those who post content on social media. The increasingly easy access of many kinds of agents to the media magnifies the importance of the dramaturgical, performative aspects of agency for those who want to stand out and exercise influence publicly (Hajer 2009).

At their best, journalists can publicize and help form public perceptions of injustice. For example, the civil rights movement in the United States relied heavily on media coverage of staged confrontations with police to publicize racial injustice in the American South in the 1960s. There is a long tradition of investigative journalism that brings injustice to light. For example, the International Consortium of Investigative Journalists that brought the 'Panama Papers' to light in 2016 showed the extent to which politicians and powerful political actors throughout the world illegally hid their wealth and evaded taxes.[9] But the structural causes of injustice and the injustice of everyday life – or 'slow violence' (Nixon 2011) – generally get little coverage by mainstream journalists. Instead, a spectacular event – a cyclone, famine, or massacre – is likely to receive much more attention, though typically the attention is transient. Aware of such windows of opportunity, civil society groups (especially those that engage in service delivery, such as Médecins Sans Frontières and Oxfam) will use the window to appeal for funds.

Yet there can be a cost to both justice and democracy in relying on spectacle, as journalistic representation typically involves painting those affected by repression or a disaster as helpless victims with a claim on the consciences of the better off, as opposed to competent agents demanding justice (Curato 2019: ch. 3). Journalists are generally less interested in success stories in which communities become healthier, more secure, more sustainable, or less vulnerable to tragedy. Good news perhaps sells better in social media, where Facebook, for example, privileges 'likes' and so positive expressions. However,

---

[9] See www.icij.org/investigations/panama-papers.

reinforcement via likes does not enable space for argument or controversy across competing views.

Sensation, personality, scandal, drama, and conflict are generally more newsworthy than reasoned deliberation. Even coverage of citizen deliberative processes tends to highlight dramatic moments of conflict involving advocates (i.e. not the citizens themselves), while downplaying what the citizens involved actually do (Parkinson 2006).

What journalists (and public writers more generally) can write or say also depends who they work for. Authoritarian regimes can and do exercise direct control. Media moguls (notoriously, Rupert Murdoch) have their own political agendas that they impose on their employees (Girard 2015). Those agendas often involve protecting inequality, hierarchy, and privilege, and ridiculing those who seek redistribution or broader recognition of the standing of vulnerable groups, or who challenge an unjust political economy.

The Media and the SDGs

A Lexis Advance search for 'SDGs' or 'Sustainable Goals' reveals a major upswing in late 2015 followed by a large number in 2016 (1,009 articles in 2014, to 6,453 in 2015, to 8,626 in 2016). What this suggests is that journalists were not very active as the SDGs were being formulated, only swinging into action once they were about to be adopted in 2015, when there was a dramatic spike in coverage (see also Rios 2015). This apparent absence in the formation of the SDGs may perhaps be forgiven in light of journalists' long-standing role in publicizing some of the injustices that the SDGs address.

There were some high hopes for social media to play a prominent role in the development of the SDGs. As the ubiquitous Jeffrey Sachs (who we already encountered under experts and public intellectuals) put it:

New social media and information technology have given the world an unprecedented opportunity for inclusive, global-scale problem solving around the main sustainable development challenges … The pathways to sustainable development will not be identified through a top-down approach, but through a highly energised era of networked problem solving that engages the world's universities, businesses, nongovernmental organisations, governments, and especially young people, who should become the experts and leaders of a new and profoundly challenging era. (Sachs 2012: 2211)

The UN's Global Pulse initiative was designed to use big data in the service of development and has tried to harvest and analyse opinions from social media data in, for example, content analysis of tweets.[10] The MyWorld survey (which we will discuss in Chapter 6) was available online. Those who favoured a relatively short, simple, and readily communicated list of goals and targets were fond of saying that the SDGs should be 'tweetable', in the words of a delegate to the OWG that finalized the SDGs.[11] Tweetability lends itself to short, striking statements consistent with 'fast' thinking – not necessarily to the slow thinking that deliberation requires. The long and complex final form that the SDGs took would appear not to be especially tweetable. Fast thinking on Twitter may have a role in mobilizing publics that can subsequently deliberate. However, there is no such public around the SDGs comparable to (for example) the #MeToo movement on sexual harassment or #BlackLivesMatter. The striking icon that each goal has can perhaps be deployed in simple and vivid communication.[12] A host of celebrities contributed to a short video, 'We the People for the Global Goals', promoting the SDGs on YouTube, which as of 2018 had over a million views.[13] The video covers all seventeen goals in two and a half minutes.

Sénit, Kalfagianni, and Biermann (2016) analyse the 'Rio Dialogues' conducted in association with the UN Conference on Sustainable Development in 2012, which featured facilitated online interaction that converged (via counting 'likes') on ten recommendations that were presented to the conference. They conclude that this online process reinforced established participatory inequalities as it was dominated by people from high-income countries and organized groups.

It is easy to find social media communications, campaigns, and summary analysis relevant to the SDGs, but less easy to determine how consequential they were in the larger scheme of things. As a rough judgement, the volume of social media commentary relevant to the SDGs appears to be of higher deliberative quality than one finds on (for example) climate change, where the pernicious influence of identity on cognition, demonization of the other side, and the influence of organized climate change denial are pervasive (Boykoff 2019: 40–2).

---

[10] See www.unglobalpulse.org.
[11] See www.un.org/development/desa/newsletter/dialogue/2013/05/7034.html.
[12] See https://sustainabledevelopment.un.org/?menu=1300.
[13] See www.youtube.com/watch?v=RpqVmvMCmp0.

The Media and Climate Justice

Climate change does perhaps reveal the contribution of social media to the crisis of democracy quite starkly. In its early days, social media was hailed as a democratizing force inasmuch as it provided massively expanded opportunities for ordinary people to communicate their ideas and opinions, with a very low entry cost. But that is not quite how matters played out. A vast increase in the volume of expression has brought with it a weakening of both civility and argumentative complexity, as people organize into enclaves where like-minded partisans encourage each other and when communication moves beyond enclaves, simple barbs substitute for reasoning (Vosoughi et al. 2018). The ensuring polarization means that audiences (and voters) pay little attention to the actual content of messages, following instead simple partisan invocations that associate messages with different sides (religions, ideologies, or nations) in the larger political struggle (Druckman, Peterson, and Slothuus 2013). There is as a result an increasing gap between simple solutions – including those put forward by political leaders – and the complexity of public problems. This is an environment where post-truth politics flourishes, where emotion and what American comedian Stephen Colbert calls 'truthiness' substitute for truth. In the context of climate change, Kahan, Jenkins-Smith, and Braman (2010) have shown how 'cultural cognition' has displaced reasoned evaluation, at least in the United States. There, climate change denial has become an integral part of right-wing political identity – while belief in the reality of climate change and the need to address it have become equally so for those on the left.

Reforming the Media

There are, then, a number of ways in which journalism and social media are problematic when it comes to how global justice and injustice get perceived and defined. It is straightforward to identify things that the media should do better, for example: to be better informed by relevant expertise, to translate that expertise into easily understandable form, to make sure that abstract arguments are leavened with personal stories to bring them alive, and to be more inclusive in terms of the contents and concerns that are covered (see e.g. Titus 2017, speaking explicitly of coverage of the SDGs). It is also possible to hold journalism up to democratic and deliberative norms of independence from vested interests, inclusivity, and reason-giving – if necessary through public regulation (Girard 2015). As Girard (2015) points out, relying on the free-for-all of a 'marketplace of ideas' is not enough when some of those active in that marketplace have vastly greater resources at their disposal than others. Even specifying balance is not enough: as Boykoff and Boykoff (2004) argue, balance has meant giving equal time to climate change denial, out of all proportion to its credibility in climate science, effectively paralysing governmental action on climate change (at least in US federal politics).

What else can be done? Today's media landscape features an overload of expression, as it is easier for more people to have a say (especially in social media) than ever before. The 'Rio Dialogues' described earlier yielded 'a forest of comment, blogs, articles, and discussions' in the words of a UN official (quoted in Sénit et al. 2016: 546). The sheer volume of communication made it impossible for the UN to construct any sort of deliberative accountability to social media participants.

What is in short supply in the media landscape is considered response to expression. If there is a response, it can often be a visceral one, be it as a result of the invocation of partisan identity (as on climate change questions), or in reaction to portrayals of tragedy. In Kahneman's (2011) terms, a visceral response involves 'fast' thinking, deploying shortcuts and heuristics, rather than deliberative 'slow' thinking. In the case of disasters, slow thinking is more likely to ponder the structural problems of how vulnerability to disaster in marginalized communities arose in the first place – and how those structures might be changed for the better.[14] More generally, slow thinking might extend to long-range strategies for coping with issues that have deep roots, as opposed to immediate feel-good hits (such as inundating a stricken community with aid).

It is not necessary for the media as a whole to transition from fast to slow thinking; if it did, it would hardly be the media we know. It is more productive to think about the cultivation of spaces for reflection and slow thinking, be they in the media itself, or outside it. Within the

[14] The reform in question might involve democratization. Amartya Sen (1999) has famously pointed out that no famine has ever arisen in a democracy. It is worth thinking about whether democracy provides an antidote to other sorts of cataclysms, though of course democracy versus autocracy does not exhaust the

media, investigative journalism provides such a space, though its traditional emphasis on exposing individual, corporate, and institutional wrongdoing may limit its applicability to questions of global justice. Elsewhere, reflective spaces exist mainly on the margins of politics and governance. Ercan, Hendriks, and Dryzek (2019) give several examples of such spaces. The first entails a citizens' panel interrupting campaigns for and against proposals to be put to a referendum by deliberating the question for several days. The panel then summarizes what it considers to be the best arguments for and against the referendum question, and this summary is then published in a pamphlet distributed to all voters. This 'Citizens' Initiative Review' process was pioneered in the US state of Oregon and copied elsewhere. The second example is an independent Member of Parliament in Australia organizing 'kitchen table conversations' of citizens throughout her district, as well as direct deliberative exchanges between herself and her constituents. The third involves a social movement taking a holiday from online interaction to think a bit about what they were doing and why.

Initiatives to introduce more space for reflection in social media include weDialogue[15] and (in Germany) #Ichbinhier, both of which promote civil exchange on controversial topics. Algorithms could be redesigned to recognize that social media constitutes a political sphere and not a merely social sphere. For example, crowdsourcing assessments about the quality of different news sources turns out to produce reliable collective judgements (Pennycook and Rand 2019), which in turn can be used to design algorithms that weight sources for newsfeeds by their trustworthiness, and so counteract misinformation.

The crucial role of the media in constituting and informing global publics is inescapable, but reflective spaces are currently in short supply. We will have more to say on introducing such spaces in deliberative systems in Chapter 8.

Conclusion

Global justice can benefit to the degree its definition and content are influenced by the power of words, rather than by formal authority or

---

structural questions relevant to the creation, perpetuation, and remediation of vulnerability.

[15] See https://wedialogue.world/about.

money. The meanings that global justice takes depend substantially on the words mobilized by experts, public intellectuals, advocacy groups, journalists, and those active on social media. It is important to scrutinize them in the democratic terms we have established.

In this light, we have argued for the deliberative democratization of the engagements of those who muster words and the media through which those words make themselves felt. Specifically, this would involve:

- establishing deliberative relationships between experts and policy makers such as international negotiators;
- extending these relationships to citizens through means such as deliberative policy analysis and the constitution of deliberative mini-publics alongside expert forums;
- deliberative engagement across public intellectuals advocating plural justice claims, in association with public adjudication of their disagreements;
- reminding public intellectuals to perform as though their claims required deliberative validation – as opposed to being presented as authoritative;
- securing deliberative accountability from advocacy groups to those (such as the global poor) they claim to represent;
- promoting critical engagement across advocates from different discourses (such as radical and moderate ones);
- opening advocacy group representation in global governance beyond a privileged set of Major Groups;
- applying critical standards of independence, inclusivity, and reason-giving to journalism; and
- cultivating spaces for reflection within the media and outside it.

The formative agency of those who influence the content of global justice through the words they mobilize is defensible only to the degree its operation and context are deliberative and democratic.

6 | Empowering the Many
Citizens and the Poor

We turn now to categories of agents that should be vital in democratizing global justice in theory, but whose presence on the global stage can be elusive in practice: citizens in general, and the poor in particular.

Despite the unavailability of global elections, and against sceptics who think lay citizens lack the capacity to exercise meaningful political agency at all, let alone formative agency about complex questions of global justice, we show how citizens can be effective agents. This capacity is revealed only to the degree citizens interact in deliberative settings. In this light, we assess the citizen consultations conducted to inform the Sustainable Development Goals (SDGs). For the first time in history, a global governance process actively sought citizen input. However, the consultations were problematic when they relied on surveys, while the national and thematic dialogues were only weakly and variably deliberative, and not very consequential. We show how citizen deliberation could be promoted further through transnational and global forums – most ambitiously, a Deliberative Global Citizens Assembly (a glance at climate governance shows the success of such assemblies at the national level). The consultations for the SDGs also did more to try to reach the poor than any previous global process, though again with mixed deliberative and inclusive success. We will argue that it would be best for the global poor to exercise formative agency together as a global community of interest and that democratic deliberation is needed to empower such a community to act like this. This exercise can be redeemed in both poor-led social movements and institutional design. Given the chance, the poor too can be competent deliberators and formative agents.

Citizens

Citizens are central to most accounts of democracy, such that democratizing global justice ought to involve them in a big way. Citizenship is currently popularly associated with full membership in a sovereign state, or at most only of a regional association, such as the European Union (EU). But it is also possible to think in terms of global citizenship. Global citizenship is central to cosmopolitan democracy, which seeks to secure citizen participation in global institutions (such as legal systems, legislative assemblies, and referendums) without that participation having to take place only at one remove, through national governments (Held 1995). Many national governments are not democracies to begin with. Some simply lack the capacity to ascertain the concerns of their citizens about global questions, and to transmit those concerns effectively. Even liberal democratic states often treat foreign policy – and so participation in global governance – as something for the executive branch of government, which need bear little relationship to citizen preferences and concerns. National elections are generally about national issues, such that there is no way to register citizens' opinions on global questions through electoral means. Cosmopolitan democrats look forward to an eventual directly elected global parliament (Falk and Strauss 2011), though they mostly recognize this would have to be preceded by a long series of incremental steps.

Global elections are of course currently unavailable, and at best a distant prospect. A deliberative approach to (global) democracy of the sort we have developed highlights communication rather than voting, but citizens are no less necessary for that emphasis. However, deliberative democracy has more demanding expectations of citizenship than occasionally voting in elections. Is it realistic to expect this demanding kind of citizenship at the global level, when it is hard enough to secure at the national level? We will argue that it may be hard work, but that it is achievable.

But first we have some scepticism about citizen competence in general to overcome. There is a long tradition in political science that calls into question the competence of citizens to judge anything very much when it comes to their political behaviour – let alone judge big questions of global justice. One prominent iteration in this tradition comes from Achen and Bartels (2016), who deploy evidence from opinion surveys to show that individuals generally vote on the basis of group identity, rather than their opinions on candidates or policies, and certainly not on any ethical principles. However, as Chambers (2018) points out, Achen and Bartels deploy the monological social science of survey research to answer essentially dialogical questions.[1] People may be bad when it comes to solitary reasoning, but very good when it comes to collective problem solving.

But why exactly should citizens do so much better collectively than individually? To begin, as we pointed out in Chapter 2 (following Landemore 2012), cognitive diversity across individuals can compensate for the shortcomings of any one individual. Moreover, the 'wisdom of crowds' suggests that such diversity is more important than individual ability when it comes to reaching effective solutions (Page 2007). Deliberation here enables individuals to piece together different bits of relevant information to which each of them (or some subset of them) has access, enabling a fuller picture of the relevant aspects of the problem at hand to be formed, and a collective response that is more rational than any individual's (or subset's) response could be. Each piece of information will not be decisive in supporting the collective outcome, but enough pieces when sifted and reasoned through can provide robust support for an action. In deliberation, bad arguments and erroneous assumptions can be exposed (Estlund and Landemore 2018: 120–2). This is, for example, why when faced with a crisis a good leader (e.g. John F. Kennedy) will convene a diverse advisory group to deliberate options and come up with a recommendation of the best course of action; a bad leader (e.g. Donald Trump) will fire anyone who disagrees with him and rely instead on his own 'judgement' or 'gut instinct'. Cognitive diversity can benefit from the inclusion that is central to democracy.

Stevenson (2016) applies this epistemic argument to global governance, which she believes will benefit from three moves. The first involves maximizing the number of people capable of participating in governance (she sees the SDGs and Millennium Development Goals (MDGs) as potentially instrumental to the broadening of this capacity if they advance human capabilities across the globe). The second entails maximizing cognitive diversity across participants in governance institutions; this is a problem in areas of global governance such as finance and trade dominated by neoliberalism. The third involves maximizing the opportunities to share relevant knowledge, which

---

[1] For further critiques of the same methodology and the questioning of citizens' competence, see Goodin and Spiekermann (2018: 88–92) and Lupia et al. (2007).

she thinks can benefit from meaningful participation by civil society organizations.

But why should the inclusion that fosters diversity extend to lay citizens? The answer here is that citizens have some key capacities and virtues that are otherwise in short supply in any kind of governance, global or otherwise. We have evidence from citizen forums (about which we will have much more to say later) that lay citizens are especially good when it comes to their reflective capacities, given the right deliberative conditions (Dryzek 2017a). This is why, for example, juries in criminal cases are entrusted with reflecting upon the evidence they have heard and reaching a collective decision on that basis. Members of the jury are not necessarily much good at advocacy and justification of positions; that is the task of lawyers. Given the right setting, and the chance to deliberate with each other, lay citizens can be relied upon to exercise independent critical judgement. When it comes to citizen forums convened on policy issues, we have plenty of evidence that they do so (Benson 2018). Evidence also suggests that participants in citizen forums do a much better job than other participants in other institutions (such as legislatures) in prioritizing the common good over material and sectional interests (Fishkin 2009: 109 and 142; Smith 2009: 94). These qualities are especially important when it comes to the exercise of formative agency about matters of justice for three reasons: first, to ensure that the principles justifying collective action are not used hypocritically as covers for the material interests of the powerful; second, to ensure that advocacy on behalf of *any* value or interest receives proper scrutiny; and third, to help ensure that the common good is prioritized.

In short, when it comes to participation and the exercise of formative agency in global justice governance (no less than elsewhere), it is important that citizens interact in deliberative fashion. Consulting them individually in a way that can capture only their monological reasoning is not enough.

Citizens in the SDGs

Consider in this light the MyWorld survey that was conducted ostensibly to inform the content of the SDGs. The survey could be completed online, though most respondents completed it on paper. Unlike a standard opinion survey, it did not involve a random sample, but depended on the efforts of partner organizations to reach respondents (Spijkers and Honniball 2015: 264). By the end of 2014, 7 million people had responded. The survey remained open after the adoption of the SDGs, and by 2017 the number of respondents had risen to 9.7 million (UN 2017). Most respondents were young people in low- to middle-income countries, though the survey inadvertently oversampled the highly educated; 44 per cent of respondents had post-secondary education (Fox and Stoett 2016: 566). Results from the survey were widely publicized, and communicated to the secretary general of the United Nations (UN), as well as the High-Level Panel, though the latter's report did not reflect the priorities identified in the survey (Spijkers and Honniball 2015: 265–6).

On the face of it, the MyWorld survey was an invitation to formative agency, as it asked respondents to prioritize six of sixteen issues. Specifically, the question was: 'Which six of the following global goals are of immediate concern to you and your family?' This framing of the question is problematic. Note that individuals were asked which global goals would most affect their *own* lives *immediately*, not other peoples' lives, or the lives of local, regional, national, or global communities, or even their own lives in future. There was no possibility for respondents to think about and report on the interaction between different goals (such as gender equality and access to employment; Fox and Stoett 2016: 566). This individualistic and presentist framing led, for example, to climate change receiving the very lowest priority of all sixteen issues ('a good education' was highest). This result could be highly misleading if interpreted to mean that the citizens of the world do not care about climate change. But more important than this individualistic framing of the questions is the fact that answers to them constitute unreflective preferences, with no requirement that individuals engage in the group activity that is required for effective human problem solving; let alone allow 'shaping of the terms of the debate by citizens, themselves' (Howard and Wheeler 2015: 560–1). In this light, the MyWorld survey is not an especially meaningful exercise of formative agency, which is just as well its results had no impact on the High-Level Panel, or it seems any of the other key bodies involved in formulating the SDGs. All sixteen global goals on the survey appeared in the final SDGs, which suggests the prioritization exercise of the survey was ultimately a bit pointless.

MyWorld was just one part of the 'global conversation' that preceded and was supposed to inform intergovernmental negotiations on the SDGs. MyWorld itself was linked to a 'WorldWeWant' website that was more interactive.[2] Anyone with an Internet connection could access the website and its information, as well as contribute to online discussions.

Around 100 'national dialogues' were also part of the global conversation. The national dialogues did not follow any common procedure and varied substantially in their design. Options included crowdsourcing, the use of social media, town hall meetings, surveys, focus groups, public meetings, targeted recruitment for meetings of particular groups (such as refugees), individual interviews, and radio phone-ins (UNDG 2013a). Not all of this activity could be interpreted as involving lay citizens; there were elements of stakeholder consultation, as well as expert involvement. While the UN Manual for the National Dialogues mentioned the possibility of organizing deliberative processes such as citizens' juries and citizens' panels (UNDG 2012: 53–4), there is no evidence that any such processes were held. The results of the national dialogues (in total involving thousands of people) were summarized – along with other aspects of the global conversation – in a report entitled *A Million Voices: The World We Want* (UNDG 2013b) (the 'million' includes respondents to the MyWorld survey, though as we have seen the eventual number was much higher than a million for this survey alone). This report contains plenty of conclusions about what the people of the world and its component regions are supposed to want. The national dialogues revealed commitments to environmental protection and reducing inequality much more strongly than did the MyWorld survey (Fox and Stoett 2016: 565).

Given their number and internal variety, it is hard to generalize about the deliberative qualities of the national dialogues. But even if they were deliberative, they would be limited in their value because they were separate national conversations, while global justice would benefit most from a global conversation.

The 'thematic consultations' organized under the global conversation helped to fill this gap. The eleven themes were 'conflict, violence, and disaster; education; energy; environmental sustainability; food security and nutrition; governance; growth and employment; health; addressing inequalities; population dynamics; and water' (UNDG

---

[2] See www.worldwewant2030.org.

2013a: 7). However, the thematic consultations mostly involved non-governmental organizations (NGOs), stakeholders, and sometimes government officials – not lay citizens. Again, there was no uniform approach as the eleven themes involved very different methods; in most there was an opportunity for online comments or discussion.

These more interactive opportunities for citizen participation in the formulation of the SDGs – the interactive website, the national dialogues, and the thematic consultations – were well intentioned, even in deliberative terms. They are certainly an advance on most global governance processes, which provide no opportunities at all for public participation. But they have several limitations.

The first is the thin, non-deliberative nature of much of the participation. In the MyWorld survey, but also to a degree in the other exercises, breadth of participation was sought by making questions simple and easy to answer, rendering the responses a matter of 'clicktivism' rather than reasoning (Spijkers and Honniball 2015: 294–5).

The second is the self-selection of participants. To the degree self-selection operates, participants will be unrepresentative (in the statistical sense) of any larger population. This is not necessarily a problem in ensuring that different points of view get heard, if those who do participate are sufficiently varied – but there is no guarantee such variety will ensue.

The third challenge comes in the production of summaries in the various processes. For the MyWorld survey, it is a straightforward counting of votes for different priorities. Each of the three interactive consultations received its own separate summary. The consultations yielded massive textual data bases so a UN Development Programme (UNDP) team was employed to search and summarize, developing taxonomies that could then inform frequency counts of topics, which were then interpreted cautiously to yield substantive conclusions about issues and priorities. The data summary cast a broad net, including (for example) the Participate panels we will discuss later, which were organized separately from the UN consultations. At the request of (for example) the Open Working Group (OWG), summary reports could be produced on very precise topics. The data sets were publicly accessible.

What happened in each national consultation had to be synthesized; then the resultant syntheses themselves had to be synthesized into the *A Million Voices* report (Spijkers and Honniball 2015: 275). To bring them alive, some summary reports also contained a few more in-depth accounts of individuals' views. Gellers (2016: 415) found 'considerable dissonance between the characteristics of participants in the e-discussions and those whose voices were included in the resulting summary report'. Notably, people from developed states were over-represented, people from poorer states were under-represented, and no comment was reported unless it was originally made in English.

The fourth problem is the lack of clear and uniform guiding principles for consultations. The variety of methods and procedures that took place might enable sensitivity to local or national circumstances (Fox and Stoett 2016: 563), though we suspect that this variety is more readily explained by different people in different positions of authority having different resources, or different preconceptions about the specific tools that could be used.

The fifth problem concerns the impact of the various exercises on the commanding heights of the process that produced the SDGs. The UNDP team that produced the summaries was active in promoting them in various UN forums, including the High-Level Panel. But Fox and Stoett (2016: 562) conclude that it is hard to discern any influence from the consultations on the proceedings of the High-Level Panel to which they reported. There is little evidence that these exercises had much impact on the OWG that finalized the goals (they receive only passing mention in the comprehensive insider account of Kamau et al. 2018).

The sixth problem is the lack of any mechanism for accountability to citizens from the peak-level processes that finalized the SDGs. That lack of accountability extends into implementation of the goals (Howard and Wheeler 2015: 561). Some micro-accountability to participants in the consultations was proposed in the original UN guidelines (UNDG 2012: 31–2), but this was in the form of access to summary reports and instant feedback to groups of participants about what they are saying. In the Serbian national dialogue there was a final 'validation event' to which experts and civil society representatives were invited (Spijkers and Honniball 2015: 272). Many of the summaries of the national dialogues and thematic consultations were subject to similar kinds of validation. But this kind of accountability did not reach peak-level processes.

The overall picture, then, is of well-meaning, pioneering, but haphazard and only loosely coordinated processes, with little quality control. Earlier we argued that the full potential of involving citizens in collective decision-making processes can only be achieved under deliberative conditions. The degree to which such conditions were present in the various consultation exercises that accompanies the formulation of the SDGs varied widely, and defies easy summary. So while over 10 million people participated in consultations on the 2030 Agenda (Sénit, Biermann and Kalfagianni 2017), that doesn't mean this participation effectively channelled the formative agency of citizens. Still, the glass is half-full: the process for involving citizens was better in deliberative and democratic terms than anything attempted before or since in global governance.

How to Promote Citizen Deliberation for Global Justice

How then could citizen participation be made more genuinely and systematically deliberative? If we look beyond the SDGs, there are few locations in global governance where more positive lessons might be sought. Indeed, for all its flaws, the multifaceted consultation process for the 2030 Development Agenda is the most ambitious yet when it comes to citizen participation in global governance. In the absence of clear lessons from global experience, it is necessary to be a bit more imaginative.

Citizen Forums

In national politics, there has been an explosion of interest in lay citizen forums in recent years. Thousands have been conducted around the world. There are many different models: citizens' juries, consensus conferences, deliberative polling, citizens' assemblies, planning cells, citizens' panels. Mostly they recruit through stratified random selection: an initial random sample of citizens is tweaked to make sure it contains a good spread in terms of characteristics such as age, income, and education. The number of participants can be as small as ten or as large as several hundred. They are brought together under deliberative conditions, normally under the auspices of a facilitator to promote principles such as respect for other participants, no ad hominem arguments, and listening to what others say. The principles for interaction can themselves be decided by the participating citizens at the outset of the process. Once the numbers involved get above about twenty, participants will need to be divided into smaller deliberating groups. The time involved is usually several days, during which participants deliberate with each other, as well as hearing from experts and advocates from different sides of an issue, and being able to read information on the issue at hand. The product can be a recommendation on an issue, or a report on the best reasons for and against a course of action, or even a poll of the participants. These kinds of forums have been applied to a wide variety of issues including climate change, biotechnology, nuclear waste, the design of electoral systems, biodiversity, constitutional change, abortion, immigration, and same-sex marriage.

Citizen forums have been researched extensively (Grönlund et al. 2014). What we know from this research is that given the chance and the right circumstances, lay citizens can make highly competent deliberators (or at least competent judges – they are less effective than partisan advocates and parliamentarians when it comes to making arguments and justifying positions). Citizen forums or 'mini-publics' are the best means currently available for taking advantage of the qualities of lay citizens – independence of judgement, reflective capacity, and propensity to invoke common interests – in public deliberation.

Citizens in Climate Justice

The global governance of climate change has not seen anything like the kind of organized citizen engagement of the SDGs. What it has seen is a surge in citizen forums at the national level, especially in the form of citizens' assemblies. Ireland was the pioneer in 2016, when its citizens' assembly (among other topics) spent two weekends on climate change and developed recommendations on carbon taxation and other questions that were taken up by the government.[3] In 2019 Extinction Rebellion called for a citizens' assembly on climate and ecological justice in the United Kingdom and produced a guide to citizens' assemblies.[4] Several committees of the UK Parliament combined to sponsor a citizens' assembly on climate change that was held over four weekends

---

[3] See www.climatechangenews.com/2019/06/27/irelands-world-leading-citizens-climate-assembly-worked-didnt.

[4] See https://rebellion.earth/wp/wp-content/uploads/2019/06/The-Extinction-Rebellion-Guide-to-Citizens-Assemblies-Version-1.1-25-June-2019.pdf.

in 2020, charged with making recommendations on how to reduce greenhouse gas emissions to net zero by 2050 – not quite the more radical framing that Extinction Rebellion was looking for. In France, 2020 saw the establishment of the Convention Citoyenne pour le Climat, made up of 150 people deliberating over seven weekends, with a promise from President Macron that their conclusions would be considered by his government. The convention was in part a response to the Gilets Jaunes multidimensional protest movement, and (more formally) to a request from the associated Gilets Citoyens. In all these cases the citizens' assembly was charged with making recommendations for national policy, but that did not prevent considering the global public good; though the various assemblies were not charged with considering climate justice specifically.

Global Citizen Forums

There is currently no example of a citizen forum at the global level, though in 2020 Laurence Tubiana, chief executive of the European Climate Foundation and co-president of the governing committee for the French Convention Citoyenne pour le Climat, called for a global citizens' assembly to be held before the planned Conference of the Parties (COP) 26 in Glasgow.[5] There is enough relevant experience to suggest it can be done. Lay citizen forums have been held successfully at the transnational level. The most prominent example is the Europolis deliberative opinion poll, held in 2009 over three days in Brussels. Europolis brought together 400 citizens from 27 member states of the EU to deliberate a range of questions facing the EU, including immigration and climate change. Simultaneous translation solved the problem of multiple languages.

The most prominent global exercise in designed citizen deliberation is World Wide Views, which was run first in the lead-up to the 2009 COP of the UN Framework Convention on Climate Change (UNFCCC) in Copenhagen (Rask, Worthington, and Lammi 2012). World Wide Views was multinational rather than transnational. The 2009 exercise was conducted on the same day in thirty-eight different countries, to a common deliberative model (that in practice was tweaked by local partner organizers; so, for example, in Mali the

---

[5] See https://europeanclimate.org/a-tale-of-two-citizens-assemblies.

citizen deliberation was preceded by a day of elders' presentations). Around ninety citizens in each country deliberated a set of questions about climate change and at the end completed the same questionnaire. In almost all countries (China was an exception) the citizens supported stronger action on climate change than their governments were prepared to support. The process had its limitations: a day is not really long enough for citizen deliberation on a complex issue. But World Wide Views shows logistically what is possible. The process was repeated in twenty-five countries in 2012 on biodiversity, then again in seventy-six countries on climate change and energy in 2015. In each case the summary recommendations were presented at the relevant UN COP. The welcome it received was much warmer for biodiversity than for climate change, where in Copenhagen in 2009 the organizers had to rent commercial space in the conference centre to get a platform for their message (interview evidence).

What could have been done, but wasn't, was bring together one or more representatives from each national World Wide Views exercise to deliberate together. It would be especially powerful if this were done as a 'shadow COP' in the same city and at the same time as the official COPs. Bringing together citizens from different countries in this way would have the advantage that they were already primed on the issue in question, so would be ready to go in transnational deliberation. It would have the disadvantage that the citizens in question might see themselves as representatives of their countries, as opposed to citizens of the world. In this light, it could be better to recruit directly into a global citizens' assembly. But could this be done?

A Deliberative Global Citizens' Assembly

The idea of a deliberative global citizens' assembly (DGCA) was first proposed by Dryzek, Bächtiger, and Milewicz (2011). Members of the DGCA would be chosen by random selection organized most easily at the national level, though participants would not represent countries in any sense. Each country would send a number of participants proportional to population size (though a floor of one participant per state could also be established). Random selection should ensure a good spread of participants by income, education, and gender at the global level (though not in any national delegation). The DGCA would need to be broken down into smaller deliberating groups of not more than twenty people, each containing participants from different parts of the world, so they would not be clustered by nation, region, or language. Simultaneous translation would overcome language barriers. The DGCA could vote on measures, or seek consensus among its members; or it could simply be a forum for the generation of ideas, or (consistent with what we know from research on citizen forums in general) be tasked with sorting good from bad arguments for and against proposals.

In its most ambitious conceptualization, the DGCA could act as a general-purpose body whose resolutions would have standing in international law. Alternatively, it could act as a house of review or second chamber to sit alongside the UN General Assembly. That would probably still be a bad place to start. A general-purpose chamber would run the risks of its participants becoming professionalized and so remote from the citizenry whose characteristics they are supposed to represent. More realistically, a DGCA could be convened to deliberate a specific set of issues or global goals – such as the SDGs, or a subset of the goals, or even just one of the goals. This would be consistent with existing national practice with citizens' assemblies.

However ambitious it might seem, a DGCA is more feasible than an elected global parliament. It would not require undemocratic states to hold elections on their territory and it might provoke fewer jitters on the part of Americans implacably hostile to the idea that there could be any (elected) legislative institution at a higher level of governance than the US Congress.

Smaller Forums

Short of a DGCA – and perhaps still less challenging to nervous autocrats and Americans – would be citizens' juries or citizens' panels, which could still play a part in global deliberation. Goodin and Ratner (2011) suggest convening global citizens' juries to deliberate the content of *jus cogens*, peremptory norms of international law (such as prohibitions on returning asylum seekers to where their life would be in danger, genocide, and torture) that take priority over the content of any treaty between states. One can imagine the domain of *jus cogens* extending into the SDGs, especially when it comes to the content of human rights – as we noted in Chapter 1, the SDGs are surprisingly weak when it comes to human rights.

The main difference between a DGCA and citizens' juries or panels is in representativeness and nomenclature. Representativeness is mainly a function of size: a small-scale citizen panel or citizens' jury with, say, twenty participants would find it harder than a large assembly to claim that it is statistically representative of the global population, or capture the diversity in that population. However, a small global citizens' panel could still perform the key functions associated with forums of lay citizens: notably, a capacity for independent judgement and for reflection upon the arguments that they hear. In a criminal case, a jury of 12 members probably works just as well as a jury of 100. Where a relatively small forum might fall short is in epistemic terms, if the full variety of relevant points of view is not captured. However, this shortcoming can be ameliorated through the idea of discursive representation (Dryzek and Niemeyer 2008).

We discussed discursive representation in the previous chapter as a way of making sense of many of the activities of global civil society, home to a variety of discourses, and activists of various sorts who represent these discourses. In the context of citizen forums, discursive representation could be deployed if the requirement is to constitute a relatively small deliberating group. The key here would be to start with a large group of more or less randomly selected citizens as if we were selecting the participants in a DGCA. But rather than have them participate in that larger forum, we could try to ascertain the discourses present in the large group of citizenry, and then select particularly good representatives of each discourse to participate in the smaller deliberative forum. The mapping of discourses should be done inductively in order to get a comprehensive sense of the full range of discourses present. A number of methods could be used, involving interviews, questionnaires, or Q methodology. Q methodology is well developed: it would involve each person in the larger group reacting to a set of forty to sixty statements relevant to the issue area in question (such as issues of global poverty), then sorting them into categories (around nine) from 'most agree' to 'most disagree'. The 'Q sort' that each person produces is a picture of their subjective orientation to the issue area in question. There are millions of ways to sort forty to sixty statements, so each person has substantial freedom in crafting their own position. The Q sorts of the larger group can then be subject to statistical factor analysis to identify a relatively tractable number of discourses. It is then straightforward to identify the individuals who load particularly highly on each of those discourses – and so would make good discursive representatives for inclusion in the smaller deliberating group. We could then ask the participants if our depiction of the discourses on which they (individually) loaded and who we chose to represent them made sense, and change the composition of the smaller group if it did not.

We have emphasized the constitution of bodies of ordinary citizens as the best way to integrate deliberative citizen participation into global governance. It would also be possible to enlist citizen input at the national level (perhaps through citizens' panels) in reviews of the progress (or lack of progress) of national governments in meeting their obligations under international agreements. The existing system of voluntary national review of progress toward the SDGs could be modified to involve citizens' panels. While the SDGs do not actually impose any obligations on governments, the goals and targets are a source of benchmarks. For climate change, citizens' panels could monitor progress on meeting national emissions reduction pledges made under the 2015 Paris Agreement. However, national monitoring would not give citizens the chance to exercise formative agency on the national, let alone global, stage. The same could be said for various individual complaint mechanisms that exist under UN human rights treaties.

As things stand, we are at the beginning of what we suspect is a long road when it comes to effective deliberative citizen participation in global governance. Citizens' assemblies, panels, and juries (minipublics) are just one step on that road. Their importance lies in the degree to which they can induce more effective, broad-scale public deliberative participation in global governance, not substitute for that participation.

The Poor

We turn now from citizens in general to the question of how the poor in particular might participate in global governance. In Chapter 4 we encountered good reasons for stressing the formative agency of the poor. Seeing the poor only as recipients of the largesse of others violates two approaches to justice: one for which recognition of the full humanity of the poor is central; another for which non-domination is crucial to the idea of freedom, and so to one conception of justice.

Unjust domination remains so long as the poor cannot exercise formative agency over the key questions that affect their lives. Formative agency here means democratizing the relationships of the poor with other actors in global governance. Such democratization would also help contribute to the legitimacy of any global process that is ostensibly concerned with matters of basic justice.

There are also epistemic reasons for paying special attention to the formative agency of the poor. The poor have direct or 'situated' knowledge of, and perspectives upon, the causes and consequences of poverty that nobody else has (Haraway 1988; Narayan et al. 2000). Earlier in this chapter we stressed that the effectiveness of democratic deliberation in solving any set of complex problems depends crucially on the integration of all relevant bits of information. Some of the most important bits relevant to questions of global justice are in the hands of the poor themselves; for example, concerning the kinds of individual and collective capabilities they think they need to alleviate misery.

Thinking about the formative agency of the poor puts them in a different light than approaches to justice that conceptualize the poor mainly in terms of being at the receiving end of treatment. For example, Rawls's (1971) second principle of justice famously prioritizes the 'least advantaged', though no grant of formative agency to the poor follows from this recognition, only that their interests are paramount when it comes to justifying inequalities in society. The idea that the poor should be the main beneficiaries of justice is of course also central to prominent accounts of global justice such as those of Singer (2009) and Pogge (2002), though again no agency for the poor necessarily follows.

One thinker who has stressed the agency of the poor as helping to constitute justice is Amartya Sen (1985). However, for Sen, this agency is mainly in the form of the poor exercising control over their own lives, rather than them playing a role, let alone a formative role, in larger systems of governance (though the kind of autonomy Sen stresses would facilitate the ability of the poor to exercise formative agency in larger systems). There is a larger and longer tradition of participatory development that emphasizes the agency of, if not necessarily the poor exclusively, then at least of the communities including them. That tradition and its associated literature are of limited relevance to our concern here with the poor's exercise of agency on the global stage.

The agency of the poor is explicitly promoted by those (such as Kuper 2002; Deveaux 2015) who criticize Singer and Pogge for seeing justice mainly in terms of the obligations of the rich to redistribute their income. Yet the prominence of groups such as Oxfam that advocate for the poor but have none or few poor members confirms the most problematic feature of the poor as potential agents of justice: they often lack the opportunity and capacity to exercise agency, which would require more than they currently have in the way of linguistic skills, free time, education, and access to places where their voice might be expressed and heard. Those who seek the agency of the poor sometimes fail to specify any mechanism whereby this agency might be enabled. Even Simon Caney (2013), while recognizing the claim to agency of victims of injustice, treats it only as a matter of local resistance to unjust rules.

The most obvious solution to this problem would be the direct one: provide the poor with the material conditions (education, income, etc.) that would enable them to exercise agency more effectively. The problem here is that the poor's agency would then only be the outcome of such material redistribution. The poor would not exercise any agency along the way. The alternative would require mechanisms for the poor to exercise their agency without having to wait for material redistribution and its eventual impact on capabilities that would render them no longer poor.

Such mechanisms do exist – at least locally. In India, the state-mandated *gram sabha* village assembly 'creates a space for public interaction among the dominant and the dominated, the literate and the illiterate' and is 'vested with the authority to monitor the activities of the local state and demand accountability' (Rao and Sanyal 2010: 148). Given that one of the main topics of the *gram sabha* is the administration of welfare, this institution enables the poor to be formative agents of justice. This is in stark contrast to the situation in (for example) the United States, where 'the individual beneficiary is a powerless subject' at the mercy of public officialdom (Rao and Sanyal 2010: 148). Interpreting *gram sabhas* as institutions of deliberative democracy, Rao and Sanyal (2010: 154) show that their operation does much to counter inequalities in a caste-divided society: it 'creates a relatively level discursive field. It briefly releases people from inequality traps and allows them the freedom to speak', corroborating the theoretical claim that 'participation in a deliberative democracy is expected to produce more cognitively competent and well-informed people' (Rao and Sanyal 2010: 151). Consistent with the idea that the poor's formative agency is best channelled through deliberation, Rao and Sanyal (2010: 164–7) show how this 'deliberation shapes the meaning of poverty'. At the same time, the deliberation is highly contestatory, as different groups with varying economic deprivation and caste position (the two do not necessarily coincide) make claims.

While it might seem a long way from local institutions such as *gram sabhas* to global justice, the relevant capacities ought to be transferable. It is vital that they operate at the global level, and not just local or national levels, because the poor form a global community of interest. What exactly does this mean, and what are the implications for the deliberative participation of the poor, not least when it comes to global goals?

The Poor as a Global Community of Interest

As we have noted, current accounts in global justice tend to emphasize the agency of wealthy states and individuals (Singer 1972, 2009; Pogge 2002). They are the agents bearing the duties and having the resources to address global injustice. To be sure, allocating responsibility is a crucial step in redressing injustice. However, there is a danger that such an emphasis will encourage us to think only of rich states and individuals or donors and charities as acting as formative agents of justice, and discourage any thought of the recipients of justice – the global poor – doing so. Unfortunately, nobody has a more limited access to formative agency in global governance than the global poor themselves.

There are various ways in which the global poor could act as formative agents. Of course, to some extent the global poor can already *indirectly* exercise *some* formative agency in global governance, insofar as they participate politically in local and national governments, and their government in its turn participates in global governance processes.[6] Here, however, we leave aside this modality of indirectly exercising formative agency via democratic citizenship

---

[6] Of course, their political participation at the local and national levels might be ineffective. This makes their direct participation in global governance even more important.

(whose deficiencies we noted earlier) to concentrate on the alternative, direct, and targeted ways in which the global poor could and should exercise formative agency in global governance.

Such a direct, collective exercise of formative agency on the part of the global poor would involve them *acting together* as a *global community of interest*. Recognizing the global poor as a global community of interest and allowing them to act as such is important not least because global problems like global poverty and climate change require global solutions that go past state boundaries to recognize the collective claims of a transnational group – the global poor – to global justice.

The Ideal

Both political theorists and international organizations implicitly recognize the existence of such a global community of interest, at least rhetorically, every time they use the terms 'global poor', 'world's poor', or the generic phrase 'the poor' (e.g. Pogge 2002, 2005; Risse 2005; UNDG 2013a; World Bank 2017, 2018). But it is harder to see how in practice those to which the term refers can act together under this label. On one hand, the global poor as a *collective* have an *undivided* moral claim to assistance against the rest of the world. On the other hand, the global poor are not represented as one single moral claimant in international governance. Various states may claim to defend the interests of the global poor when in fact the most they can do is to speak for 'their poor' back home.

Several objections could be raised to conceiving the global poor as a global community of interest. First, it might be pointed out that the poor from around the world cannot be a global community of interest because the experience of poverty is different in different parts of the world. There are only *national* poor communities of interest because the experience of poverty is circumscribed to each state and its socio-economic, cultural, and political environment. While recognizing the importance of the international poverty line of $1.90 a day, the Atkinson Commission's Report for the World Bank emphasized the need in the future also to focus on relative poverty lines that are country specific.[7] In being universal, the SDGs bring into focus the

---

[7] The idea would be to complement the absolute measure of global poverty (based on the poverty line of $1.90 a day) with a 'weakly relative' measure of it. The relative measure would be based on the (median) income in each country. By

same problem: while poverty is a *global* problem (in the sense that every country has poor people), the experience of poverty and the poverty line is very different for each state. Hence it makes sense for the poor inside *each state* to speak together in one voice and have their interests represented by their state's government.

Similarly, while all poor share the same *general* interest in escaping poverty, different solutions are needed in different places because the *cause* of poverty varies from one country to another. It would thus be a mistake to talk about the world's poor as constituting *one* community of interest, as if their interests were the same *on the ground*. Poor people's interests at the *concrete* level might in fact clash.

The same, however, could be said of states: the experience of poverty and causes of poverty might vary inside states as well. For example, some regions might be poor because they do not have enough water, others because of the quality of soil. If we think that under these circumstances a state can still speak for 'its' poor, then we must think there must be some way of transcending all the differences and of rendering them commensurable at the *global* scale as well. Furthermore, just as there are limited resources to address poverty and its root causes around the world, each state faces similar problems when dealing with its internal poor. If states can resolve such trade-offs between the interests of their poor inside their borders, then there is no logical problem for the global community of the poor doing likewise at a greater, global scale.

Finally, it might be objected that the *global* poor (in contrast to the poor from each country) do not have the agential capacity to speak with one single voice. After all, the global poor do not constitute a collective agent; they lack, for example, a concrete decision-making procedure allowing them to make collective decisions together (List and Pettit 2011). They also lack the more basic features of loose collectives such as a *common identity* or *shared intentions*.[8] The poor from across the world simply do not see each other as belonging to the same community of interest, it might be argued.

Allowing poor from around the globe to deliberate *together* and exercise formative agency *in the same forum* is crucial in addressing all

---

adding up these 'weakly relative' poverty counts for all countries, we end up with a different, higher estimate of global poverty (see World Bank 2017).

[8] On shared intentions, see Bratman (1993); on shared intentions and collective agency, see Collins (2019).

of these obvious objections. Through processes of democratic deliberation allowing them to exercise formative agency in global governance, the world's poor would be able to *constitute themselves* and act together as a global community of interest. Because democratic deliberation involves equal participation and equal standing, the poor would be able to recognize themselves as a *community* and *single moral claimant*. The deliberations would allow the poor to focus better on their *general* common interest in escaping poverty, as well as reconciling the potential conflicts of interest that arise at the lower level (e.g. 'Which causes of poverty should be tackled first and where?' 'Which programmes should receive funding first?' etc.). They would be able to exercise formative agency, acting as moral arbiters of competing claims to assistance, instead of letting other parties (more or less democratic and plutocratic governments, NGOs, international organizations, donors, corporations) exclusively decide on such matters concerning them.

Through democratic deliberation the poor would also be able to develop *shared intentions* that go beyond generality to form concrete plans and priority lists for donors and the global rich. In other words, global deliberative forums involving poor from different countries would allow them to develop collective agency and assert their moral claims more successfully. By deliberating and exercising formative agency together, the global poor would finally be able to act as a global community of interest.

It should be clear by now that our account is unapologetically *cosmopolitan* in emphasizing global consultations, and we defend it as such. By enabling *cosmopolitan consultation* processes allowing global poor from various parts of the world to exercise formative agency together, international organizations like the UN or World Bank can build global conversations *across* national boundaries rather than inside these boundaries.

But wouldn't *national* consultations be enough? For example, if deliberative forums allowing their poor to exercise formative agency were to be organized in each state, wouldn't that be a perfectly good way of empowering the 'global' poor? Our answer would be 'no'. Because ultimately such forums allow only the poor *inside* each national community to act together and reconcile their competing claims to aid. But they cannot help towards reconciling the competing moral claims emerging among the poor from different states around

the world. Such conflicts remain an issue, and while the poor themselves are left without any means of arbitrating among and having an
input into reconciling these claims, bureaucrats, political elites, and
unelected representatives (like NGOs) speaking on their behalf will be
tasked with such moral work, exercising formative agency where the
poor themselves should.

The Limits of State-Focused Processes

To what extent did the SDG process realize such aspirations to
empower the poor?

A key stage in the process were the national dialogues organized by
the UNDP in cooperation with government officials and civil society
representatives in 83 of a total of 193 member states.[9] Besides the
obvious fact that such consultations did not take place everywhere,
there are several problems with this approach. One is the extent to
which the poor themselves (instead of NGOs speaking on their behalf)
were able to participate in these meetings. Second, we can doubt to
what extent such consultations adopted a deliberative-democratic
format like the one we advocate here. All this means that not all global
poor will have exercised *equal* formative agency – their capacity to do
so depended crucially on where they resided and the efforts that were
put there into ensuring their participation. And of course, as argued
earlier, such state-based processes cannot enable the global poor to
exercise formative agency and act together as a global community of
interest. Only a genuinely global conversation among the poor from
different states would allow the global poor as a group to exercise
formative agency in important areas of global governance, which are
currently dominated by state and non-state actors.

The SDGs process also saw a more active participation of states in
the formulation of the goals, by comparison to the MDGs. It was
important for the new goals not to be perceived as being imposed on
states 'from above' by the UN Secretariat (as the MDGs had been), but
instead to be endorsed and promoted by the states themselves (interview evidence). In negotiations over the SDGs, *large mid-income*

---

[9] Governments were of course free to organize their own consultations in countries
where the UNDP did not organize national dialogues. To what extent they
actually did so, is another question.

developing states played a more active role. This was in part justified by pointing to the sheer large numbers of people living in poverty in these countries, which put these states in an especially strong position as advocates for the poor (interview evidence).[10] Since those states have a larger share of the global poor in their population than do other states, they should have more input into the negotiations.

Such was the claim. But does it have merit? Suppose we define severe poverty, crudely, as 'living on less than $1.90 a day (PPP adjusted)'. By that standard Brazil had 6,943,246 people living in poverty in 2014. Its neighbour Surinam, in contrast, had only 128,215. Brazil thus represents a much larger share of the global poor than does Surinam.[11] How *many* of the global poor a state represents is one thing, however. How *well* they represent them can be quite another. As an indicator of the amount of influence that a country's poor can exert on the policy of their state, we might take the *proportion* of the country's population that is constituted by its poor.[12] In that connection, it is a telling fact that the $1.90-a-day poor represent only 3.4 per cent of Brazil's total population, whereas they represent 23.4 per cent of Surinam's. Following the reasoning just outlined, the poor in Brazil are therefore likely to have much less influence on the policy positions of the government of Brazil than are the poor of Surinam on Surinam's policies. Hence if we ask, 'Which state's government *better* represents the global poor?' (as opposed to, 'Which represents *more* of the global poor?'), the answer is more likely to be Surinam than Brazil.

Or for another example, consider the case of China versus Nepal or Laos. China had 9,549,890 people living on less than $1.90 a day in 2014. In terms of absolute numbers, Nepal and Laos had far fewer:

[10] The World Bank (2018: 29) has noticed this trend in a recent report stating that many of the countries with high poverty numbers (e.g. Bangladesh, India, Indonesia, Kenya, and Nigeria) have become over the last years mid-income economies; meaning two-thirds of the global poor now reside in mid-income countries.

[11] These calculations and those that follow are based on: World Bank, 'World Development Indicators: Poverty Rates at International Poverty Lines', available at http://wdi.worldbank.org/table/1.2#; and World Bank, 'Population Total', available at https://data.worldbank.org/indicator/SP.POP.TOTL.

[12] If anything, that constitutes an overestimate of the power that the poor can actually exert over government policy, given that the poor are typically less politically active than the rich (see e.g. Schattschneider 1960; Goodin and Dryzek 1980; Ansolabehere, de Figueiredo, and Snyder 2003; Lukes 2005; Solt 2008).

4,248,486 and 1,492,842 respectively. But the poor thus defined constituted only 0.7 per cent of China's total population, whereas they constituted 15 per cent of Nepal's and 22.7 per cent of Laos's. So, once again, while China may have represented *more* of the global poor, it is likely that Nepal or Laos represent them *better*.

Putting the point in democratic terms (which are more appropriate to some of the countries just discussed than others, of course), since democratic governments care about getting elected, they will try to first satisfy the interests of their median voter. But in populous mid-income countries, the median voter might not be so poor after all, even when that country has a large number of poor by comparison to other states. Politically, these countries' elites have thus an incentive to better represent the interests of their growing middle class, which is also likely to decide the results of the elections, rather than their poor people's interests.

Of course, even where the poor constitute a large proportion of a state's population, the state has many other interests to pursue than representing the interests of the poor specifically. And any given state might pursue policies that would promote the interests of *its* poor at the expense of equally poor people in other states. In favouring their own poor over others who are equally poor, states can promote only a *subset* of the fragmented interests of the global poor overall. No agent promotes their interests as a global community, nor thinks of these interests and reconciles them in a global, systemic way. For all these reasons, it would be better to empower the global poor as a single community of interest, one that can exercise formative agency through democratic deliberation in a global forum.[13]

It may be thought that democratic deliberation among elected and non-elected representatives of the global poor from each country is the most we can hope from global *intergovernmental* processes. To some extent the SDG OWG fostered such engagement among representatives (elected and otherwise) of the global poor. Yet deliberation among state and non-state actors, as representatives of the global poor, is no substitute for direct global democratic deliberation among the poor themselves. Only the latter would allow the global poor to fully

[13] In Chapter 2 we argued that inclusive and equally participative processes of democratic deliberation among all affected parties can overcome the bias that comes from self-interest, ensuring thereby that the interests of the entire constituency of global poor are represented impartially.

exercise formative agency and arbitrate among their own competing claims and interests. Only the latter guarantees against paternalistic intervention of other agents on their behalf as well as against the hypocritical rhetorical invocation of their interests by other agents such as states, NGOs, or other stakeholders. Furthermore, only such engagement can allow the global poor from different parts of the world to participate together as *equals* in realizing global justice on the ground. Despite their equal sovereignty, different states will always deploy different amounts of power in global governance. This power is, as international relations theorists argued a long time ago, determined by various factors such as their economy, their military capacity, and the size of their territory and population (Morgenthau 1948; Waltz 1993; Mearsheimer 2001).

Since states have a different status and power on the world scene and in international negotiations, equality among the global poor's interests cannot be achieved if only *states* as representatives of the poor act as formative agents of justice. Were we to institute *global forums* enabling the poor to deliberate together on matters of justice and global governance, they would provide a means of bypassing the division between rich and poor states, donor and recipient states, since poor from all countries would be united together in one deliberative body. The framework we propose is an explicitly cosmopolitan one: it postulates the 'global poor' as a global community of interest that transcends national boundaries. States cannot properly represent the interests of such a cosmopolitan, transnational community for the reasons we have already mentioned.

The Global Poor and the SDGs: A Closer Look

We have argued that the formative agency of the poor needs to be exercised in a deliberative way that would construct a global community of interest. Let us now take a closer look at the way the poor participated in the development of the SDGs in light of that requirement. In formulating the SDGs, perhaps for the first time in history, the organizers of a major global process did recognize the need to involve the poor directly, rather than through states' representatives. Even so the poor's participation remained wanting in one respect or another: its scope or its mode. As we will see, some of that participation was global but not deliberative, some was (weakly) deliberative but not global, some was more strongly deliberative but didn't quite succeed in reaching the crucial global level. None of this participation was especially consequential in affecting the content of the goals, despite the best intentions of the UN and its agencies to involve the poor directly (Spijkers and Honniball 2015: 260).

To begin, *global but not deliberative* participation of the poor can be found in the MyWorld survey. The sixteen global goals in the survey were based in part on the results of previous research into priorities of poor people (UN n.d.). One reason for the use of paper ballots was that access to the Internet is rare among the poor. However, the definition of who is poor and who therefore needed extra support to respond to the survey appeared to be arbitrary (Spijkers and Honniball 2015: 264). But as discussed earlier, a survey based on simply selecting six from sixteen goals is not very meaningful; and skewing participation in the survey in favour of the poor (to the extent this was achieved – as we noted earlier, it was in practice skewed in favour of the highly educated) would do little to make it more meaningful.

A very different kind of global but in the end not very deliberative participation was sponsored by ATD Fourth World (All Together in Dignity to Overcome Poverty), which organized testimony in New York by people living in poverty. The individuals in question spoke before the UN's Commission for Social Development (in 2014) and other events, but not directly to key bodies such as the High-Level Panel and OWG. They did not deliberate with each other.

Weakly deliberative but not global participation of the poor can be found in the national dialogues. Their guidelines stressed the need to 'amplify the voices of the poor and other marginalized in formal negotiation processes ... support citizens from the Global South to actively engage in the discussions towards a post-2015 development agenda ... to create avenues through which voices of the marginalized can be amplified and acted upon' (UNDG 2012: 13). The fact that it was the *national* (and not transnational or global) dialogues where participation of the poor and marginalized would be sought was confirmed in the Initial Input Report that the UN secretary-general prepared for the OWG in 2012. The enormous variety in the way the national dialogues were conducted probably meant that some proved better at channelling the concerns of the poor than others. 'The consultations involved inter alia street children, indigenous people and people living with HIV in the Asia Pacific region, the homeless and prisoners in Brazil, and gang members in El Salvador' (Fox and Stoett 2016: 563), but there was no systematic logic behind these selections. Even if the poor participated effectively in a national dialogue, their concerns still had to be represented in global processes by somebody else.

The most *strongly deliberative* effort to involve the poor in the SDGs began in 2012 with the founding of Participate, a network of research organizations active in twenty-nine countries, whose mission was 'to bring the perspectives of those left behind into the post-2015 debate'.[14] This was done by carrying out and summarizing participatory research on the perspectives of the poor, and through trying to influence UN bodies to develop mechanisms for those voices to be heard. Participate also developed exhibitions and films targeted at participants in the SDGs process, including ordinary citizens (Shahrokh and Wheeler 2014). The research itself was participatory in that it involved members of poor communities in co-design. Reacting to the early activities of the High-Level Panel, Participate (2013) issued a mixed evaluation, arguing that 'a "people-centred" agenda is one in which the transformation of societies is led by citizens themselves – including the poorest and most marginalized, such that participation in research is itself empowering. This must be the guiding principle that underpins the new global development framework'. Participate produced numerous reports and videos on the conditions and perspectives of marginalized people around the world.

Participate offered all twenty-seven members of the High-Level Panel the chance briefly to live with marginalized people. None of the twenty-seven accepted the offer (Chambers 2014: 5). This refusal is perhaps symbolic of the difficulty in getting those in positions of power to take seriously the kinds of knowledge that Participate was trying to generate. As Shahrokh and Wheeler (2014: 20) point out, 'While Participate was premised on the challenges of mobilising the poor and marginal into policy discussions, through this process we became more cognisant of the challenge of mobilising policymakers to step outside of their own margins and towering heights'. We will have more to say on this kind of linkage between the poor and the powerful when we address deliberative systems in Chapter 8.

---

[14] See participatesdgs.org/about.

By way of highlighting the limitations of the UN's High-Level Panel, Participate sponsored a series of Ground-Level Panels of ten to fourteen people with a mix of experiences drawn from poor communities, along with local political leaders. Panels were held in Egypt, Brazil, India, and Uganda. The panels produced conclusions strikingly at variance with the content of the SDGs. For example, the Brazilian panel saw economic growth (treated as desirable in the SDGs) as 'part of the "death plan". For the Brazilians, the critical issue is not "poverty" per se, but "misery" and dignity' (Burns 2014: 42). Burns (2014: 42) summarizes the common themes emerging from panels in different countries: 'People want to feel that they have meaningful control over the influences that impact their lives. In all cases structures for equal participation were highlighted as foundational. In almost all of the panels there was a recurring theme of "self-management". People don't want aid. They want the means to generate and sustain their own livelihoods.' Participate emphasized the power dynamics and intersecting and reinforcing inequalities and discriminatory norms that can get in the way of good intentions in the implementation of the SDGs.

Perhaps alone among the various inputs into SDGs, Participate combined deliberative principles with direct participation of the poor. Burns (2014: 42) points out that though deliberative principles informed the design of the Ground-Level Panels, they could find no existing deliberative designs whose 'material for discussion was to be the life experiences of the participants'. The panels mixed lay citizens with community activists. They did not, however, include those living in the most extreme poverty (for which the week-long process might be too demanding). Participate did try to get the powerful to hear the voice of the poor, producing summary reports and a documentary, organizing outreach days (Newell 2014: 30), and sending speakers to public events. The powerful did not necessarily listen.

Participate constituted a small step along the road to the establishment of a deliberative global community of interest of the poor exercising formative agency. This sort of deliberative participation by the poor will not necessarily be welcomed by the states to which the poor belong, nor can those states be relied upon to communicate the reflective concerns of the poor to the global level. The problem is compounded to the degree global governance is intergovernmental (see Chapter 3) and so made up largely of the very states that can be such poor transmitters of the real concerns of their own poor. This consideration drives home the need to think in terms of a global community of interest of the poor, and of the roles that non-state actors and institutions can play in global governance; if necessary in a way that will restrain ineffective, corrupt, or incompetent states. Two possibilities here involve the organization by the poor of global social movements and global institutional design. These two, which we now examine, correspond respectively to the distinction between 'insisted' and 'invited' participation (Carson 2007).

Enhancing the Global Deliberative Participation of the Poor

Poor-Led Transnational Social Movements

Deveaux (2018) points to the importance of 'poor-led social movements' in promoting global justice (acting as global justice entrepreneurs, in our terms). Most of her examples are national or sub-national (landless workers in Brazil, landless poor in Bangladesh, and pavement dwellers in India). Such movements can challenge oppressive laws and practices, struggle for political recognition, and seek redistributive social policies. They can also shape the meaning of poverty and identify its causes in oppressive social, economic, and legal structures, as well as raise the individual and collective capabilities of the poor to control their own lives. The one globally active such movement Deveaux considers is La Via Campesina (LVC), which began in South America, but is now a global peasants' movement. As Deveaux (2018: 6) points out, LVC has had some success in influencing policy and (in our terms) exercising formative agency. In 2018 the UN General Assembly adopted the Declaration on the Rights of Peasants and Other People Working in Rural Areas after years of lobbying from LVC and others.

LVC was founded in 1993. It is multinational (more than eighty countries) and multilingual (see Martinez-Torres and Rossett 2010 for its history), and makes massive use of simultaneous translation at its meetings. Central to its global agenda is the idea of food sovereignty, meaning environmentally sustainable local participatory control over food systems, as opposed to corporate or market control and subordination to the neoliberal global political economy. Food sovereignty resonates with Target 2.3 in the SDGs: 'By 2030, double the agricultural productivity and incomes of small-scale food producers, in particular women, indigenous peoples, family farmers, pastoralists and fishers, including through secure and equal access to land, other productive resources and inputs, knowledge, financial services, markets and opportunities for value addition and non-farm employment.' However, as written this target embodies a lot of ambiguity on the key question of concern to LVC: the reference to 'financial services' and 'markets' could mean tighter integration into the global economy, rather than food sovereignty.

Elizabeth Mpofu (2018), general coordinator of LVC, lauds the commitments of the SDGs on poverty, food security, and sustainable agriculture, but says agroecology with land reform is necessary. In a presentation to the High-Level Political Forum she praises the content of Goal 2 ('End hunger, achieve food security and improved nutrition, and promote sustainable agriculture') and argues for a radical interpretation of what its targets should mean. At the same time, she worries that it will be overridden by the broader commitment of the SDGs to conventional economic growth and free trade and the domination of their implementation by corporations and global financial institutions, and regrets that the key concepts advanced by LVC – 'food sovereignty, agroecology, and popular and integral agrarian reforms' – find no mention in the SDGs.[15]

LVC has also been present in the activist gatherings that flourish on the fringes of the UNFCCC negotiations. 'Peasants can cool the planet', because agroecology is much more climate-friendly than industrial agriculture (Cormier 2010). LVC opposes measures that will affect peasant livelihoods, such as emissions mitigation schemes that involve carbon trading and forestry and that threaten to displace peasants from the land. It joins with other climate justice organizations to try to ensure that the voices of some of those most vulnerable to the impacts of climate change, as well as vulnerable to mitigation measures, are heard.

LVC's urban counterpart is Slum Dwellers International (SDI), a global network founded in 1996 and active in at least thirty-three countries, mostly in developing countries. SDI is perhaps less radical than LVC, working with local and national governments and large foundations, such as the Gates and Ford Foundations. Target 11.1 of

---

[15] See https://sustainabledevelopment.un.org/content/documents/ 24933elizabethmpofuzimsoff.pdf.

the SDGs is: 'By 2030, ensure access for all to adequate, safe and affordable housing and basic services, and upgrade slums'. While SDI founder Jockin Apurtham recognizes the relevance of Goal 11 to its vision of 'slum-friendly cities',[16] SDI appears not to have been very active in the SDG process.

There are or have been other movements of the vulnerable (if not necessarily poor), for example the World Council of Indigenous Peoples, which dissolved in 1996 (amid claims its international reach was not comprehensive and groups with more limited remit taking over some of its functions; see Kemner 2011). The year 1996 did, however, also see the founding of the International Indigenous Forum on Biodiversity; more limited in scope than the World Council, as its name suggests, and active in connection with the UN Framework Convention on Biodiversity (CBD).[17] As such it is not quite as radical as LVC, seeking instead recognition of the role of indigenous people in conserving biodiversity and the importance of involving indigenous peoples in any global biodiversity strategy, given how much of the world's biodiversity is located in areas they inhabit. The World Forum of Fisher Peoples is a federation of national organizations representing small-scale fishers.

Poor people's movements are, then, thin on the ground in global governance. Poor groups are often not organized (Zuijderduijn, Egberts, and Krämer 2016: 32). In their absence, advocacy groups and activists sometimes claim to speak for the poor. As we saw in Chapter 5, that role can be problematic (though we also showed how some of the more problematic aspects could be alleviated). Most of the participants in the World Social Forum, perhaps the most high-profile global forum devoted to the concerns of the poor and marginalized, are relatively radical NGOs, social movement organizations, and activist groups, as opposed to grassroots transnational poor people's movements (though some national movements participate).

Institutional Design for the Participation of the Poor

The Participate initiative discussed earlier involved attempts to develop some structures for the poor to deliberate and get their voice heard,

---

[16] See www.iied.org/what-might-slum-dwellers-want-sdgs.
[17] See https://iifb-fiib.org.

with some institutional innovation in the Ground-Level Panels. It is possible to push institutionalization a bit further.

Earlier we saw how ordinary citizens could be recruited into transnational and global citizen forums, such as the Deliberative Global Citizens' Assembly. It would be possible to constitute such forums based not on random selection, but targeted to recruit the poor (though even random selection if done properly should yield a significant representation of the global poor in any assembly).

In the context of the Post-2015 Development Agenda, Wisor (2012: 126) proposed assemblies along these lines at multiple levels (from the local to the global) whose composition would 'stack the deck for social justice' by oversampling the poor. Wisor (2012: 128–9) points out that the effective participation of the poor (and even illiterate) could be promoted by support for building the capacities of participants, financial compensation for time spent, and anonymity (to enable individuals to speak freely about the particular injustices to which they have been subjected). A proposal for the Post-2015 Development Agenda to deploy deliberative assemblies along these lines was made to the UNDP in 2012 by the group Academics Stand Against Poverty,[18] but it had no impact.

In our earlier discussion of citizens, we suggested that it would be possible to bring together selected participants from national citizen forums in a global process. The same logic could apply to the participation of the poor: people who have developed their capabilities and knowledge in local processes, such as Ground-Level Panels, could be recruited to global processes.

Transnational social movements and institutional designs for the direct participation of the poor can both help in the construction of a global community of interest of the poor, and help render that community consequential in global governance. Movements and institutions both have roles to play in deliberative systems, about which we will have more to say in Chapter 8.

Conclusion

The democratization of global justice ought to enhance the formative agency of the citizens who are central to any democracy and the poor whose well-being is central to most conceptions of global justice. This agenda could be advanced by:

---

[18] For which one of us (Dryzek) provided some advice.

- conducting global public engagements with citizens in thickly deliberative fashion, as opposed to the thin forms of consultation that have dominated to date;
- establishing the principle that global governance processes should be accountable to the global citizenry;
- establishing global citizens' assemblies and other kinds of transnational citizen forums;
- validating the global poor as a community of interest by providing opportunities for the transnational interaction that would give such a community tangible form;
- recognizing the ability of transnational poor-led social movements to facilitate deliberative inclusion of the least advantaged;
- designing institutions at all levels from the local to the global for the direct deliberative participation of the poor; and
- ensuring that institutions for the deliberative participation of citizens in general and the poor in particular have meaningful and consequential voice in global governance.

The participation in global governance of citizens in general, and the poor in particular, should not be seen merely as a matter of consultation whose outcomes those in power can choose to accept or ignore as they see fit. Participation can start with consultation, but should not end there. Meaningful and empowered participation must be deliberative, inclusive, and consequential if citizens, and the poor specifically, are to be effective formative agents of justice. That effectiveness also depends on how they are joined with other actors in deliberative systems, but before attending to that question in Chapter 8, we will look at others often absent in global justice governance: future generations and non-humans.

7 | Democratizing Intergenerational, Interspecies, and Ecological Justice

The Role of Moral Imagination in Deliberation

In the previous chapters we have discussed the ways in which individual or collective agents exercise formative agency in global justice governance. We defined formative agents as those deciding which principles of justice are suited in any given socio-economic, political, and cultural context, and what these abstract principles require in practice, on the ground. They thus 'translate' various theories of global justice into policies, programmes, or procedures taking effect in the real world. The inclusive exchange of arguments and reasons among free and equal deliberators – democratic deliberation – is, as we have argued, supportive of such processes (see Chapter 2). The processes of reflection and moral reasoning should thus be central to the exercise of formative agency.

Global justice policies and institutions have long-lasting and wide-ranging effects across time and space. They can, for example, affect the welfare of *future individuals* as well, by reducing or enhancing the various available resources and opportunities that they will enjoy. Moreover, such policies and institutions can also (more or less) negatively affect *ecosystems, animal species*, and ultimately Earth in its entirety. The welfare of future generations, non-human animals, and ecosystems is especially affected by policies addressing global poverty and climate change, both of which figure prominently in the Sustainable Development Goals (SDGs). While tackling these problems is a matter of justice owed to present people, it should be done in a way that is respectful of *intergenerational,*[1] *interspecies,* and *ecological* justice. Guaranteeing food security and access to energy, promoting

---

[1] 'How can we get a grip on (or quantify) intergenerational justice?' we might ask. The ecological footprint and early-life conditions (as measured by child poverty levels) are two indicators of intergenerational equity. Together with fiscal burdens (as measured by public debt levels per child) and pro-elderly bias in social spending, they give us a good image of the levels of intergenerational justice at the domestic or global levels. See Vanhuysse (2013) for a cross-national

global equality, and maintaining existing levels of prosperity for present people should thus not come at undue cost to biodiversity and the well-being of future generations.

Various individual and collective agents – from the global poor to states to corporations – can act as formative agents of justice influencing global governance agendas. Since future generations, non-human animals, and ecosystems are also deeply affected by these agendas – morally as well as legally[2] – their interests should also figure prominently in them. The United Nations (UN) Sustainable Development Agenda should be no exception to that. One problem is, of course, that future individuals, non-human animals, or ecosystems cannot themselves exercise formative agency in global governance.[3] They cannot be actors in global governance or engage in the reasoned exchange of arguments and reasons to defend their interests. Given that fact, how can their interests be given due consideration by the *other* formative agents in the course of global justice deliberations? How can we ensure a better representation of these silent interests in global governance?

To be sure, the neglect of these silent interests might be due to a multitude of factors. In this chapter we focus on one in particular – *moral imagination* – which hasn't been on the radar of scholars of global governance or deliberative democracy. We argue, first, that moral imagination plays an important role in the exercise of formative agency and thus also in any deliberative process supporting this agency. We argue, second, that the difficulty of taking into account the interests of future generations, non-human animals, and ecosystems might be due to a *failure* of moral imagination on the part of those who *can* exercise formative agency. If deliberators have trouble imagining the stakes that ecosystems, animals, and future generations

comparison of the Organization for Economic Cooperation and Development (OECD) states along these lines.

[2] Legally, in virtue of international treaties protecting animal species and ecosystems, such as the Convention on Biological Diversity (1992) and the Cartagena Protocol on Biosafety to the Convention on Biological Diversity (2000).

[3] While recent work in a number of biological fields has uncovered quasi-agency in communicative and cooperative action in non-human species and systems, and even plants (see Calvo 2016), that does not mean non-humans can be seen as *formative* agents of justice, because formative agency requires a capacity to shape the meanings of abstract principles.

have in their decisions and how their well-being might be affected by the alternative courses of action under consideration, then they will end up inadvertently privileging their own interests over the course of the deliberations.[4] Finally, we suggest that while deliberation is eminently talk-centric, the use of arguments, narrative, or testimony might not be enough to stimulate the formative agents' moral imagination. We point out that the use of *visual imagery* and *experiential prompts* might be more impactful in this respect. If so, then visual and experiential inputs including those enabled by technological advancement – pictures, projections, and holograms – should be more widely used in deliberative settings to evoke mute non-present, non-human interests, where they are at stake in the decisions being made. Visual and immersive technologies stimulating moral imagination can thus complement talk-centric democratic deliberation to maximize its potential.

Background

One might think that because sustainable development is a forward-looking concept it simply cannot overlook the interests of future generations. After all, the Brundtland Commission defined sustainable development as 'meeting the needs of the present generation *without compromising* the ability of future generations to meet their own needs' (World Commission on Environment and Development 1987: 8, emphasis added). Yet global governance decisions are political decisions, taken here and now by present generations and their representatives. Sustainability thus risks being understood in the short term as sustainability across one, two, or three generations.[5] It is less likely that global governance decisions will focus on *perpetual* sustainability: sustainability at the *species* level of all mankind, in the long term.

---

[4] Notice that because of their planetary scale, we might have trouble grasping or keeping them present in the back of our mind when deciding the various effects that such policies would have on these three different categories of interests.

[5] Because they take into account their own interests, the interests of their children, and their grandchildren. It's harder, however, for them to think beyond that. This is clear from the UN secretary general's report on future solidarity, which dedicates a section to 'children and young people'. It also states that 'few would question the responsibilities that the world owes to its *children and grandchildren*, at least in the moral sense if not strictly in law. Our political thinking, mirroring these concerns, speaks to those obligations' (UN 2013: 2, emphasis added).

Such an expanded time frame for sustainability is harder to invoke and justify, first, because it entails higher costs for present people and their immediate descendants and, second, because in some areas we lack the scientific instruments that would allow us to see that far into the future. There are of course exceptions: at present we know already that those born ten or twenty generations into the future will be most affected by the decisions we now make, especially regarding climate change mitigation and environmental protection (UN 2013: 5).

While we could not identify any particular institution or mechanism that was specially dedicated to representing the interests of future generations in the SDGs negotiations themselves, it was a topic being much discussed in prior and parallel international discussions. Rhetorically at least, the 2012 document emerging from Rio+20 – 'The Future We Want' – places a strong emphasis on the future. It states in its first paragraph that countries should renew their 'commitment to sustainable development and to ensuring the promotion of an economically, socially and environmentally sustainable future for our planet and for present and *future generations*' (UN 2012). There was also a proposal supported by the Group for Children and Youth at the Rio+20 conference to establish a UN High Commissioner for Future Generations, but it was removed at the last moment from the outcome document (Offerdahl 2013). The proposed high commissioner was supposed to emulate the Ombudsman for Future Generations, an institution found in several countries. Furthermore, an Expert Panel on Future Generations made up of only five experts was also convened in 2013 with the purpose of informing the secretary general's report.

The 2013 report of the secretary general entitled *Intergenerational Solidarity and the Needs of Future Generations*, mandated by the Rio+20 Conference, was endorsed by the General Assembly in its resolution 66/288. Its aim was to put forward ways of 'institutionalising concern for future generations' within the UN system, as well as showing how intergenerational solidarity was 'embedded in the concept of sustainable development' (UN 2013: 2).

A positive development is the report's adoption of a more expansive conception of *intergenerational solidarity* that includes future generations who do not yet exist. That constitutes acknowledgement that the appropriate time frame for some governance decisions (such as those affecting the climate and the environment) is that of the entire *species* rather than any given generation. This is premised on the view of the report that humanity forms an 'intergenerational community' (UN 2013: 3).

Tellingly, the document's title uses the word 'solidarity' instead of 'justice'. The aim is thereby to motivate the present generation to take into account the interests of future generations on the grounds that they are both part of the same community of interest, rather than because the present generation *owes* something to future generations (e.g. for inflicting harm through their actions on future generations). And indeed, the report emphasizes early on that 'all members [of humanity'] must care and respect one another in order to achieve the 'common goal of survival of humankind' (UN 2013: 3). The language of justice (and rights talk) comes to the fore in the section on ethical dimensions, which draws on moral philosophical thinking. But it does not figure in the title, summary, or recommendation of the report, which stresses, in a vague and not so helpful way, the need for 'suitable mechanisms to promote intergenerational solidarity for the achievement of sustainable development, taking into account the needs of future generations' (UN 2013: 18).

The report also recognizes that conflicts between the interests of present and future generations should be reconciled through 'open, reasoned processes and not by means of closed or indirect systems of decision-making' (UN 2013: 5). This reads of course as a rhetorical endorsement of deliberative democratic processes of the sort we argue for in this book. To what extent the UN practically tried to secure intergenerational justice through such processes is another issue, however. While the report endorsed the establishment of an Ombudsman or High Commissioner for Future Generations, recommending that states 'may wish' to invite the High-Level Political Forum to consider such arrangements, in the end no such institution or similar mechanism was adopted.

Environmental advocacy groups as well as animal welfare and animal rights non-governmental organizations (NGOs), were more actively involved in the SDGs negotiations. Despite this, the SDGs remain largely anthropocentric and do not make any reference to animal welfare, to the disappointment of animal advocacy groups. When it comes to environmental groups, whenever they influenced states to support goals that were environmentally or species-friendly, they did so by emphasizing that this would be in those states' interest rather than being a matter of interspecies or ecological justice, recognizing animal species and ecosystems as moral claimants (interview evidence). And finally, another downside is that the goals do not explicitly recognize the importance of the Earth system and planetary boundaries, as already pointed out in Chapter 1.

We can only hope that future processes aimed at developing successors to the goals before they expire in 2030 will be better at acknowledging the interests of animals, ecosystems, and future generations, and at developing special institutions for representing them. In what follows, we identify the particular obstacles a future decision process would face in that respect.

Moral Imagination

Imagination is the capacity to form a mental representation or image of things that we do not perceive: absent objects and people, events, or experiences. As such, imagination is standardly distinguished from other mental states like perceiving, remembering, believing, desiring, or anticipating (Gendler 2018). Importantly for our purpose, imagination plays a central role in moral judgement (Gendler 2018). The term 'moral imagination' refers to the imaginative processes that support moral reasoning or are deployed to answer moral dilemmas; for example, when evaluating the fairness of different possible outcomes.[6] In virtue of this important function in moral reasoning, moral imagination is also an essential component of formative agency.

Lacking any secondary rules and principles governing their own application, abstract moral rules and principles must be interpreted in light of specific circumstances. The process of applying abstract rules to the real world – of putting principles into practice – is in large part a creative and imaginative one (Larmore 2001: 47–64). Moral imagination can help us determine '*which* moral principles are relevant to the case at hand and *how* those moral principles apply in the present context' (Johnson 1985: 266, original emphasis).[7] We often use imagination in moral deliberation whenever we recognize how any given moral rule or principle (such as the categorical imperative) is

---

[6] A cognate concept of moral imagination is 'moral creativity': creativity used in moral reasoning for solving complex moral problems (see Grisanti and Gruber 1993).

[7] Of course, coherence tests and inference may also be used in this task of deciding which principles are relevant and how they would apply to any given context.

relevant to any given situation, or assess how that situation is similar or dissimilar to other situations to which we applied the same rule or principle (Johnson 1985: 276). The development of 'mid-level norms' that bridge general principles and norms to particulars – 'specification' in Henry Richardson's words – rests on moral imagination (Richardson 1990; Biss 2014: 16). Assessing the feasibility and desirability of different options also requires moral imagination. It entails mentally representing potential states of affairs as a way of figuring out which option should be pursued.

Furthermore, moral imagination helps us better understand others around us (Kekes 1991). By enabling perspective-taking and stimulating empathy (Rabinowitz and Heinhorn 1985),[8] morally sympathetic imagination allows us to stand in relationships of justice with others and show concern for their rights, interests, and well-being.[9] Through moral imagination we can depict in our minds the lives of differently situated individuals in time and space, but also different possible worlds that we could have inhabited (counterfactuals) or that we might inhabit in the future: 'Imagination is the means for *going beyond ourselves* as presently formed, moving transformatively toward imagined ideals of what we might become … moral imagination is our capacity to see and to realize in some actual or contemplated experience possibilities for enhancing the quality of experience both for ourselves and the communities of which we are a part' (Johnson 1993: 209, emphasis added). In being able, through moral imaginative processes, to envisage possibilities beyond our immediate context, and thereby endorse a comparative perspective, we can also better evaluate our immediate context and its possibilities, and improve them (Kekes 1991: 104).

---

[8] See also Johnson (1993: 200): 'Reflecting in this way [through empathic imagination] involves an imaginative rationality through which we can participate empathically in another's experience … Morally sensitive people are capable of living out, in and through such experiential imagination, the reality of others with whom they are interacting, or whom their actions might affect.'

[9] Empathy refers to those capacities allowing us to know what others are thinking and feeling, and to share those thoughts and feelings. It is thus instrumental in enabling us to promote others' well-being (Stueber 2019). We use the terms 'empathy' and 'sympathy' interchangeably here. Before the term 'empathy' was introduced in English in 1909, the term 'sympathy' was used to refer to the same capacities (Stueber 2019). While analytically distinct, moral imagination can enable empathetic thinking.

Moral Imagination and Formative Agency

Since applying moral principles to particular cases requires moral imagination, moral imagination will play an equally important role in the exercise of formative agency. Formative agents called upon to deliberate about how abstract principles of global justice should translate into policy will have to imagine the consequences of the various policies under consideration.

They will have to imagine not just how those policies would affect them, but also how they would affect others living in a very different environment. Those 'others' include not just other present humans, but also future generations, ecosystems, and animals whose sensorial perception of this world is very different from their own. In other words, the exercise of formative agency through external collective, democratic-deliberative processes will require individuals not only to put themselves in other people's shoes – some in the very distant future – but also to take the perspective of other, *non-human* objects of moral concern, such as animal species or ecosystems. Since these groups cannot exercise formative agency and act as equal deliberators in their own right, the moral success of these democratic-deliberative processes, and their potential to include this vast array of affected interests, will depend on those who can exercise formative agency. It will depend primarily on their capacity to act as *impartial* deliberators and decision makers, placing adequate weight on these groups' interests. But decision makers' impartiality hinges in turn on their moral imagination – their capacity to imagine and relate to future generations, animals, and ecosystems, and to how their interests will be affected by their decisions.

When decisions entail potential trade-offs between our self-interest and others' well-being, deficiencies of moral imagination can lead us to adopt biased decisions that favour our own immediate self-interest. Both climate change and global poverty are complex global problems – 'perfect moral storms' in Gardiner's (2006) words – that entail trade-offs between the (short-term) interests of present individuals and their political representatives and the (long-term) interests of future generations, animals, and ecosystems. Next we point out that global governance decisions may fall prey to the logic of self-interest and short-termism due to the limited moral imagination of current stakeholders and deliberators.

The Triumph of Short-Term Self-Interest: A Problem of Moral Imagination?

Since imagination plays an essential role in moral reasoning, an enlarged moral imagination is better able to ensure collective outcomes that are just among all affected parties – human and non-human alike. On the other hand, deficits in moral imagination or obstacles to it can distort moral reasoning, leading to suboptimal moral outcomes. The phenomenon of *imaginative resistance* points to such limitations. Imaginative resistance occurs when an individual cannot (or is unwilling to) imagine something, for example, out of fear that the imagination process might challenge her beliefs (Gendler 2018).

As Steven Cooke (2017: e1) remarked, despite the powerful arguments put forward by animal rights advocacy and conservation groups, nothing much has changed over the last years for animals themselves. According to a report by the World Wide Fund for Nature (WWF), since the 1970s humans have wiped out 60 per cent of the world's mammals, birds, fish, and reptiles (Carrington 2018). Furthermore, according to the International Union for the Conservation of Nature (IUCN), some 26,000 species are currently under threat (Watts 2018).[10] Cooke (2017) argues that moral psychology plays an important role in the failure to realize animal rights – or to ensure species conservation, we might add. He points out that sympathy is a motivating force and that moral imagination is a constitutive element of the process of feeling sympathy for others. Yet animals pose a special challenge to moral imagination, because it is very difficult – indeed, perhaps impossible – for humans to take the perspective of 'essentially alien beings' (Cooke 2017: e8).[11] Take, for example, the philosophically notorious case of bats – since these creatures experience the world very differently from us, we may have trouble fully understanding their experiences and hence situate those in the context of moral reasoning (Nagel 1974; Cooke 2017: e12).

---

[10] The organization is best known for compiling and publishing the IUCN Red List of Threatened Species, which assesses the conservation status of species worldwide.

[11] This is not to say the problem arises *only* in the case of animals. It may arise of course, to a lesser or greater extent, also when trying to imagine the life of humans living through events we've never experienced (e.g. Aleppo under siege) or in the case of those with severe disabilities.

In consequence, the decisions we make as individuals and communities will be insensitive to animal interests. We face the same or perhaps greater challenges when trying to contemplate the interests of ecosystems and the environment overall. Humans have so far managed to wipe out 571 plant species (likely a gross underestimate) (Carrington 2019). Together with the extinction of so many animal species, this accelerated extinction of plant species is considered by scientists the 'sixth mass extinction of life on Earth' (Carrington 2019). Ecosystems and plants also suffer from the sharp drop in the number of insects that are vital plant pollinators, as a result of human activity and development (McCarthy 2017). In contrast to animals, however, it is even harder to empathize with forms of life (plants and ecosystems) that cannot feel pain (or pleasure) and are not endowed with cognition and consciousness.[12] This failure to feel sympathy for alien others – whether animals or ecosystems – prevents us from reaching judgements that are impartial as between animal, ecosystem, and human interests.

A Challenge for Deliberative Democracy?

Deliberations about global justice seeking to include the interests of future generations, non-human animals, and ecosystems, will thus have to cope with two separate (but related) obstacles. First, these groups will not be able to speak for themselves,[13] to defend their interests in deliberation, and act as formative agents of justice. Second, those (humans) who can act as formative agents of global justice and participate in deliberations may be unable – owing to a deficit of moral imagination or imaginative resistance – to impartially take into account the interests of these groups in their deliberations and judgements.

Just outcomes are *impartial* outcomes – outcomes that place appropriate weight on all affected parties' interests. Of course, different theories of justice define 'appropriate' in different ways. But we do not need to adopt any given substantive conception of justice to know

---

[12] Different scholars of plant neurobiology might of course disagree with this statement to various degrees. To get a sense of the disagreement among plant scientists, see Gabbatiss (2017).

[13] Of course, while they cannot speak human language, ecosystems send plenty of tell-tale signs that can communicate their condition and needs to humans. Even so, humans can be very bad at recognizing these signals.

that in the minimal sense justice requires diligently taking into account others' interests alongside one's own, *without* (self-interested) bias or prejudice.[14] This is what we mean by 'just' and 'impartial' outcomes here.

Deliberative democrats emphasize that democratic deliberation, being inclusive and equally participative, promotes impartial thinking through the exchange of reasons and considerations that other deliberators can accept. But this impartiality is largely the by-product of the fact that by participating in the deliberation, all those individuals are equally capable of defending – through argument – their own interests and those of people similar to themselves (and who by extension have similar interests). The deliberative outcome is thus impartial across the subset of deliberators and the groups they represent; it may nonetheless fail to be impartial with respect to groups whose interests are not directly or indirectly represented in the deliberation.[15] Since future generations, non-human animals, and ecosystems cannot directly participate ('speak for themselves') in deliberations, they are surely disadvantaged.

To that we might reply that, insofar as others can speak for these groups, their interests should appropriately be represented in deliberation, and deliberations may reach a decision that is impartial across all present and future individuals, as well as non-human animals and ecosystems. That is the point, after all, of political innovations such as the Ombudsman for Future Generations – an institution several polities have or had at one point.[16] But there are two limitations when it comes to this strategy, both of which have to do with a lapse in moral imagination.

First, we might worry that the spokespersons themselves may not be fully able to represent the interests of these groups, due to limitations of

[14] The term 'appropriate' is meant to leave open the question of *which* theory of justice should guide us in weighing the interests of present and future generations, animals, and ecosystems.

[15] Our observation draws on Sen's (2002) distinction between 'open' and 'closed' impartiality. He points out that devices such as Rawls's veil of ignorance would be able to achieve closed impartiality – a partial type of impartiality across existing members of the decision-making community – but would fail to ensure an open, universal type of impartiality across all interests and perspectives, notably those found outside any given political community or other decision-making group.

[16] For example: Israel, Wales, and Hungary.

their own moral imagination. This may happen especially when the spokespersons would be chosen among bureaucrats, political representatives, and other professionals who have spent their entire lives serving people rather than trying to understand the non-human world. Or, even if they themselves succeed in fully internalizing the interests of those groups, they may nonetheless have trouble conveying to the rest of the deliberators the full extent of the effects their decisions will have on future generations, non-human animals, and ecosystems.

Second, deliberators might experience imaginative resistance, or might simply find it difficult to fully empathize with these groups in a way that allows them to be impartial decision makers, despite the goodwill of the spokespersons and the arguments that they advance. As Cooke (2017) points out, this is the point we are at right now, at least when it comes to the interests of non-human animals and ecosystems. Advocacy groups and biodiversity experts have been vocal and clear in communicating the extent of damage done to animals and ecosystems, as well as how development policies and climate change affect them. However, what seem like powerful and persuasive arguments to researchers and scientists still fail to have a desirable impact on the minds and judgements of either political representatives or the general public.

Future generations are in a weak position as well. They lack powerful social movements or NGOs promoting their interests. There is no organization equivalent to Greenpeace, Oxfam, or Save the Children devoted to protecting the interests of distant future generations alone. Our interviewees confirmed that intergenerational justice was not one of the main talking points during the SDGs negotiations, with discussions focusing on states' short-term development over the next ten years or so. Only a limited number of small organizations focusing exclusively on future generations (such as the World Future Council and the Oxford Martin Commission for Future Generations) were involved in the discussions (either in the Expert Panel on Intergenerational Solidarity organized by the UN Department of Economic and Social Affairs (DESA) or in the Open Working Group (OWG) discussions).

Perhaps the interests of future generations could benefit from present generations' concern for their descendants.[17] Since present generations

---

[17] Such is the mechanism behind Rawls's (1971) principle of 'just savings'.

are interested in their children's welfare, and their children will be interested in their own children's welfare, present generations have a *derivative* interest in their grandchildren's interests and so on for all successive generations. Such a 'daisy chain' of interests means that at any given point in time the interests of the next two generations might be taken into account. However, it is less likely, at any given point in time, for the interests of *all* future generations (especially those far in the future) to receive adequate weight in moral deliberation.

This doesn't mean that strong arguments favouring the interests of future generations are never voiced in global governance. Certainly they are, as we mentioned at the start of this chapter. The problem is that they have minimal to no impact on stakeholders and political decision makers. If not even persuasive arguments and facts, testimony and storytelling are enough to counter deficits in moral imagination and imaginative resistance, what else can we do to ensure that formative agents of global justice will deliberate and decide in an impartial fashion, duly taking into account the interests of future generations, non-human animals, and ecosystems?

Moral Imagination and One's Own Future Self

Notice, however, that the same obstacles we encounter when making moral judgements involving others can also arise when deciding for *ourselves*. When facing decisions with effects that fall only in our own distant future, we often fail to properly take into account the interests of our future self, compared to those of our present self. This failure to relate to our future self and internalize its preferences and interests is also due to a deficit of moral imagination.

Thankfully, as we point out in what follows, there are solutions to this problem. Moreover, the solutions for expanding our moral imagination vis-à-vis our future self could be used equally for broadening our moral imagination with respect to others, be they future generations, non-human animals, or ecosystems. Next, we point out how these solutions, involving the use of visual and experiential prompts, should be incorporated in deliberations about global justice to help formative agents internalize the interests of their future selves, but also those of future generations, animals, and ecosystems, and thereby reach decisions that are impartial across all affected interests (past and present, human and non-human).

How to Relate to the Future Self

We standardly assume each individual is the best judge of his or her own interests. Democratic theorists agree: we should each be given a vote because each is the best judge of his or her own interests. In practice, however, we often fail to be so. That is in part because we are prone to procrastination (Andreou and White 2010) and hostages to short-term thinking (or present bias) (Loewenstein and Elster 1992).[18]

Both procrastination and short-termism arise from a failure to internalize the preferences and interests of our future selves when making decisions.[19] And this incapacity to relate to our future self may itself be due to a confined moral imagination (Rawls 1971, sec. 45; Parfit 1984: 161; Schelling 1984).[20] We will then be partial in our judgements and privilege the present self to the detriment of our future self. In other words, we will fail to make a decision that is impartial across the interests of both our present and future selves. Saving patterns are a good example in this respect. Our decisions are skewed in favour of our present self. We prefer spending more of our disposable income than we should *now* instead of investing in our retirement (see e.g. Munnell, Webb, and Golub-Sass 2009). More generally, such patterns emerge from our natural tendency to prefer immediate or short-term gains to long-term ones – a tendency that is at least in part due to our inability to relate to and empathize with our future self.[21]

The solution is to find ways of expanding our moral imagination in order to 'connect' with our future selves. In turn, this should allow us to make impartial decisions that take into account *both* our present

[18] Of course, there may be other reasons for failure, such as an inability to understand one's own interests due to misinformation, false consciousness created by ideological identification, and so forth.

[19] Insofar as procrastinating entails pushing costs into the future.

[20] Ramsey (1928: 543) famously dubs pure time discounting a 'practice which is ethically indefensible and arises merely from the weakness of the imagination'.

[21] Certain forms of discounting found by behavioural economists are not only imprudent but also inconsistent. However, policy makers can use this to nudge people the right way. For example, they can encourage people to 'save more tomorrow' – to pre-commit to increase their savings toward retirement as their salaries increase. The success of such policy resides again in that the future ('tomorrow') rather than the present self will have to save more, allowing the present self to keep the same spending level (see Thaler and Benartzi 2004).

and future selves' interests. Luckily, psychology research has shown, first, that our moral imagination can be expanded in significant ways and, second, that this indeed allows us to relate to our future self in a more just and impartial way. Importantly for our argument, this expansion of moral imagination occurs as a result of *visual* and *experiential prompts* rather than in response to verbal cues, such as arguments.

Scholars have tested whether allowing people to interact with age-processed rendering of themselves changes their spending behaviour (Hershfield et al. 2011). They tried to fill the gaps in moral imagination with the use of technology – immersive virtual reality – that allows participants to have a visual representation of their aged face and body. The results showed that those directly exposed to their aged selves preferred long-term over short-term spending, choosing to allocate more money towards their retirement (Hershfield et al. 2011). Other studies using the same technology had been shown to influence consumer behaviour, health behaviour, and financial decisions (Yee and Bailenson 2007; Fox and Baileson 2009; Ahn and Baileson 2011).

From Future Self to Future Generations, Animals, and Ecosystems: The Role of Visuals and Experience

By stimulating moral imagination, visual imagery was therefore successful in nudging people to be more considerate toward their future selves. But there is no reason why it shouldn't have similar effects in helping to nudge people to be more considerate toward others instead. Visual imagery could be used in deliberative processes for the same purpose of expanding the moral imagination of deliberators vis-à-vis those who cannot themselves directly participate in those processes: future generations, non-human animals, and ecosystems. This would enable deliberators acting as formative agents of justice to properly internalize these groups' interests.

Visual prompts and holograms can be used not only to 'make present' in deliberations future generations, non-human animals, and ecosystems, but also to give decision makers an idea of how their different options might impact the welfare of these affected parties. They can 'anchor' experientially talk-centric decision processes. Computer-aided visualization, for example, has already been used in such ways in climate change mitigation (Appleton and Lovett 2003;

Nicholson-Cole 2005; O'Neill et al. 2013). Climate change is often seen as a remote problem of no personal concern. In consequence, many people don't feel the tug of any duty to act in response to climate change or support mitigation policies. Visualizing scenes of the future ('futurescapes') is used as a tool to raise people's awareness and motivate them to take action. Furthermore, virtual reality technology – already used in decision making about land use – brings an extra, experiential bonus, immersing individuals into a simulated environment and thereby allowing them to better assess the consequences of different options at hand (Stock and Bishop 2002).

Sometimes all the arguments in the world cannot make up for first- (or even just second-) hand visual and experiential contact with the objects of our moral concern. To be sure, in the case of future generations, such contact would have to be *simulated* with the help of technology. But just sometimes, direct contact might be possible – at least in the case of animals and ecosystems – provided decision makers are willing to get out of the meeting room.[22] The study of the Bloomfield Track deliberations in North Queensland is a case in point in this respect (Niemeyer 2002). A citizens' jury was convened in 2000 to discuss policy options regarding the Bloomfield Track – a track running through the Daintree rainforest accessible only by four-wheel-drive vehicles. A key moment came when deliberators went on a bus trip to inspect the rainforest (Niemeyer 2002: 138). This allowed them direct contact with one object of moral concern for the deliberators, the Daintree rainforest, which up to that point they had discussed purely in the abstract. As one deliberator acknowledged, 'being in the rainforest itself (especially when the bus driver turned off the engine)' had the most impact on her judgements of anything that she heard or experienced over the course of the deliberation. Another testified that 'the site visit was good in terms of *seeing* the current state of the road, thinking about the big picture issues' (Niemeyer 2002: 138, emphasis added). Being able to listen to the sounds of nature, see the rainforest for themselves, and revel in the majestic greenery of the place was an *experiential anchor* for the deliberators. It allowed them to connect and relate to the rainforest on a deeper level that heightened not only their sense of moral duty, but also their capacity to feel empathy for a non-human subject and to

---

[22] When not, virtual reality could be used instead.

internalize its interests. The deliberative process 'properly' started only afterwards (Niemeyer 2002: 139). The Bloomfield Track citizens' jury is thus one example of a deliberative process that successfully combined verbal and experiential inputs.

Avoiding Misrepresentation

When representing and speaking for an absent party in a decision process, it's important for the representative or spokesperson to have the consent of that party. To avoid any misrepresentation, this consent should extend to the way in which that absent party will be portrayed and its interests presented by its spokesperson to other decision makers. Ideally, those who are 'made present' by others, discursively or through the use of visuals, should have a means of participating in the production economy of those discourses or visuals. The problem is that because future generations, animals, and ecosystems are unable to undertake such participation, the use of visuals portraying them, or the use of arguments used in their defence cannot be so easily 'democratized'. Others' moral imagination stimulated by those visuals and arguments cannot therefore be directly responsive to these affected parties.

But this does not mean that there can't be any type of accountability. Importantly, any visual and experiential prompts should be grounded in scientific research in order to anchor deliberators' moral imagination in a way that avoids distortions or misrepresentations. The reliance on evidence and the involvement of the scientific community in the production of visual imagery would ensure that imagined scenarios are as plausible as possible and that they accurately reflect how the interests of animals, future generations, and ecosystems would be impacted by various policies. This would of course impose some constraints to how widely deliberators' own imagination can roam, but welcomely so insofar as we do not want deliberators to engage in (self-serving) flights of pure fantasy. Those constraints are also welcome insofar as they can prevent deliberators' imagination from being contaminated by their own biases (think of how prevalent wishful-thinking scenarios would be in the absence of scientifically informed prompts).

Some might nonetheless object that visual and experiential technologies carry the risk of manipulation. Images in particular have a powerful impact, by eliciting emotion and thereby impacting reason. Visual imagery has a long history of being used to influence individual behaviour, whether we are talking about commercial advertising or political propaganda. The informational content of visual imagery is limited and images can easily be taken out of their context and weaponized politically or otherwise. Hence many would worry that using visual and experiential prompts in deliberations about global justice would risk doing more harm than good. We have already pointed out that such prompts would be informed as much as possible by scientific research and would be developed by global expert communities. Furthermore, words are not immune to manipulation either. They can be and are easily taken out of context and weaponized. And, of course, they can easily convey false information – something we've increasingly been aware of over the past few years of post-truth politics. So words, just as much as images, require us to exercise epistemic vigilance and diligence, as well as a fair degree of scepticism. Images just as words can be used to either inform or manipulate. *Truthfulness* should thus operate as a background condition for any decision-making process at both domestic and global levels, whether it relies on arguments or images or both.

Nonetheless we believe that visual and experiential prompts aided by new technologies can improve talk-centric democratic deliberation, especially when it comes to the inclusion of the 'silent' interests of future generations, animals, and ecosystems. By helping deliberators expand their moral imagination so as to overcome bias, visual imagery and virtual reality can help arguments and facts have the impact they deserve.

Ecological Justice: A Caveat?

For the purpose of this chapter we have grouped together future generations, animals, and ecosystems. We have argued that if an enlarged moral imagination can help us internalize the interests of our future selves, then by extension it might be able to help us do the same for the interests of all these groups. But does the argument extend *equally* well to all three categories? As humans we share more with future generations than we do with animals or ecosystems. We also have more in common with some animals than with others, and speciesism easily leads us to value some animal lives and some species (especially those with complex cognition and consciousness) more than others. Finally, how could we take an ecosystem's perspective or the environment's perspective if 'perspective-taking' implies *consciousness*? Can we imagine what it is like to be an ecosystem threatened by climate change? Or the entire environment or Earth system at the mercy of human whims? The worry is that if moral imagination can play a role in achieving intergenerational and even interspecies justice, it is not a solution for achieving ecological justice.

Before answering this question, we want to clarify what is at stake in ecological justice and what our focus was all along in this chapter. At stake in ecological justice is not *humanity's* interest in a (clean, safe) environment but *the interest of the Earth system* in its own right. While the first interest is expressed loud and clear in the SDGs, the second interest is absent. The aim of the goals is to promote the 'sustainable *use*' of forests, oceans, land, and marine resources. Employment of the noun 'use' is telling: we are talking about production and consumption goods that first and foremost must advance human welfare and development, not about natural items that have interests *independently* of our own, and that deserve protection *as such*.

Equally well, we cannot play the epistemic card of ignorance and say that we do not or cannot know what these interests are. We have enough scientific knowledge about our surrounding environment to know what the *functional needs* (i.e. interests) of any given ecosystem are (that is, under which conditions it can thrive and under which conditions it will decline). And yet the welfare of ecosystems matters in the SDGs only insofar as it is interlinked with human welfare and human development.

Some might admit that ecosystems and natural items have needs and interests at least in a functional sense (they can thrive or decay in virtue of some factors), and yet deny that these needs and interests can give rise to *moral* standing and *moral claims* to protection. The question of whether natural items can have moral standing is a thorny one in environmental ethics (Brennan and Lo 2016). So is the issue of whether they can have value in their own right (intrinsic versus instrumental value). We cannot do justice to these complex questions here. Instead we assume, following others who have discussed such issues at length, that the answer to both these questions is positive (Leopold 1949; Naess 1973, 1984; Rolston 1975; Routley and Routley 1979; Norton 1986). Our premise is that at least *living* natural items and ecosystems can have 'morally considerable interests' that give rise to moral claims – they can thus be harmed in ways that are morally wrong (Goodpaster 1978; Goodin 1996).

We also acknowledge that *fully* empathizing with natural items or ecosystems might be impossible because of insurmountable phenomenological barriers. Perhaps we cannot fully appreciate 'what it's like' to be a forest or an ecosystem.[23] But equally perhaps we do not need to know that exactly in order to understand the freestanding needs and interests of forests and ecosystems, and how they may be affected by our actions. Visual and experiential prompts might get us closer to this understanding. The Queensland citizens' jury we mentioned earlier is a case in point: being in the rainforest had more impact on the deliberators' judgements than simply hearing from others what the rainforest is like and how it might be affected by the policies under review. The reason is that experiencing first-hand the rainforest ('being in communion' with it) helped them expand their moral imagination in ways words could not.

Furthermore, ecosystems and the environment have ways of *communicating* their needs as well as their distress to us. Such communication is not verbal, of course. But it is information that most of the time can be conveyed *visually*, or through other types of experience. We must *see* and *experience* what the environment and ecosystems (and parts of them) are communicating, whether through birds' chants in a luscious rainforest, withered foliage, or dried-up riverbeds.

Some have even argued that such non-verbal communication can justify natural items and the environment being given legal standing in their own right (Stone 1972: 471). If states, corporations, estates, and infants can have legal rights without being able to speak, then natural objects should have them as well, they argue (Stone 1972: 464). Through guardians, they should be able to press those claims and seek redress for wrongs done to them. But how could the natural items communicate to their guardians their needs? For some this is a simple matter:

Natural objects can communicate their wants (needs) to us, and in ways that are not terribly ambiguous. I am sure I can judge with more certainty and meaningfulness whether and when my lawn wants (needs) water, than the

---

[23] Jackson (1982, 1986) once argued similarly that someone who has never seen the colour red may not be able to fully imagine what it is like to see red.

Attorney General can judge whether and when the United States wants (needs) to take an appeal from an adverse judgment by a lower court. The lawn tells me that it wants water by a certain dryness of the blades and soil – immediately obvious to the touch – the appearance of bald spots, yellowing, and a lack of springiness after being walked on; how does 'the United States' communicate to the Attorney General? For similar reasons, the guardian-attorney for a smog-endangered stand of pines could venture with more confidence that his client wants the smog stopped than the directors of a corporation can assert that 'the corporation' wants dividends declared. We make decisions on behalf of, and in the purported interests of, others every day; these 'others' are often creatures whose wants are far less verifiable, and even far more metaphysical in conception, than the wants of rivers, trees, and land. (Stone 1972: 471)

In the case of domestic companions, such as cats and dogs, their owners are often pretty confident that their needs can be communicated to them. Indeed, domestic companions are sometimes beneficiaries of bequests from their deceased owners, which are managed in their interests by human guardians or trustees (see e.g. BBC 2007; Hooper 2011). The challenge is ensuring that the same empathy and concern we have for the interests and welfare of our domestic pets extends to animals we have no association with, as well as animate natural items and ecosystems.

The passage cited above was written in the 1970s, a period known for progressive advocacy. In 2017, after 140 years of petitioning, a court in New Zealand has granted legal personhood to Whanganui River and appointed two guardians to act on its behalf and protect its interests (Ainge Roy 2017b).[24] Perhaps in ten years' time similar recognition will be given to ecosystems and animals species at the *global* level as well. A more visual and experiential approach might go some way toward achieving that.

Some Thoughts on Institutional Design

Several institutional design proposals have been advanced in the last years to promote intergenerational justice. In this section we discuss how our own proposal for the use of visual imagery can serve to address the shortcomings of such proposals by expanding deliberators'

[24] Mount Taranaki was granted a similar standing (Ainge Roy 2017a).

moral imagination, in anticipation of the future negotiations that will review the 2030 Development Agenda.

One proposal is the establishment of a commission or similar institution that would act as 'guardian for future generations' (Caney 2016). Such a commission would have multiple members, which would allow greater diversity of opinion. Caney (2016) argues, for example, that a Commission for Future Generations would have several strengths: it would be representative, both geographically and demographically; it would be independent in delivering a neutral perspective; it would be authoritative, its message being heard and respected; and it would be inclusive and transparent in its procedures. Furthermore, the commission would tap into resources from across civil society. Its activities would comprise data collection and analysis, research as well as advocacy. The details would of course all have to be determined by UN member states.

Others have already discussed at length the limitations of such institutions for representing future generations (e.g. Karnein 2016). Besides the fact that such representation would lack any authorization and accountability to those represented, it would be limited by several obstacles. The main ones are that (1) epistemically, present people may not know the subjective interests and preferences of future generations; (2) these interests and preferences would themselves be, to a great extent, influenced by the choices of present generations; and (3) different future generations might have different, even conflicting interests, which means present generations would have to arbitrate among a plurality of diverse interests and preferences. And there is always the danger that the representatives of future generations might selfishly betray the interests of future humans (Karnein 2016: 86–7).

To those standing concerns we want to add some worries of our own. While any initiatives to advance the interests of future generations, animal species, and ecosystems are welcome, we cannot help but notice the lack of any hard or soft *accountability* mechanism to ensure that the decisions of a Commission (or High Commissioner) for Future Generations would be heard or respected by states.[25] In the absence of any such mechanism, we can only hope that stakeholders –

---

[25] Beckman and Uggla (2016) argue that this may in fact be a strong point of these institutions, on the grounds that they are less threatening and therefore more acceptable by parliaments and governments.

primarily state governments as representatives of present generations – will be persuaded by, and will internalize, the goals of the commission/ high commissioner.

While it is good to have special institutions devoted to representing the interests of future generations, these institutions may ultimately be powerless if they cannot overcome the bias that naturally clouds the judgements of present generations and their representatives. Institutions for future generations will thus have to resort to a wider range of devices to ensure that their decisions and proposals are taken up by those who must actually bear the costs of their implementation. Democratic deliberative processes that have a visual and experiential component, and that rely on technologies to expand the moral imagination of present generations and their representatives, would arguably be one such device these new institutions could adopt.

A plethora of alternative institutions and mechanisms have been recommended. Among them are ombudsmen or commissions for future generations (Caney 2015; Beckman and Uggla 2016), manifestos for the future, parliamentary committees, councils for the future and 'visions of the future' national days (Caney 2016), or national and global mini-publics on intergenerational justice (Niemeyer and Jennstål 2016). Regardless of which we are talking about, the most serious obstacle to ensuring that proper weight in decision making, not just representation, will be given to the interests of future generations, non-human animals, and ecosystems is present generations' *self-interest*. Because current decision makers can clearly see their self-interest, but (because of inadequate imaginative capacity) fail to clearly perceive others' concerns and thereby weigh them adequately in moral deliberation, their self-interest wins by default in their judgements. It is not that they weigh their own interests too heavily on purpose but rather that, because of an impoverished moral imagination, they do not weigh those other moral considerations as heavily as they should.

Those politically empowered (citizens and their political representatives) are the ones who will ultimately have to exercise impartial judgement in order to authorize and implement laws and policies promoting the welfare of future generations, non-human animals, and ecosystems, but that might clash with their own interests. Epistemic and cognitive limitations, such as deficits in moral imagination, might prevent them from doing so, even if the goodwill exists.

This is why it is important to take such structural deficits into account when thinking about potential solutions.

Images, Human Cognition, and Moral Reasoning

The impact of images on human behaviour has been studied extensively. Sometimes visual prompts can serve as a surrogate for real human interactions, and elicit the same type of pro-social, empathetic response. The 'watching eyes' effect is a good example: in the presence of images of watching eyes, people are more likely to take others' interests into account, which, for example, makes them more likely to donate to charity, transfer money to others in economic games, and litter less (Burnham 2003; Haley and Fessler 2005; Ernest-Jones, Nettle, and Bateson 2011; Powell, Roberts, and Nettle 2012). These effects are independent of local norms and hold even when nobody is around to notice their behaviour (Bateson et al. 2013).

In this chapter we argued that where words and arguments have failed, images and experiences may succeed. But why should the human mind respond better to imagery and what role do images play in moral reasoning? And, by extension, what role would they play in the exercise of formative agency and moral judgement?

In recent years scholars of cognition have considered more carefully how visual – in comparison to verbal – thinking influences moral judgement (Amit, Gottlieb, and Greene 2014). They have suggested that visual imagery stimulates *deontological* moral judgement: a concern for averting harm rather than maximizing good, a concern for the means rather than then end. On the other hand, both deliberation time and reflection have been seen to encourage *utilitarian* judgements (Paxton, Ungar, and Greene 2011; Suter and Hertwig 2011). But morality consists in the union of the right and the good – in the union of utilitarian and deontological thinking (Ross [1930] 2002). A conjunction of talk and visuals can give us that.

These findings are important for those studying deliberative process. First, because one central claim is that deliberation improves the quality of moral judgements by promoting reflection. Yet if reflection promotes utilitarian thinking, then deliberative theorists might have to implicitly accept utilitarianism as the *superior* moral principle when arguing that deliberation improves moral judgements. Many may have trouble accepting this implication of what is by now a classic claim of deliberative democracy.

To be sure, deliberative democrats could easily reply that utilitarian moral judgements are better than no moral judgements at all. At least deliberation forces people to take *a* moral perspective, rather than *no* moral perspective. True. And perhaps we shouldn't worry about these effects in the case of more mundane deliberations. But in the case of agents whose main task is identifying, precisifying, and arbitrating between different principles and conceptions of global *justice*, we may rightly think otherwise. We should ensure that the moral judgements of formative agents deliberating on global justice are not skewed in one direction (utilitarianism) simply because deliberation is *talk*-centric par excellence.

That brings us to the second point: these findings are important because they not only make deliberative theorists aware of some (moral) limitations of the practices that they support, but also because they offer a solution to these limitations. We can balance out the effects of talk-centric practices on moral judgement (the tendency toward utilitarian thinking) by incorporating visual and experiential prompts into deliberation, which prioritize deontological concerns.

Another advantage would be that visual representations are also more likely to trigger an immediate response because things that are perceived visually are likely to conceived as 'here and now' (Amit et al. 2014: 346). Many global problems (global poverty, climate change, environmental destruction, etc.) are *objectively* 'here and now' problems: they are manifest and require an immediate response. But verbal arguments and representations of these issues make it more likely that they will be perceived as distant in both time and space, and not requiring any immediate response (at least at the deeper cognitive level) (Amit et al. 2014: 346). This is another reason for including visual imagery in deliberations about global justice.

Conclusion

Political theorists have already pinned short-termism and procrastination as the main reasons why we haven't already successfully advanced the interests of future generations (González-Ricoy and Gosseries 2016). They say that deliberative institutions and processes may be a solution (e.g. Mackenzie 2016; Niemeyer and Jennstål 2016).

Yet they fail to explain what the root causes of short-termism and procrastination at the *individual* level are and how deliberation could address these root causes.

In this chapter, we offered a more elaborate explanation for short-termism and procrastination as arising from deficits of moral imagination, which may prevent deliberators taking the perspective of future generations, non-human animals, and ecosystems. In consequence, we put forward a more nuanced argument about the role of democratic deliberation, one that acknowledges the limitations of talk-centric approaches and the importance of incorporating visual and experiential prompts into talk-centric deliberative processes. By bridging gaps in moral imagination, these prompts may enable those who *can* exercise formative agency in global justice to place appropriate moral weight in their moral judgements on the interests of those who – as a matter of logical and practical possibility – cannot exercise formative agency. Where words have failed, images and experiences may succeed.

Moral imagination necessary to enhance formative agency when it comes to the interests of future generations, non-human animals, and ecosystems can be promoted through:

- confronting individuals with images of their future selves in order to induce thinking beyond the present;
- using visual imagery and 'futurescapes' in designed deliberative forums and other decision-making processes;
- providing experiential inputs to deliberative processes;
- grounding visual and experiential prompts in scientific research;
- applying a truthfulness standard to such prompts;
- listening more effectively to communications from the non-human world;
- recognizing natural entities such as landscapes and ecosystems in legal terms; and
- ensuring that institutional innovations to represent the interests of future generations are accompanied by visual and experiential prompts.

In this light, the 2030 negotiations surrounding the Sustainable Development Agenda should take a more pluralist approach toward the sort of inputs they entertain, in order to ensure that global justice incorporates a proper concern for intergenerational, ecological, and interspecies justice. In the next chapter we will say more about how these concerns can be integrated into deliberative systems for global justice governance, along with all the agents we analysed in previous chapters.

8 | *Global Justice in the Deliberative System*

As should be clear from the preceding chapters, global justice is the work of many agents. No single category of agents currently has, nor should have, a monopoly when it comes to establishing what global justice can and should mean. We have argued throughout that formative agency needs to be exercised in democratic ways. Our focus in Chapters 3–6 was on specific categories of agents. In this chapter, we will take a broader view of democracy in global justice governance to show how different sorts of agents (along with the interests of future generations and non-humans as analysed in Chapter 7) can be integrated into a more effective system of governance. We will deploy the idea of a global deliberative system. Systemic thinking can pinpoint ways to enhance the democratic agency of different kinds of actors and help make agency more consequential. It can cast a different light on how different conceptions of justice can be reconciled, and on how formative activity in the domain of global justice can most profitably be organized.

Earlier chapters contained some suggestions about how different categories of agents might interact in ways that could benefit global justice. For example, we argued in Chapter 5 that more effective engagement of experts and publics could increase the legitimacy of expert advice about matters of justice in global governance. In Chapter 4 we suggested that for broadly epistemic as well as democratic reasons, foundations could engage more effectively with those at the receiving end of their charitable activities, thus enabling decisions to take advantage of the contextual knowledge of the poor and disadvantaged.

In this chapter we will show how a deliberative systemic perspective allows us to think more comprehensively about how to democratize global justice governance, and how to enable different categories of actors to be more effective formative agents of justice, individually and especially jointly. We will make the argument in the context of an interpretation and analysis of the process that yielded the Sustainable Development Goals (SDGs).

This process featured multiple venues and networks for communicating about the content of these global goals, forums for dialogue, decision-making bodies, consultation exercises, and different negotiating tracks. The whole complex process was pervaded by norms of public participation. This process can be described and evaluated in terms of the agents present and what they did (and failed to do) – this is how we organized our discussions in earlier chapters. Coming to grips with the system in its entirety is a much bigger challenge, which we shall attempt to meet in this chapter.

Deliberative System

Thinking about deliberative democracy in terms of a system rather than in the image of a forum is rooted in the recognition that imposing all the burdens of deliberative and democratic decision making on one location (such as an assembly of citizens, or a legislature) is too demanding. These burdens include: inclusion of all affected actors; the validation of actors' political standing; problem recognition; agenda setting; securing dialogue across deep difference; producing good arguments, reflection upon principles, upon practices, and upon preferences for action; and collective decision. Like any system, a deliberative system consists of a set of differentiated yet linked components that can be interpreted in light of some common purpose. The purpose in question could be (in our case) the specification of what global justice means, or effective response to the problem of (for example) climate change, or ensuring that collective decisions are reached in democratically legitimate ways. We can interpret any real-world political process – such as that which yielded the SDGs, or similar processes in global climate governance – as a *potentially* deliberative system. That is, we can hold the real-world system up to a template and ascertain the degree to which it measures up.

Deliberative systems can operate at any level, from the local to the global (Mansbridge et al. 2012: 8). A general scheme (modified from Dryzek 2010), applicable at any level, has the following elements:

- *Public space*, a relatively informal communicative realm where ideas, perspectives, and discourses are generated and interact with each other. Public space can be home to social movements, political activists, global justice entrepreneurs, old and new media, public intellectuals, and citizens. Ideally public space should feature meaningful engagement across different discourses.

- *Empowered space*, yielding authoritative collective decisions. Empowered space will often contain – or even be coterminous with – some formal body producing decisions. However, such a body is not absolutely necessary. For instance, networks of public and private actors can yield collective decisions (e.g. on greenhouse gas emissions standards) without the need for validation by any government.
- *Transmission* of concerns, ideas, principles, and discourses from public space to empowered space. The means of transmission might include argument, demonstration, disruptive protest, the provision of evidence, rhetoric, and testimony.
- *Accountability* of agents in empowered space to those in public space. Accountability is arguably strongest if those in public space can sanction those in empowered space if they are not satisfied (as is supposed to happen in electoral democracy, when a government is voted out). Accountability at its weakest means simply giving an account – what Mansbridge (2009) calls 'narrative accountability'. Deliberative accountability is achieved when those in public space can question agents in empowered space and the latter give justifications in terms acceptable to the former.
- *Reflexivity*, the ability of a deliberative system to assess its own performance and if need be change in response to that assessment. Reflexivity can involve meta-deliberation; that is, deliberation about the deliberative qualities of the system itself.

In addition, hybrid spaces can be acknowledged, involving interchange between (for example) governmental and civil society actors, or international organizations and experts.

Deliberation can occur within empowered space, within public space, within hybrid space, in transmission, and in accountability. Of course, non-deliberative interactions can occur in all four of these locations too, and it may be the case that a non-deliberative interaction can have positive deliberative consequences for the system as a whole; for example, if the ridicule of power-holders induces them to reflect upon and take into account concerns they had otherwise ignored. A systemic account of deliberative governance recognizes that formative agency can be distributed across multiple sites, actors, and institutions. It is the deliberative capacity of the entire system that matters most, rather than that of any given unit, actor, process, or site within the system. Interaction across categories of agents in a deliberative system can compensate for any limitations in each category. Ideally a deliberative system should be authentic (in terms of featuring meaningful deliberation), inclusive (of all affected interests), and consequential (in making a difference when it comes to collective outcomes – maximally in determining their content).

In a way, the process that yielded the SDGs recognized the need for a system by establishing multiple venues, decision-making groups, consultations, and negotiation tracks, all infused with participatory norms. We will now examine that process through a deliberative systems lens. The process was of course established without reference to deliberative systems logic (or indeed any clear overall logic) – but it can still be evaluated in these terms.

The Deliberative Health of Public Space

Public space surrounding the 2030 Development Agenda and formulation of the SDGs was crowded. In previous chapters we met advocacy organizations, grassroots social movements, public intellectuals, experts, corporations, and foundations – all much more active and visible than the citizens of the world.

The United Nations (UN) created and discharged many of its participatory obligations in the form of consultation, which we will subject to closer examination later in this chapter when we contemplate transmission from public space to empowered space. From a deliberative systems perspective, a healthy public space should generate its own activity – and not have that activity engineered, and its terms established, from empowered space. There are too many actual and potential engagements in public space to cover comprehensively, here we identify some potentially deliberative ones that are significant when it comes to the individual and collective exercise of formative agency.

Ideally, public space would be constituted by vibrant exchanges within and across different sorts of advocacy groups, public intellectuals, experts, and citizens. We should expect a plurality of views within each of these categories. If we examine public space surrounding the development of the SDGs in these terms, there are some positives and some negatives.

The (qualified) positives include:

- *Encounters across advocacy groups.* Such groups advocated for different values. Their concerns did though interact and overlap. Many civil society organizations concerned with the global development agenda coalesced in the Beyond 2015 Coalition, founded in 2010, and renamed Together 2030 in 2015. Around 1,500 organizations eventually joined. The initial intent was to push for something like the SDGs to be adopted; the coalition was also committed to an inclusive and participatory approach (Kamau et al. 2018: 127–8). This initiative really took the form of a campaign rather than a setting for engagement across different groups, though one of its declared purposes is to rectify the imbalance in capacity between organizations from the Global North and Global South.[1]
- *Limited encounters of public intellectuals with broader publics.* Public intellectuals such as Jeffrey Sachs, Bjørn Lomborg, and Joseph Stiglitz did try to reach broad publics, though the size of their attentive audience is hard to ascertain (see Chapter 5).
- *Relative online civility.* The kind of vituperation that one finds in social media exchanges on climate change was largely absent when it came to the SDGs (see Chapter 5).
- *Deliberation by the poor.* The Participate initiative organized deliberations in Ground-Level Panels on the SDGs in many poor communities (see Chapter 6).

The negatives include:

- *Advocacy enclaves.* The relationships between different kinds of advocacy groups were not necessarily happy ones. In particular, the Major Groups recognized by the UN since 1992 became used to their privileged access to power and could regard other civil society groups as interlopers – notably 'local communities, older persons, persons with disabilities, migrants, LGBT groups, human rights organizations, humanitarian aid groups, and volunteer organizations', although with time the relationship improved (Kamau et al. 2018: 124). There was also a disconnect, and some hostility,

---

[1] See www.helpage.org/what-we-do/post2015-process/post2015-coalitions/ #Beyond2015.

between non-governmental organizations (NGOs) concerned with development and aid on the one hand, and corporations and business associations on the other (interview evidence).

- *Absent poor peoples' movements.* These movements were not very active on the SDGs. As we saw in Chapter 5, this absence could be only partially compensated by other advocacy groups doing their best to facilitate the voice of the poor.
- *Disconnected experts.* Experts did a good job in connecting with empowered space. They did not do so well in connecting with publics. Indeed, given how closely it interacted with empowered forums such as the Open Working Group (OWG), and the fact that it reports to the UN secretary general (though it is not a UN body), the expert-based Sustainable Development Solutions Network (SDSN) can be seen as operating in hybrid rather than public space. In public space, it did not engage extensively with lay citizens and their perspectives – especially those of the poor and marginalized. The SDSN was set up with the intent of involving businesses and civil society organizations, but in the end proved to be mostly an enclave of experts (with a shared position on what the content of the goals should be), leaving broader public participation for elsewhere in the system (Spijkers and Honniball 2015: 253).
- *Missing encounters across public intellectuals.* As we saw in Chapter 5, the deliberative and democratic processing of disagreement across divided public intellectuals – such as those broadly supportive of the SDGs and those more critical – was elusive.
- *Weak consideration of future generations, animals, and ecosystems* (see Chapter 7).
- *Expressive overload.* The sheer volume of communication in global public space surrounding the SDGs made it hard for any participant to grasp all the information, arguments, and considerations relevant to their position.

Public Space in Perspective

One way to think about the deliberative health of public space is in terms of the effective and productive engagement of different discourses. As we pointed out in Chapter 1, in any situation involving plural justice claims, those claims are best deliberated to some kind of resolution; and public space is one place to start. It is neither necessary nor desirable for deliberation to finish in public space – for empowered space awaits. Deliberative public space should feature the sharpening of positions in their engagement and contestation with others, and certainly not consensus. Public space can, however, yield a normative meta-consensus in which there is agreement on the content and validity of different normative principles of justice. Such a meta-consensus would require that each discourse survive – and ideally prosper from – encounters with other discourses. But this is not what happened in the case of the SDGs. Notably, looking at all the interactions we have canvassed in previous chapters, there was no encounter between neo-liberalism and the discourses of the poor themselves (let alone discourses that would highlight future generations and non-humans), or indeed between neoliberalism and any of its competitors. Criticism from a distance does not count. The picture that emerges is of a fragmented public space that was not very good at processing differences and producing the social learning that would result from better engagement. This is not necessarily fatal for the deliberative system, but it does mean that such processing had to be left to empowered space in the system, to which we now turn.

The Deliberative Health of Empowered Space

The formulation of the SDGs took place in an empowered space that was more crowded and complicated than is normally the case for global governance processes – for example, when a treaty is negotiated by representatives of states. In the case of the SDGs, states and multiple international organizations played a role in the early days; Colombia played a pivotal role in ensuring that the SDGs would be broadened into sustainability from the Millennium Development Goals' (MDGs) narrower stress on poverty. The agreement to proceed required cooperation from sixty UN agencies under the leadership of the UN Development Programme (UNDP) (Kjørven 2016). The UN secretary general established in 2012 a High-Level Panel of Eminent Persons to drive the post-2015 Development Agenda. The OWG with 30 seats shared by 70 states finalized the content of the goals, which then had to be formally adopted by a UN summit (representing 193 countries). Implementation was to be overseen by the High-Level Political Forum established in 2013. Experts played a less central role in the SDGs than in the MDGs – though as we noted above, the experts organized into the SDSN could be interpreted as constituting a hybrid space, with a foot in empowered space, given their closeness to the OWG in particular.

For empowered space, the positives included the following:

• Compared to most multilateral processes, the ratio of deliberation to bargaining was quite high; we saw in Chapter 3 that the OWG had procedural features conducive to deliberation.
• The fact that that the whole process was geared to the production of a statement of principles (the goals themselves) without the imposition of financial costs on any state meant that the role of financial interest was weakened.
• The fact that the locus of authority in the process was not initially very clear meant that especially in the early days of the process (before the OWG was confirmed as the key venue), there had to be a lot of persuasion across different actors – not least to get the idea established that there should be a more comprehensive set of goals to succeed the MDGs (see Chapter 3).

The negatives included the following:

• Material interest was in some cases decisive in overriding aspects of justice. In Chapter 3 we saw, for example, that China kept any mention of democracy out of the goals, while Saudi Arabia successfully de-linked energy and climate change, and the United States curbed any strong commitment to international redistribution.
• Conflicting interests and values were not necessarily deliberated to any resolution, but rather accommodated in different places in the long list of goals and targets (see Chapter 3).
• Limited moral imagination was on display when it comes to the long-term future, non-humans, and the Earth system.

Any assessment of the deliberative qualities of empowered space cannot be reached just by looking at the content of interactions – such as those that took place in the OWG. It is entirely possible that seemingly deliberative interactions are heavily constrained by limitations in the discourses present – at an extreme, there could be discursive hegemony, of the sort we see in the way neoliberalism dominates global financial governance. There was no such hegemony of a single discourse in the case of the SDGs, but the discourses present were mostly confined to neoliberalism (which ensured a commitment to conventional economic growth and an assumption that the market is a force for good), human development (which is the dominant anti-poverty discourse that carried over from the MDGs), sustainable development (which of course gave the goals their name), and results-based management (which led to the specificity in targets and indicators). At the same time there were important absences: notably, discourses that challenged the easy accommodation of market capitalism on the one hand, and social justice, poverty alleviation, and environmental protection on the other (Carant 2017). So even if there were important moments of deliberation in empowered space, that does not mean the deliberative system as a whole was successful. For that to happen (and assuming public space is in good condition), effective transmission of concerns and discourses from public space to empowered space is necessary, as well as effective accountability, so we need to examine these two key aspects of deliberative systems.

The Condition of Transmission

The multiple public consultations conducted on the SDGs (see Chapter 6) signify plenty of good intentions in connecting public space and empowered space, though the consultations do not assume that there is already a well-developed public space in which putatively deliberative interactions occur. Certainly, the rhetoric of needing to hear from ordinary citizens, and especially the most disadvantaged, pervaded the whole process that yielded the SDGs, starting with the UN's guidelines for national consultations (UNDP 2012: 13). The High-Level Panel was ostensibly committed to hearing the voices of civil society, corporations, and especially the Global South. Speaking of a 2013 meeting of the panel, Sen (2013) concludes that it 'did exactly what it was expected to do: bringing distinguished members of the HLP [High-Level Panel], on the one hand, and a plethora of grassroots' representatives and CSOs [civil society organizations] across the Global South, on the other, for an evidence-based, face-to-face interaction'. But as we saw in Chapter 6, citizen consultations eventually proved to have little impact on the High-Level Panel to which they reported, and it is not obvious that organized civil society fared much better – though as we will see, organized civil society did much better when it came to the OWG.

Our summary judgement in Chapter 6 was that the various consultations conducted for the SDGs did not do an especially good job in achieving the *deliberative* inclusion and impact of the voices of citizens in general and the poor in particular. As we pointed out, much of the consultation was monological rather than dialogical (think of the MyWorld survey), participants were mostly self-selected so highly unrepresentative, and some processes (notably the thematic consultations) did not involve many ordinary citizens, let alone the least advantaged. And it was hard to discern any real influence of the consultations in empowered space, especially when it came to influencing state negotiators in the OWG and elsewhere (Zuijderduijn et al. 2016: 21). It is not as though negotiators were going to wade through materials on the websites and elsewhere in a search for ideas to incorporate into the SDGs. It could be said that the agenda of the OWG partially reflected the areas of the thematic consultations (Zuijderduijn et al. 2016: 23); though of course those areas were defined by the organizers of the consultations – not by those consulted.

There were some more deliberative engagements involving the poor – notably the Ground-Level Panels organized under the Participate initiative. The organizers of Ground-Level Panels were aware of the need to try to influence the SDG process, and tried to both sponsor interactions between the panels and policy makers, as well as produce a documentary intended to influence decision making (empowered space, in our language) (Shahrokh and Wheeler 2014: 111). The panels featured 'outreach days' where their conclusions were presented (Newell 2014: 30). However, it is not easy to discern any significant influence on empowered space; Participate got lost in the crowd, as did the testimonies by poor individuals organized by ATD Fourth World. Still, something similar to Participate on a much larger scale would have been better in deliberative terms than the consultations conducted under the banner of the global conversation – showing what that conversation could have been.

Organized civil society – notably as recognized in the Major Groups by the UN – fared somewhat better than ordinary citizens and the poor in reaching empowered space with their concerns, though one of our interviewees believed advocacy groups spent too much time with each other, and not enough time on communicating with diplomats and negotiators. The Major Groups were present in force at the OWG, and there were daily meetings with state negotiators (Kamau et al. 2018:

125–6); though sometimes few states showed up (Kamau et al. 2018: 125), and while positions of the Major Groups were supposed to be funnelled into the OWG, there was no formal mechanism for this to happen. The Women's Major Group was especially active (Gabizon 2016: 105). Civil society representatives were present in the negotiating room, even when not allowed to speak; but all those in the room could and sometimes did communicate with each other via Twitter. However, midway through its proceedings, the OWG co-chairs made some procedural changes that limited the influence of Major Groups by requiring that group representatives rotate on a monthly basis, ostensibly so that the same old voices did not dominate, but in practice depriving the Major Groups of nuance, experience, and influence as the OWG moved to its conclusion (interview evidence). In the context of the OWG and beyond (including at home), some states are open to input from NGOs, while others (generally the less democratic states) are closed. NGOs can have relevant expertise that non-specialist negotiators lack, and sometimes negotiators recognize that they can learn something useful from their interactions with NGOs.

The activities of public intellectuals were arguably more influential still, at least in one sense: the discourse of human development that informed the MDGs and was carried over into the SDGs owes much to one particular public intellectual, Amartya Sen. More radical public intellectuals were marginalized, as we saw in Chapter 5. In the SDGs, experts were arguably more influential than public intellectuals (though there is considerable overlap between the two categories). We have already noted the influence of the SDSN network of experts.

Business corporations did well too, beginning with the strategic alliance between the UN secretary general and business on the SDGs we described in Chapter 3. The SDG experience confirmed the more general over-representation of the rich, corporations, and big foundations in global governance. Corporate lobbying was successful in getting conventional economic growth validated by the SDGs, avoiding any challenge to neoliberalism or the basic structure of the global political economy, and making sure that business was enlisted as a seeming force for good in the implementation of the goals.

Just as our summary judgement of the deliberative health of the public sphere was based on the engagement of different discourses, so can the effectiveness of transmission be based on an assessment of the kinds of discourses that made it through to empowered space – and those that did not.

Discourses that made it through from public space quite successfully were (as noted in our earlier discussion of empowered space) neoliberalism, human development, sustainable development (in moderate form), and results-based management. However this is not really a case of discourses being generated in the public space surrounding the SDGs making a successful struggle to be incorporated, because all of them were already prominent in empowered spaces in either the MDGs (human development), global environmental governance (sustainable development), global economic and financial governance (neoliberalism), or in bureaucratic governance more generally (results-based management).

Discourses that were present in public space but largely ineffective in making themselves felt in empowered space included more radical pro-poor discourses as featured in, for example, the World Social Forum (Carant 2017); the discourses of the poor themselves (such as the agroecology and food sovereignty emphasized by La Via Campesina (LVC)); the discourse of limits and boundaries that is so prominent among Earth scientists; and green radicalism. It is not as though these discourses were deliberated in public space and found unworthy of transmission to empowered space, or given due consideration in empowered space and reflectively overruled for good reasons. They simply received little or no response from their competitors in public space, and were not considered seriously in empowered space.

The Condition of Accountability

We can find moments of accountability in the process of developing the SDGs; for example, when negotiators had to report back to their governments. However, the key kind of accountability required from a deliberative systems perspective is the accountability of empowered space to public space.

In global governance there is generally little scope for any kind of punitive accountability such as the kind central to electoral democracy (punishing perceived poor performance by voting against incumbents). There is plenty of narrative accountability associated with the SDGs as a communications effort swung into action to publicize the process itself (see Chapter 5), though the limited media attention meant that most of the world's population probably wasn't reached in any significant way. Social media does not necessarily help accountability; when it does come into play, the volume of communication makes it hard to construct deliberative accountability to participants. Once the process was concluded, another media campaign sought to disseminate the content of the goals and targets.

Accountability in the implementation of the SDGs relies mostly on voluntary mechanisms, notably the Voluntary National Reviews (for which a UN handbook provides guidance). Many states have undertaken these (forty-seven in 2019). However, some states have complained that 169 targets makes comprehensive monitoring impossible (Mingst, Karns, and Lyon 2018: 221). Narrative accountability can also be found in the requirement that corporate members of the Global Compact produce an annual report on their progress in implementing the principles of the Compact, which after 2015 include the SDGs (see Chapter 4). Some deliberative accountability can be found in the participation of civil society in the meetings of the High-Level Political Forum where Voluntary National Reviews are presented, including in the 'VNR Labs' that take place at the meetings.

An accountability agenda for the SDGs has been pushed by the Center for Economic and Social Rights, which wants the implementation of SDGs to be held accountable in terms of how they affect established international standards for human rights. An early 2016 assessment is sceptical: 'The strong human rights content of Agenda 2030 risks being undermined by the weakness of its accountability infrastructure and its limited means of implementation.'[2]

The Condition of Reflexivity

Deliberative systems in global justice governance no less than elsewhere need reflexive capacity – an ability to reflect on and if need be restructure themselves in light of that reflection. In this light, there is clear reflexivity in the move from the MDGs to the SDGs. The narrow, expert-driven process of the MDGs was discarded in favour of the much more participatory and open process that yielded the SDGs. The

---

[2] See www.cesr.org/accountability-left-behind-sdg-follow-and-review. As we pointed out in Chapter 1, human rights have a stronger presence in other text in the 2030 Agenda than in the SDGs themselves.

very existence of the process that yielded the SDGs arguably owes much to reflection within the UN system on its own recent failures (such as the 2009 Conference of the Parties (COP) of the UN Framework Convention on Climate Change (UNFCCC)) (Kamau et al. 2018: 28–46). However, that reflexivity had its limits: it meant opening up the system, but what emerged as a result of this opening had no organizing logic at the systemic level, and proved to be a haphazard agglomeration of institutions and processes that evolved through a series of strategic moves as well as thoughtful designs, which few people could even grasp in its entirety. Within this institutional redesign there were moments of reflexivity – notably in the design of the OWG, though even that had a large accidental component. As we noted in Chapter 3, the OWG was much more successful in deliberative terms than typical multilateral negotiation processes, due to devices such as the sharing of seats within 'troikas' of countries, and the institutionalized daily consultation with civil society groups. However, the reason for the seat sharing was not that it would promote deliberation. Rather, the number thirty had been established in 'The Future We Want' document that was one outcome of the 2012 UN Conference on Sustainable Development, when it was not even clear that the OWG would be composed of state negotiators, as opposed to (for example) experts. When it was decided that the OWG would be a forum for inter-state negotiation, the problem arose that seventy countries expressed interest in joining; the seat-sharing troikas were an ingenious solution to the problem of there being more countries than seats (Kamau et al. 2018: 50–4).

Turning from moments of reflexivity before the 2015 adoption of the SDGs to reflexivity after their adoption, at the time of writing there is no institutionalized reflexivity that would learn either positive or negative procedural lessons from how the SDGs were formulated. But that would perhaps be premature, as the time to seek such reflexivity would be before the SDGs expire in 2030, with the search for successor goals in mind. Reflexivity in the implementation of the SDGs can be sought earlier, especially if it involves learning from the Voluntary National Reviews.

Did the System Advance Global Justice?

We have argued that though the word 'justice' was not invoked frequently in the process that yielded the SDGs, they can still be treated as the most comprehensive attempt the world has yet seen to advance global justice. We have interpreted that process as a potentially deliberative and democratic system.

The degree to which the SDGs do in fact promote global justice will depend on many factors in their implementation. A full audit would need to wait until 2030, when the goals expire, though interim assessments are possible. But an important prior question is: did the goals advance the meaning of justice in defensible fashion?

Adherents to different meanings of justice will answer this question in different ways. But given our agnosticism on the precise content of justice – though not on the need for the democratic nature of its determination – our evaluation stresses the way different ideas about justice were processed.

In this light, the SDGs have several problems. The first is the sheer number of goals and targets: the easiest way to resolve any controversy was to assign potentially competing principles (e.g. between climate change and economic growth) to different goals or targets, rather than deliberate their relative merits (see Chapter 3). Thus competing framings of justice – and (in some cases) their underlying material interests – were accommodated rather than resolved.[3] Second, inserting the adjective 'sustainable' or 'inclusive' was also a way to mollify objections – with no necessary substantive content to accompany the adjective. The third problem is the lack of priority among the goals and targets. It is not clear, for example, whether pursuing effective, accountable and inclusive institutions (Goal 16) is more or less important than sustainable consumption and production (Goal 12). (This does not of course imply that any priority would be better than none, only that priority should have been deliberated.) The fourth is the lack of any temporal sequence: are some goals or targets (e.g. inclusive and sustainable industrialization, Goal 9) logically prior to others (e.g. reduce inequality, Goal 10) in time when it comes to any particular setting (such as a country)?

Despite the proliferation of goals and targets, their content responds more effectively to some discourses of global justice than to others. The deliberative system should have responded to the full range of concerns

---

[3] Resolution could arguably be left to the national level, where formative agency can be exercised in the implementation of the goals. However, the implications of the goals for the meaning of *global* justice can be found mainly in any resolution – or lack thereof – at the global level.

and discourses relevant to a domain such as global justice. This does not mean that the SDGs should have mirrored all these concerns and discourses; that would be undesirable, given the need for principles to survive deliberative scrutiny, and impossible, for opposing discourses and principles (e.g. libertarian versus radical feminist discourses) need to be reconciled. Rather, what it means is that the process as a whole should have acted on the basis of defensible considerations or good reasons.

If a concern or discourse is represented in the content of the goals, then it ought to have survived a reflective process of justification and judgement. Arguments grounded in it should have been made and heard, and arguments against should have been made, given due weight, and received a response in terms that make sense to those who think differently. In contrast, if the concept is present because the discourse that underpins it dominates as a matter of discursive hegemony that serves a limited range of powerful interests or is imposed upon the formative process in unreflective fashion, then the deliberative system has failed.

If a concept is absent because it has been considered and rejected, and a justification for that rejection provided in terms that make sense to its proponents, then that is fine. If a concept has not been advanced or heard because it is suppressed by a dominant discourse, or if no justification is provided that makes sense to proponents of the idea of justice in question, then again the deliberative system has failed.

Earlier in this chapter we noted that the conceptions of justice that fared particularly well in the SDGs were human development (capabilities), weak sustainable development, weak cosmopolitanism (in the 'for all' language), neoliberalism, and feminism. But there were some notable absences.

Significant Absences

- *The discourses of the poor.* Poor-led social movements were scarcely visible in public space surrounding the SDGs. And in large part, the consultations that tried to reach the poor did so in non-deliberative fashion (see Chapter 6). The problem here may be in discourse formation as well as in discourse transmission in the deliberative system; the Participate initiative alone could be seen as an effective means of discourse formation involving the poor themselves.

- *Strong cosmopolitan redistribution* in the goals was opposed by the world's wealthier states, motivated by their material self-interest. Now, we should not conclude that a deliberative process with more effective participation of the poor would necessarily endorse this redistribution. In Chapter 6 we reported on the Ground-Level Panels organized by the Participate initiative, which rejected aid in favour of the means to secure livelihoods – which has more in common with a capabilities or human development approach to justice than to strong cosmopolitan redistribution. Clearly though the Ground-Level Panels did not achieve an effective voice in the deliberative system, meaning the absence of strong cosmopolitan redistribution can be attributed to the opposition of wealthier states.

- *Justice as recognition.* Women's groups were successful in securing a goal that recognizes the social and political standing of women and girls (Goal 5, 'Achieve gender equality and empower all women and girls'). Beyond that, the language of 'for all' was much more prevalent than recognition of the standing of particular disadvantaged groups. The Ground-Level Panels composed of the poor highlighted the need for dignity, which is one aspect of justice as recognition. But there was no effective mechanism for that demand to be transmitted to the negotiating process for the SDGs.

- *Ecological justice*, or indeed any recognition of the possibility that the Earth system is in serious trouble (Hajer et al. 2015). This absence of concern with the condition of the Earth system could perhaps be explained by the fact that many environmental groups and Earth scientists devote their advocacy to the ongoing climate change and biodiversity negotiations, with little energy to spare for the SDGs. Environmental groups were present at the SDGs – but not in force. This made it easy to exclude strong notions of sustainability that would challenge some powerful economic interests and entrenched ideas.

- *Intergenerational justice.* The absence of explicit concern for future generations is not excusable by the fact that the goals run only fifteen years ahead (2015–2030), and perhaps surprising in light of the fact that the well-being of future generations was built into the definition of sustainable development by the landmark 1987 Brundtland report.

- *Rights discourse.* Human rights in the abstract are endorsed in the *Transforming Our World* document, but as we noted in Chapter 1, specific rights are surprisingly absent from the SDGs and their associated targets.

Justice as recognition, ecological justice, and intergenerational justice failed in the transmission of these concerns to empowered space (though weak presence in public space also contributed). Strong cosmopolitan justice failed because of the ability of wealthier states to avoid accountability for their self-interested strategizing in the SDG process.

In addition, dominant discourses can marginalize radical challenges at many places in the system. *Neoliberalism*'s hegemonic status in the global political economy spilled over into the SDG process; many of the participants would have been socialized into neoliberal discourse. There is an argument to be made for the neoliberal approach, even when it comes to the most disadvantaged; the trickle-down effects of market-led economic growth in China have been massively successful in pulling tens of millions of people out of poverty. But there are also plenty of arguments against this kind of growth – not least in terms of how it undermines equity, is ecologically unsustainable, and ignores the long term future – which did not feature prominently in the process.

The other dominant discourse to make itself felt was *weak sustainable development*, which has long been the main discourse in global environmental affairs. Sustainable development has always had a 'social' dimension (that is largely about justice) as one of its 'pillars' (along with economic development and environmental protection). By 2015 its weak, de-radicalized form was long dominant, and this is the form that infuses the SDGs. Its presence in the SDGs is a result of some clever discourse entrepreneurship on the part of key actors associated with the 2012 UN Conference on Sustainable Development (see Chapter 3). In the ensuing process, it received no effective challenge from those who believe that economic growth and ecological sustainability cannot be reconciled, especially under dominant capitalist conditions; or that capitalist markets necessarily produce injustice.

In short, the deliberative system that yielded the SDGs did a highly incomplete job in ensuring the deliberative inclusion and sifting of different discourses of justice.

Some Ideas for the Deliberative System

The SDGs are done and dusted. However, 'governing through goals' in the international system may just be beginning. Moreover, there should be a process to develop global goals that are successors to the SDGs, which expire in 2030. In this light, it makes sense to think about how a deliberative system for the promotion of global justice could look. Here are some suggestions.

Public Space

We have identified the need to improve engagement of different discourses in public space. In part the idea here is to resist any unwarranted discursive hegemonies. More generally, such engagement should increase the weight of reflective and defensible opinions in public space, and in the system as a whole. But how might such engagement be promoted in practice?

Most obviously, different civil society organizations could interact in more deliberative fashion with each other – and with any constituencies they claim to represent. To an extent deliberation across advocacy groups already happens. Relatively radical groups gather in the World Social Forum (though no collective attempt to influence the content of the SDGs was part of this). Relatively moderate groups joined in the Beyond 2015 Coalition, which became Together 2030. More interchange across radicals and moderates would perhaps enable radicals and moderates alike to sharpen their positions. When it comes to interactions between advocates and constituencies, we noted in Chapter 6 that it is important for groups claiming to advocate on behalf of the poor to cultivate the agency of the poor themselves.

The interchange between expert and lay perspectives and knowledges could be advanced in several ways. The first would involve translation from expert language to lay terminology. But translation should not be conceptualized in one-way terms, of experts becoming better communicators (and so more like successful public intellectuals). It is more productive to think of a reciprocal and deliberative interchange across experts and publics. This might involve (for example) convening citizen forums in conjunction with expert meetings or assessments. It would have been instructive (for example) for the Participate initiative's Ground-Level Panels to meet with experts from the SDSN.

Experts themselves do not of course speak with one voice, and there are many different sorts of expertise relevant to issues of global justice. It would be salutary, for example, for economists (not just neoliberal ones) to engage with ethicists and ecologists. There are inevitably plural justice claims relevant to any situation, local or global, and their relevant merits need to be deliberated. And that deliberation should not involve just the experts and public intellectuals themselves, but also those they are trying to persuade – citizens, activists, and publics.

Public space is highly mediatized, in the sense that many of its interactions take place through the media – increasingly, social media. As we saw in Chapter 5, that can lead to an overload of expression, without necessarily being accompanied by much in the way of reflection. Social media algorithms currently work to make sure that individuals mostly receive news and interpretations that corroborate rather than challenge their existing viewpoints. In Chapter 5 we also recommended cultivation of reflective spaces for slow thinking, be they as part of the media itself (slow journalism), or beyond the media. Such reflective spaces might be found in citizens' forums or Ground-Level Panels. It is in these reflective spaces that expansion of the moral imagination could be sought, along the lines we set out in Chapter 7 in our discussion of future generations and non-humans. We have plenty of evidence that this expansion can and does happen already to a degree in citizen forums, even when it is not planned (as our Chapter 7 example from the Bloomfield Track citizens' jury suggests). The larger mediated public sphere would benefit to the degree reflections occurring in these spaces are fed back into the media system – by publicizing what they did, what they concluded, and why.

Empowered Space

There are well-established deliberative principles that can be applied to the operation of any forum, be it composed of high-level international negotiators, lay citizens in local government, or anything in between. These principles include using a facilitator rather than a chair, equal chances to speak, respectful listening, no ad hominem arguments, no threats or coercion, a search for mutually acceptable outcomes and constructive proposals consistent with the interests of more than one party, communication in terms acceptable to those who do not share one's framework, and connecting particular proposals to more general interests. These principles should not be especially controversial, and indeed if given a chance to think for themselves about procedural rules, most forums would probably come up with a list something like this. Deliberative negotiators also need the flexibility to change their positions in light of what they have heard – as opposed to being under strict instructions to stick to the position of the state (or other entity) that they represent (though they would then need to justify that change in deliberation within their state). Newly established forums have the advantage that their participants are not necessarily socialized into the non-deliberative distributive bargaining paradigm described by Hopmann (1995: 24), and so might be more open to these kinds of principles. Of course, deliberative procedural norms by themselves do not prevent principles of justice being introduced strategically to benefit the material self-interest of the actor advancing them (as we saw in Chapter 3, this is common on issues of climate justice). But these procedural norms do make it more likely that any such strategic moves will be recognized and called to account.

Compared to many multilateral processes, the OWG that finalized the SDGs was a 'minilateral' success story, in part because of its composition – thirty seats shared among seventy countries (see Chapter 3). But it would be possible to do even better in deliberative terms when it comes to composition. The seventy countries were self-selected. In the end they reinforced the pattern we have described in which the SDG process was dominated by the discourses of neoliberalism, human development, and moderate/compromised sustainable development – to the exclusion of more radical anti-poverty and environmental discourses, as well as a scientific discourse of limits and boundaries. Finding states to represent these marginalized discourses could be a challenge. At the time of the OWG, the best representatives of radical challenges could probably be found in Latin America: Bolivia, Cuba, and Ecuador. Bolivia and Ecuador were part of one troika in the OWG (along with Argentina), Cuba was not present. So their voice constituted two-thirds of one-thirtieth of the OWG. If states can be found to represent these discourses, they should be granted a prominent place by bodies such as the OWG, though getting the body in question to see the need for its own expansion could be hard. If such states cannot be found, then other means of discursive representation should be considered. Limits/boundaries could be represented by designating a representative (or representatives) of the Earth system itself, perhaps drawn from a scientific organization. Radical discourses could be represented by groups such as LVC.

Ground-Level Panels could be a source of discursive representatives with a lived experience of poverty.

Discursive representation would promote more inclusive advocacy or justification in empowered space. But also needed in any deliberative system is reflection. In the case of the SDGs, the World Resources Institute (a think tank based in the United States) convened retreats attended by national representatives and individuals from the UN system (Kjørven 2016). These took place early in the process, to discuss what kind of overall shape the SDGs should take; including the key question of whether they should broaden the anti-poverty agenda of the MDGs, which was mostly specific to poor countries. Retreats did involve members of the OWG, and were useful in generating reciprocal understandings across their participants. Retreats of this sort would have been useful toward the end of the process, to reflect upon the arguments that had been made by different representatives and advocates. Whether early or late in the process, such retreats would also provide ideal venues for the expansion of moral imagination, including the use of visual imagery and experiential prompts as described in Chapter 7, which would enable fuller consideration of future generations and non-humans.

We know from experience with national and sub-national citizen's forums that they are especially good when it comes to the deliberative virtue of reflection (Dryzek 2017a). They are not so good when it comes to developing good justifications for positions. But there are plenty of actors in deliberative systems around the SDGs that specialize in justification or advocacy; reflection is in much shorter supply. That is especially the case in an empowered space currently populated mainly by professional advocates and strategists. Currently there are no reflective bodies involving lay citizens in empowered space in global governance (nor in most other levels of government). However, we have shown how it is possible to think about institutional innovations such as a deliberative global citizens' assembly (or other kinds of transnational mini-publics) that could give citizens a role in empowered space. That role need not involve decision making. Logically, reflection should follow justification in a temporal sequence in any deliberative system. This sequence means that mini-publics should be seen not only as providing citizen inputs into decision making from public space; they should also have a place in reflecting upon the advocacy that already occurs within empowered space

(Dryzek 2017a). This role resonates with the old idea that in parliamentary systems, an upper house should function as a house of review. Given no such bodies currently exist in the international system (and often fail in national systems – think of the US Senate), global governance provides an ideal place to experiment with the idea of a citizens' assembly as a house of review. (It would also be possible to establish citizens' panels or mini-publics to review progress in the implementation of the SDGs and their associated targets, in conjunction with the High-Level Political Forum, but that would take us beyond the sphere that is our concern.)

Transmission

We have described how the concerns of ordinary citizens and the poor in particular were transmitted to empowered space in highly imperfect fashion, the good intentions of those who organized the public consultations for the SDGs notwithstanding. The core need is for the transmission of reflective preferences as generated in inclusive public deliberation. From a deliberative systems perspective, unreflective preferences (such as those sought and registered in the MyWorld survey) lack value, however important they may be in motivating action in reality.

In Chapter 6 we described how citizens' assemblies and citizens' juries could be deployed in global governance to good deliberative effect. These are not exactly transmission mechanisms because they do not take well-formed opinions and then seek to make them known in empowered space. Rather, they help citizens see through the distortions that can pervade the public sphere, and so help create reflective public opinion. As such, these forums can be located in public space, in empowered space (as we suggested earlier in the chapter), and – most consistent with the idea of transmission – in hybrid space that spans public and empowered space.

For the SDGs, consultations with citizens and with experts proceeded on separate tracks. It would make sense to integrate the two tracks, not just for the sake of rendering citizen opinion more informed, but also bringing to bear lay knowledge on expertise. As we saw in Chapter 6, there are good epistemic reasons for involving the diversity of citizen voices in collective decision. In practice, such integration could be accomplished by the simple device of expert forums being constituted in conjunction with citizen forums. This conjunction would be an obvious fit in cases such as climate change where there is an established scientific assessment body (the Intergovernmental Panel on Climate Change (IPCC)).

Another way of thinking about transmission would involve ensuring that the provisional outcome of the engagement of discourses in public space somehow makes its way into empowered space. We have seen that some discourses present in public space, notably radical anti-poverty and environmental discourses, a scientific discourse of limits and boundaries, and the idea of justice as recognition, were not effectively transmitted to empowered space. One solution, described earlier, is the direct representation of these discourses in empowered space. Alternatively, it is possible to think how advocacy on behalf of these alternative discourses could be enhanced.

We have two suggestions. One is a forum that would function as a high-visibility 'chamber of discourses' that could bring together representatives of excluded discourses – as well as ones that fared better in the official process. It would need to be called something different; unfortunately the simple 'Global Forum' name is already taken by a corporate organization (for a similar proposal for a Global Climate Forum, see Stevenson and Dryzek 2014: 197–200). We have in mind something a bit different from the World Social Forum, which features only a restricted range of radical discourses, and something a bit more geared to specific processes, such as that which yielded the SDGs. Given its character as a deliberative chamber, the main entry requirement would be a willingness to reflect upon preferences, values, and judgements.

Finally we note that one form of transmission that can sometimes be effective involves protest and disruption. Such protests are visible around climate change. Their effectiveness has long been hard to discern, though the Extinction Rebellion protests and school children's strikes beginning in 2018 did receive responses from national governments (and UN Secretary General António Guterres endorsed the strikes in 2019[4]). Protests have been both visible and effective when it comes to global economic governance – which was otherwise long immune to influence from public space of any sort (except from

---

[4] See www.theguardian.com/commentisfree/2019/mar/15/climate-strikers-urgency-un-summit-world-leaders.

neoliberal public intellectuals). Stiglitz (2002) credits anti-corporate globalization protests with changing the operating principles of the World Bank. As a goal-setting exercise, the SDG process did not attract protests of this sort; protests are usually against something, and in the case of goal-setting there is not anything tangible to be against (except inaction, which is what climate protests can be against).

Accountability

We noted earlier that there is no scope for punitive accountability in connection with the SDGs and similar global processes. Currently there is some narrative accountability, but no deliberative accountability. It is best to think of deliberative accountability not as something that occurs when a process is complete, as a retrospective summary judgement on what was decided (and perhaps implemented). Rather, deliberative accountability can be thought of as iterative, involving decision makers being accountable to decision takers at many steps along the route to decision (Roche 2003). State negotiators could establish deliberative accountability procedures in connection with briefings to journalists and civil society representatives from their own country. It would be straightforward to establish accountability platforms on social media, where those in empowered space could interact with diverse publics (though it would be important to prevent such interactions degenerating into the abusive free-for-all that is all too common on social media). It would also be possible to collectivize accountability by constituting a civil society body to act as a counterpart to collective multilateral or minilateral bodies. Along these lines, a Civil Society 20 or C20 group was established in 2013 to shadow the minilateral G20 group of major economies (with some relevance to the SDGs in their discussions).[5] C20 is recognized by G20 as an 'engagement group', though that does not imply any significant accountability from G20 to C20.

Howard, Franco, and Shaw (2018) develop the idea of 'participatory accountability', which begins with participatory processes at the local level among marginalized groups that sharpen the terms in which accountability should be sought. With the help of 'translocutor' organizations (such as partners of the Participate initiative) committed to

[5] See https://civil-20.org/c20-faqs/.

empowerment of the marginalized, 'duty bearers' can then be called to account. Translocutors should themselves be accountable to the marginalized. While Howard et al. (2018) reference the SDGs, the duty bearers they have in mind and the examples they give are mostly local (and sometimes national) officials. However, it is possible to think of translocutors extending their reach to global goal-setting processes, thus establishing accountability links from locally empowered marginalized groups to global processes, though where the resources to do this might come from is a major challenge.

Reflexivity

There is a reflexivity paradox at the heart of the SDGs. The title of the 2030 Agenda of which the goals are a part is *Transforming Our World*. Yet the goals themselves are static: there is no mechanism for changing them over the fifteen years until they expire in 2030. This assumes that the world will not become transformed enough in the meantime for the goals themselves to change. But fifteen years is plenty of time for catastrophic climate change to make itself felt with a vengeance, or for global ecosystemic collapse to accelerate, or for the international system to regress into war, or for devastating pandemics to be unleashed as a consequence of reckless human intrusion on nature.

In this light, instead of seeing the goals and targets as fixed yardsticks for results-based management, why not interpret them as a providing a 'living framework' that is a focus for ongoing global deliberation? (See Dryzek and Pickering 2019: 152–4 on living frameworks more generally.) This does not mean that all goals and targets have to be open to revision all the time – that would undercut the whole idea of governing through goals. But there ought to be some mechanism for opening up particular aspects such as the level of national ambitions or the precise content of targets in light of new evidence of threats (such as recognition that the Earth system has entered the Anthropocene, while the SDGs are essentially Holocene constructs), new opportunities (such as gene-editing technology that could eradicate diseases – but at considerable risk), or new conjunctions (e.g. climate change and violent conflict).

Such deliberation could be triggered in a number of possible ways. The UN's High-Level Political Forum that is charged with overseeing implementation of the 2030 Agenda might have as part of its mandate the ability to trigger deliberation in light of periodic review. But such triggering could also come from below, via (for example) a global dissent channel (as proposed in Dryzek and Pickering 2019: 159–60). A global dissent channel could be sponsored by the UN, and its substance could be restricted to complaints about the adequacy of particular goals or targets in light of changing circumstances. The volume of communication in the channel could be restricted by requiring deliberative crowdsourcing of complaints, with some kind of filter (such as a citizen panel) to check against frivolous organized campaigns. Should they be adopted, global citizens' assemblies could have as part of their review function the capacity to trigger deliberation on a specific topic.

One word of caution: just as in a deliberative systems approach it is conceivable that intrinsically non-deliberative acts can have positive systemic consequences (as we noted at the outset of this chapter), so it is also conceivable than intrinsically deliberative practices can have negative systemic consequences through the interactions they induce. An example might be the establishment of a deliberative oversight body (such as a supreme court) that frees legislators to behave irresponsibly in the knowledge that the oversight body will correct their excesses. While it hard to envisage any such negative consequences arising from any of our proposals, we should be alive to such possibilities (likely to be revealed by empirical analysis rather than the anticipation of the normative theorist), especially if the reform in question would be put into practice. Such possibilities drive home the need for reflexive capacity in deliberative systems that can reveal and correct any such unintended negative consequences.

Conclusion

From a deliberative systems perspective, we have argued that any global process such as that which yielded the SDGs could be improved by:

- more deliberative interchange across civil society organizations, especially radicals and moderates;
- deliberative forums involving experts, public intellectuals, and lay citizens;

- the integration of consultation tracks involving experts, citizens, and the poor;
- more direct representation by the poor themselves (as opposed to their advocates) in global process;
- cultivation of reflective moments and spaces in the media, in forums, and in retreats;
- expansion of moral imagination through visual imagery and experiential prompts in reflective spaces;
- the application of deliberative principles and procedural norms to multilateral and minilateral negotiations;
- discursive representation by states (and others) in international negotiations;
- a deliberative 'chamber of discourses' in civil society to crystallize and represent discourses;
- recognizing the potentially positive role of protest and disruption;
- the establishment of global assemblies of lay citizens, of two kinds – one would have a mandated review function in empowered space, the other would be in public space and help create and transmit informed public opinion;
- deliberative accountability platforms;
- translocutor organizations establishing accountability links from local marginalized groups to global processes;
- institutional mechanisms (including a global dissent channel) to trigger a re-opening of deliberation on goals and targets.

This list is not exhaustive. But it would, we believe, help redeem the necessarily democratic character of formative agency in global governance by bringing agents into more productive relationships with each other, and with the system of global governance that they constitute.

9 | Conclusion

Formative agency exercised under deliberative and democratic conditions is key to global justice. We showed that the pursuit of global justice can benefit from the fresh perspective developed here on the problematic relationship between justice and democracy. In a world where the content of justice is not simple, obvious, universally accepted, and easily implemented, formative agency is necessarily integral to justice itself – not an optional extra. Formative agency's promise can be redeemed, and its problematic aspects overcome, to the extent agents engage with each other in truly inclusive, deliberative, and democratic interaction.

Thus global justice must be deliberated rather than simply analysed, asserted, and advocated. Deliberation about the content of global justice should include the full range of agents with affected interests, notably those whose concerns are often not heard or suppressed: the poor and disadvantaged, future generations, and social-ecological systems. For other actors, such as corporations, foundations, and the wealthy, the exercise of formative agency can be more problematic. Sometimes the problematic aspects can be overcome. For example, deliberative credibility mechanisms can control the pervasive tendency of powerful actors to define and advance justice in terms that serve their material self-interest, thereby preventing self-interested definitions from being accepted by governments or included in international agreements. Sometimes the problematic aspects mean a category of actors should be heavily restricted in their exercise of formative agency; we have argued that corporations generally merit such treatment.

Deliberative inclusion is necessary in order for the world to know what justice should actually mean on any issue and in any given context. Further, participation in democratic deliberation can improve the epistemic competence of all agents and decision makers, thereby enabling ensuing collective outcomes to be both more effective responses to collective problems and more just.

While we focused our discussion in particular on the Sustainable Development Goals (SDGs) and climate governance as it pertains to climate justice, we believe that the basic principles articulated here about the interaction of justice and democracy have broader applicability, not just when it comes to global goals.

These principles are not just philosophical. They also provide guidelines for the analysis and evaluation of the formative activities of different kinds of agents, in isolation and in their interactions with other kinds of agents in a deliberative system. We hope to have demonstrated the fruitfulness of bringing normative political theory into sustained engagement with the empirical analysis of, and practice within, real-world cases.

Our account is not meant to imply, however, that democracy guarantees justice. We argue simply that global deliberative democratization is necessary for, and indeed integral to, the pursuit of global justice. While we have offered plenty of ideas about how this pursuit can be organized and advanced, in terms of general principles as well as institutional design and the activities of specific actors, we offer no grand normative model for global politics. The principles we have articulated admit considerable variety when it comes to both institutional structure and more informal practice. These principles are applicable to the activities of various agents, the forums in which they meet, and the systems that join them – in all the settings where we now see that justice needs to be deliberated in order to be advanced. The configuration of global governance should always be a work in progress. And the reflexivity that enables such reconfiguration to proceed in defensible and productive fashion can itself be enhanced by global deliberative democratization.

How realistic is it to expect that global deliberative democratization will lead to the pursuit of global justice? Idealism has its place in normative political theory, which among other things should be in the business of articulating ideals. However, we developed our theory with an eye on the real world (in our major and minor cases and beyond), and with the aim of showing that there are realistic, feasible moves that can be made to improve it. Some of these moves involve building on the already-observable qualities of previous institutions and initiatives, such as the deliberative aspects of the Open Working Group (OWG) we analysed in Chapter 3, or the inclusion of the poor and marginalized in meaningful deliberation in the Ground-Level

Panels of the Participate initiative that we described in Chapter 6. Some would involve more innovative institutional designs, such as the citizen forums sketched in Chapters 6 and 8, but we would argue that even those are more feasible than proposals to introduce electoral democracy into global governance. Some would involve actions that would build on what many actors already accept that they probably should do, such as the expansion of the horizontal and vertical democratic engagements of advocacy groups we outlined in Chapter 5. Some would involve improving the connections between existing practices, such as the activities of civil society, experts, and negotiators, as sketched in Chapter 8. The deliberative systems framework we applied in Chapter 8 shows how reforms that might seem individually marginal could combine to yield significant momentum.

If we look around at the condition of the world today, we see national electoral democracy under threat and in retreat in many countries. Democracy has been undermined by populist demagogues who position a pure people (defined on ethnic, national, or religious grounds) against a corrupt elite, corrupt outsiders, and corrupt transnational and global institutions. This kind of discourse can capture a substantial proportion of the citizenry. Pluralism yields to toxic identity politics that requires negation of the identity and voice of those with whom one disagrees. Democracy's epistemic qualities are undermined when demagogues offer simplistic solutions to complex problems (build a wall, expel immigrants, leave the European Union), and disabled when post-truth politics means that cascades of lies dominate the public sphere. Once elected, authoritarian leaders can refuse to abide by constitutional norms (or change the constitution to suit themselves), extend control over the media, rig electoral systems so that they cannot lose, and restrict the political liberties of their opponents, sometimes imprisoning them.

Deliberative democracy does not have to yield before these developments, and can indeed fight back. One aspect of the fightback can be the cultivation of alternative sites of democratic deliberation outside the state structures where authoritarians (sometimes) flourish. Democracy is not just the preserve of some states, it can also be found outside, beyond, against, and across states. In this light, global democratization can be part of the response to the contemporary crises of democracy, and international organizations can help here. In the same years in which democracy at the state level seems in many places to be in retreat, the global level appears to tell a different story. Populist discourse has no significant resonance in global governance. In global politics, we see moves (however halting and incomplete) toward inclusion, participation, and deliberation. We have charted these moves in the context of the SDGs. However far short they may fall in relation to democratic ideals, especially when it comes to the final content of collective decisions, they do represent substantial advance over global governance processes that feature only negotiation between the representatives of states (including authoritarian states), or the decisions of unaccountable international organizations (such as the International Monetary Fund (IMF) and World Trade Organization (WTO)). Global deliberative democratization can be seen in terms of the steps that would follow these incipient openings.

It would be an exaggeration to suggest that democracy's future and salvation lies at the global level. One long-standing argument is that democracy's natural home is the nation state, on the grounds that the kind of social solidarity possible within the nation state is unavailable in global governance. We wouldn't go so far as inverting this argument. Instead, we would argue only that global democratization can be *one significant* part (among others) of the response to contemporary challenges to democracy.

Does this mean that we should accordingly emphasize the global level rather than the national when it comes to questions of justice as well as democracy? Certainly the contemporary attenuation of democracy within nation states is often accompanied by some glaring injustices: to religious or national minorities excluded from citizenship, to demonized members of ethnic minorities, to refugees locked up rather than resettled, to those silenced by social media storms, to social movements denied the right to protest, to all those now restricted in their ability to exercise political speech, to indigenous peoples expelled from their land, and (in some cases) to an Earth system whose well-being is treated as a false concern promoted only by environmentalists and globalists. Some of these injustices lie beyond the reach of global justice, but not all of them. Global principles such as those embedded in the Universal Declaration of Human Rights and global goals such as those embedded in the SDGs, and various international conventions and regimes, can sometimes constrain states and do provide some resources for those fighting to combat national injustices. However, many national injustices lie beyond the reach of global norms (and authoritarian and populist leaders do of course want to keep it that way). We would argue only that global governance provides one venue for the pursuit of democracy and justice in a world where both are under attack in many (though of course not all) states.

Irrespective of what goes on within nation states when it comes to both democracy and justice, the pursuit of global justice remains an ethical imperative. And if we are right in our argument, that means global democratization is equally such an imperative. While it would be an overstatement to say there can be *no* global justice without global deliberative democracy, the pursuit of global justice does now require global deliberative democratization.

References

Abbott, Kenneth W., Philipp Genschel, Duncan Snidal, and Benhard Zangl, eds. 2015. *International Organizations as Orchestrators*. Cambridge, UK: Cambridge University Press.

Abouharb, M. Rodwan and David Cingranelli. 2007. *Human Rights and Structural Adjustment*. Cambridge, UK: Cambridge University Press.

Achen, Christopher H. and Larry M. Bartels. 2016. *Democracy for Realists: Why Elections Do Not Produce Responsive Government*. Princeton, NJ: Princeton University Press.

Adams, Barbara and Gretchen Luchsinger. 2015. Are FfD3 and Post-2015 Striking the Right Public–Private Balance? *Global Policy Forum*, 16 April. Available at www.globalpolicy.org/home/271-general/52754-are-ffd3-and-post-2015-striking-the-right-public-private-balance.html.

African Centre for Biodiversity. 2019. Civil Society Denounces the Release of GM Mosquitoes in Burkina Faso. Available at www.grain.org/en/art icle/6277-civil-society-denounces-the-release-of-gm-mosquitoes-in-bur kina-faso.

Ahn, Sun J. and Jeremy N. Bailenson. 2011. Self-Endorsing versus Other-Endorsing in Virtual Environments. *Journal of Advertising* 40: 93–106.

Ainge Roy, Eleanor. 2017a. New Zealand Gives Mount Taranaki Same Legal Rights as a Person. *Guardian*, 22 December. Available at www .theguardian.com/world/2017/dec/22/new-zealand-gives-mount-tara naki-same-legal-rights-as-a-person.

2017b. New Zealand River Granted Same Legal Rights as Human Being. *Guardian*, 16 March. Available at www.theguardian.com/world/2017/ mar/16/new-zealand-river-granted-same-legal-rights-as-human-being.

Amit, Elinor, Sara Gottlieb, and Joshua D. Greene. 2014. Visual versus Verbal Thinking and Dual-Process Moral Cognition. In Jeffrey W. Sherman, Bertram Gawronski, and Yaacov Trope, eds., *Dual-Process Theories of the Social Mind*, pp. 340–54. New York: Guilford Press.

Ananthapadmanabhan G., K. Srivinas, and V. Gopal. 2007. *Hiding behind the Poor: A Report by Greenpeace on Climate Injustice*. Bangalore: Greenpeace India.

Anderson, Mark. 2017. NGOs: Blessing or Curse. *Africa Report*, 29 November. Available at www.theafricareport.com/777/ngos-bless ing-or-curse.

Andreou, Chrisoula and Mark D. White. 2010. *The Thief of Time: Philosophical Essays on Procrastination*. Oxford: Oxford University Press.

Anscombe, Gertrude E. M. 1957. *Intention*. Oxford: Basil Blackwell.

Ansolabehere, Stephen, John M. de Figueiredo, and James M. Snyder, Jr. 2003. Why Is There So Little Money in U.S. Politics? *Journal of Economic Perspectives* 17 (1): 105–30.

Appleton, Katy and Andrew M. Lovett. 2003. GIS-Based Visualisations of Rural Landscapes: Defining 'Sufficient' Realism for Environmental Decision-Making. *Landscape and Urban Planning* 65: 117–31.

Arneson, Richard J. 1989. Equality and Equal Opportunity for Welfare. *Philosophical Studies* 56: 77–93.

2000. Welfare Should Be the Currency of Justice. *Canadian Journal of Philosophy* 30: 477–524.

2006. Justice After Rawls. In John S. Dryzek, Bonnie Honig, and Anne Phillips, eds., *The Oxford Handbook of Political Theory*, pp. 45–64. Oxford: Oxford University Press.

Bächtiger, André, John S. Dryzek, Jane Mansbridge, and Mark E. Warren. 2018a. Deliberative Democracy: An Introduction. In André Bächtiger, John S. Dryzek, Jane Mansbridge, and Mark E. Warren, eds., *The Oxford Handbook of Deliberative Democracy*, pp. 1–31. Oxford: Oxford University Press.

eds. 2018b. *The Oxford Handbook of Deliberative Democracy*. Oxford: Oxford University Press.

Bäckstrand, Karin and Jonathan W. Kuyper. 2017. The Democratic Legitimacy of Orchestration: The UNFCCC, Non-state Actors, and Transnational Climate Governance. *Environmental Politics* 26 (4): 764–88.

Bäckstrand, Karin, Jonathan W. Kuyper, Björn-Ola Linnér, and Eva Lövbrand. 2017. Non-state Actors in the New Landscape of International Climate Cooperation. *Environmental Politics* 26 (4): 561–79.

Barandiaran, Xabier E., Ezequiel Di Paolo, and Marieke Rohde. 2009. Defining Agency: Individuality, Normativity, Asymmetry, and Spatio-Temporality in Action. *Adaptive Behavior* 17 (5): 367–86.

Barry, Brian. 1977. Justice between Generations. In Peter M. S. Hacker and Joseph Raz, eds., *Law, Morality and Society: Essays in Honour of H. L. A. Hart*, pp. 268–84. Oxford: Clarendon Press.

Bateson, Melissa, Luke Callow, Jessica R. Holmes, Maximilian L. Redmond Roche, and Daniel Nettle. 2013. Do Images of 'Watching Eyes' Induce Behaviour That Is More Pro-social and More Normative? A Field Experiment on Littering. *PLoS ONE* 8: e82055.

BBC. 2007. Lucky Dog Inherits $12m Fortune. Available at http://news.bbc .co.uk/2/hi/americas/6969648.stm.

Beckman, Ludvig and Fredrik Uggla. 2016. An Ombudsman for Future Generations: Legitimate and Effective? In Iñigo González-Ricoy and Axel Gosseries, eds., *Institutions for Future Generations*, pp. 117–34. Oxford: Oxford University Press.

Benson, Jonathan D. 2018. An Epistemic Theory of Deliberative Democracy. PhD Thesis, University of Manchester.

Bernstein, Steven. 2017. The United Nations and the Governance of Sustainable Development Goals. In Norichika Kanie and Frank Biermann, eds., *Governing through Goals: Sustainable Development Goals as Governance Innovation*, pp. 213–39. Cambridge, MA: MIT Press.

Bessette, Joseph M. 1979. Deliberation in Congress. Paper presented at the Annual Meeting of the American Political Science Association, Washington, DC.

Biss, Mavis. 2014. Moral Imagination, Perception, and Judgment. *Southern Journal of Philosophy* 52: 1–21.

Bosco, David. 2014. *Rough Justice: The International Criminal Court in a World of Power Politics*. Oxford: Oxford University Press.

Boykoff, Maxwell T. 2019. *Creative (Climate) Communications: Productive Pathways for Science, Policy and Society*. Cambridge, UK: Cambridge University Press.

Boykoff, Maxwell T. and Jules M. Boykoff. 2004. Balance as Bias: Global Warming and the US Prestige Press. *Global Environmental Change* 14: 125–36.

Brassett, James and William Smith. 2010. Deliberative Democracy and Global Civil Society: Agency, Arena, Affect. *Review of International Studies* 36 (2): 413–30.

Bratman, Michael E. 1993. Shared Intention. *Ethics* 104 (1): 97–113.

2000. Reflection, Planning, and Temporally Extended Agency. *Philosophical Review* 109 (1): 35–61.

2007. *Structures of Agency: Essays*. Oxford: Oxford University Press.

Brennan, Andrew and Yeuk-Sze Lo. 2016. Environmental Ethics. In Edward N. Zalta, ed., *The Stanford Encyclopedia of Philosophy*, winter 2016 ed. Available at https://plato.stanford.edu/archives/win2016/entries/ ethics-environmental/.

Brennan, Geoffrey, Lina Eriksson, Robert E. Goodin, and Nicholas Southwood. 2013. *Explaining Norms*. Oxford: Oxford University Press.

Brennan, Geoffrey and Philip Pettit. 1990. Unveiling the Vote. *British Journal of Political Science* 20: 311–33.

Brennan, Jason. 2016. *Against Democracy*. Princeton, NJ: Princeton University Press.

Brooks, Thom, ed. 2020. *The Oxford Handbook of Global Justice*. Oxford: Oxford University Press.

Broome, John. 2014. A Philosopher at the IPCC. *Philosopher's Magazine* 66: 11–16.

Brown, Chris. 2006. From International to Global Justice. In John S. Dryzek, Bonnie Honig, and Anne Phillips, eds., *The Oxford Handbook of Political Theory*, pp. 621–35. Oxford: Oxford University Press.

Brown, Chris and Robyn Eckersley, eds. 2018. *The Oxford Handbook of International Political Theory*. Oxford: Oxford University Press.

Brown, Phil. 1992. Popular Epidemiology and Toxic Waste Contamination: Lay and Professional Ways of Knowing. *Journal of Health and Social Behavior* 33 (3): 267–81.

Burnham, Terence C. 2003. Engineering Altruism: A Theoretical and Experimental Investigation of Anonymity and Gift Giving. *Journal of Economic Behavior and Organization* 50: 133–44.

Burns, Danny. 2014. Reflections on the Ground Level Panels. In Thea Shahrokh and Joanna Wheeler, eds., *The Participate Anthology*, pp. 41–2. Brighton: Institute of Development Studies.

Calvo, Paco. 2016. The Philosophy of Plant Neurobiology: A Manifesto. *Synthese* 193: 1323–43.

Campbell, Thomas D. 1974. Humanity before Justice. *British Journal of Political Science* 4: 1–16.

Caney, Simon. 2012. Just Emissions. *Philosophy and Public Affairs* 40 (4): 255–300.

2013. Agents of Global Justice. In David Archard, Monique Deveaux, Neil Manson, and Daniel Weinstock, eds., *Reading Onora O'Neill*, pp. 133–56. Abingdon, UK: Routledge.

2015. *Meeting the Needs of Future Generations*. Dublin: Mary Robinson Foundation.

2016. Political Institutions for the Future: A Fivefold Package. In Iñigo González-Ricoy and Axel Gosseries, eds., *Institutions for Future Generations*, pp. 135–55. Oxford: Oxford University Press.

Carant, J. Briant. 2017. Unheard Voices: A Critical Discourse Analysis of the Millennium Development Goals' Evolution into the Sustainable Development Goals. *Third World Quarterly* 38 (1): 16–41.

Carrington, Damian. 2018. Humanity Has Wiped Out 60% of Animal Populations Since the 1970s, Report Finds. *Guardian*, 30 October.

Available at www.theguardian.com/environment/2018/oct/30/human ity-wiped-out-animals-since-1970-major-report-finds.

2019. 'Frightening' Number of Plant Extinctions Found in Global Survey. *Guardian*, 30 June. Available at www.theguardian.com/environment/ 2019/jun/10/frightening-number-of-plant-extinctions-found-in-global-survey.

Carson, Lyn. 2007. Creating Democratic Surplus through Citizens' Assemblies. *Journal of Public Deliberation* 4 (1): article 5.

Chambers, Robert. 2014. Foreword. In Thea Shahrokh and Joanna Wheeler, eds., *The Participate Anthology*, p. 5. Brighton: Institute of Development Studies.

Chambers, Simone. 2018. Human Life Is Group Life: Deliberative Democracy for Realists. *Critical Review* 30 (1–2): 1–13.

Chasek, Pamela and Lynne M. Wagner. 2016. Breaking the Mold: A New Type of Multilateral Sustainable Development Negotiation. *International Environmental Agreements* 16 (3): 397–413.

Chasek, Pamela S., Lynn M. Wagner, Faye Leone, Anna-Maria Lebada, and Natalie Risse. 2016. Getting to 2030: Negotiating the Post-2015 Sustainable Development Agenda. *Review of European, Comparative and International Law* 25 (1): 5–14.

Cimadamore, Alberto. 2016. Global Justice, International Relations, and the Sustainable Development Goals' Quest for Poverty Reduction. *Journal of International and Comparative Social Policy* 32 (2): 131–48.

Cohen, Gerald. A. 1989. On the Currency of Egalitarian Justice. *Ethics* 99: 906–44.

Coke, Edward. 1610. *Thomas Bonham v. College of Physicians*, 8 Co. Rep. 107; 77 Eng. Rep. 638.

Collins, Stephanie. 2019. *Group Duties: Their Existence and Their Implications for Individuals*. Oxford: Oxford University Press.

Cooke, Steve. 2017. Imagined Utopias: Animal Rights and the Moral Imagination. *Journal of Political Philosophy* 25: e1–18.

Cormier, Zoe. 2010. Peasants Cool the Planet! *New Internationalist*, 7 December.

Curato, Nicole. 2019. *Democracy in a Time of Misery: From Slow Violence to Deliberative Politics*. Oxford: Oxford University Press.

Curtis, Mark. 2016. *Gated Development: Is the Gates Foundation Always a Force for Good?* London: Global Justice Now. Available at www .globaljustice.org.uk/sites/default/files/files/resources/gjn_gates_report_ june_2016_web_final_version_2.pdf.

Dahl, Robert A. 1979. Procedural Democracy. In Peter Laslett and James Fishkin, eds., *Philosophy, Politics & Society*, fifth series, pp. 97–133. Oxford: Basil Blackwell.

1999. Can International Organizations Be More Democratic? A Skeptic's View. In Ian Shapiro and Casiano Hacker-Cordón, eds., *Democracy's Edges*, pp. 19–36. Cambridge, UK: Cambridge University Press.

Darwall, Stephen L. 2006. *The Second-Person Standpoint: Morality, Respect, and Accountability*. Cambridge, MA: Harvard University Press.

Davidson, Donald [1963] 1980. Actions, Reasons, and Causes. In Donald Davidson, *Essays on Actions and Events*, pp. 3–20. Oxford: Clarendon Press.

1982. Rational Animals. *Dialectica* 3 (4): 317–27.

Deveaux, Monique. 2015. The Global Poor as Agents of Justice. *Journal of Moral Philosophy* 12 (2): 125–50.

2018. Poor-Led Social Movements and Global Justice. *Political Theory* 46 (5): 698–725.

Dowding, Keith, Robert E. Goodin, and Carole Pateman, eds. 2004. *Justice and Democracy: Essays for Brian Barry*. Cambridge, UK: Cambridge University Press.

Doyle, Michael W. and Joseph E. Stiglitz. 2014. Eliminating Extreme Inequality: A Sustainable Development Goal, 2015–2030. *Ethics and International Affairs* 28 (1): 5–13.

Druckman, James N., Eric Peterson, and Rune Slothuus. 2013. How Elite Partisan Polarization Affects Public Opinion. *American Political Science Review* 107 (1): 57–79.

Dryzek, John S. 1990. *Discursive Democracy*. Cambridge, UK: Cambridge University Press.

1996. *Democracy in Capitalist Times: Ideals, Limits, and Struggles*. Oxford: Oxford University Press.

2000. *Deliberative Democracy and Beyond*. Oxford: Oxford University Press.

(with Simon Niemeyer). 2010. *Foundations and Frontiers of Deliberative Governance*. Oxford: Oxford University Press.

2012. Global Civil Society: The Progress of Post-Westphalian Politics. *Annual Review of Political Science* 15: 101–19.

2013a. The Deliberative Democrat's Idea of Justice. *European Journal of Political Theory* 12: 329–46.

2013b. *The Politics of the Earth: Environmental Discourses*, 3rd ed. Oxford: Oxford University Press.

2015. Democratic Agents of Justice. *Journal of Political Philosophy* 23: 361–84.

2017a. The Forum, the System, and the Polity: Three Varieties of Democratic Theory. *Political Theory* 45 (5): 610–36.

2017b. The Meanings of Life for Non-state Actors in Climate Politics. *Environmental Politics* 26 (4): 789–99.

Dryzek, John S., André Bächtiger, and Karolina Milewicz. 2011. Toward a Deliberative Global Citizens' Assembly. *Global Policy* 2: 33–42.

Dryzek, John S. and Jonathan Pickering. 2019. *The Politics of the Anthropocene*. Oxford: Oxford University Press.

Dryzek, John S. and Simon Niemeyer. 2008. Discursive Representation. *American Political Science Review* 102: 481–93.

Dunlap, Riley and Aaron McCright. 2011. Organized Climate Change Denial. In John S. Dryzek, Richard B. Norgaard, and David Schlosberg, eds., *The Oxford Handbook of Climate Change and Society*, pp. 144–60. Oxford: Oxford University Press.

Dworkin, Ronald. 1977. *Taking Rights Seriously*. Cambridge, MA: Harvard University Press.

2000. *Sovereign Virtue*. Cambridge, MA: Harvard University Press.

Elster, Jon. 1986. The Market and the Forum: Three Varieties of Political Theory. In Jon Elster and Aanund Hylland, eds., *Foundations of Social Choice Theory*, pp. 103–32. Cambridge, UK: Cambridge University Press.

1998. Introduction. In Jon Elster, ed., *Deliberative Democracy*, pp. 1–18. Cambridge, UK: Cambridge University Press.

Ercan, Selen, Carolyn M. Hendriks, and John S. Dryzek. 2019. Public Deliberation in an Era of Communicative Plenty. *Policy and Politics* 47 (1): 19–36.

Ernest-Jones, Max, Daniel Nettle, and Melissa Bateson. 2011. Effects of Eye Images on Everyday Cooperative Behaviour: A Field Experiment. *Evolution and Human Behavior* 32: 172–8.

Erskine, Toni. 2004. 'Blood on the UN's Hands'? Assigning Duties and Apportioning Blame to an International Organisation. *Global Society* 18 (1): 21–42.

Estlund, David and Hélène Landemore. 2018. The Epistemic Value of Democratic Deliberation. In André Bächtiger, John S. Dryzek, Jane Mansbridge, and Mark E. Warren, eds., *The Oxford Handbook of Deliberative Democracy*, pp. 113–31. Oxford: Oxford University Press.

Falk, Richard and Andrew Strauss, eds. 2011. *A Global Parliament: Essays and Articles*. Berlin: Committee for a Democratic UN.

Feinberg, Joel. 1973. *Social Philosophy*. Englewood Cliffs, NJ: Prentice-Hall.

1980. The Rights of Animals and Unborn Generations. In Joel Feinberg, ed., *Rights, Justice, and the Bounds of Liberty: Essays in Social Philosophy*, pp. 159–84. Princeton, NJ: Princeton University Press.

Finnemore, Martha and Kathryn Sikkink. 1998. International Norm Dynamics and Political Change. *International Organization* 52: 887–917.

Fischer, Frank. 1990. *Technocracy and the Politics of Expertise*. Newbury Park, CA: Sage.

Fischer, Frank and Piyapong Boossabong. 2018. Deliberative Policy Analysis. In John S. Dryzek, André Bächtiger, Jane Mansbridge, and Mark E. Warren, eds., *The Oxford Handbook of Deliberative Democracy*, pp. 584–94. Oxford: Oxford University Press

Fisher, Andrew. 2011. *Big Hunger: The Unholy Alliance between Corporate America and Anti-hunger Groups*. Cambridge, MA: MIT Press.

Fishkin, James. 2009. *When the People Speak: Deliberative Democracy and Public Consultation*. Oxford: Oxford University Press.

Floridia, Antonio. 2017. *From Participation to Deliberation: A Critical Genealogy of Deliberative Democracy*. Colchester, UK: ECPR Press.

Follett, Mary Parker. [1925]1942. Constructive Conflict. In Henry C. Metcalf and Lyndall Urwick, eds., *Dynamic Administration: The Collected Papers of Mary Parker Follett*, pp. 1–20. New York: Harper.

Ford, Liz. 2015. Sustainable Development Goals: All You Need to Know. *Guardian*, 19 January. Available at www.theguardian.com/global-development/2015/jan/19/sustainable-development-goals-united-nations.

Forester, John. 1999. Dealing with Deep Value Difference. In Lawrence Susskind, Sarah McKearnan, and Jennifer Thomas-Larmer, eds., *The Consensus Building Handbook*, pp. 463–94. Thousand Oaks, CA: Sage.

Forst, Rainer. 2015. Noumenal Power. *Journal of Political Philosophy* 23 (2): 111–27.

Fox, Jesse and Jeremy N. Bailenson 2009. Virtual Self-Modeling: The Effects of Vicarious Reinforcement and Identification on Exercise Behaviors. *Media Psychology* 12: 195–209.

Fox, Oliver and Peter Stoett. 2016. Citizen Participation in the UN Sustainable Development Goals Consultation Process: Toward Global Democratic Governance? *Global Governance* 22: 555–74.

Frankfurt, Harry. 1971. Freedom of the Will and the Concept of a Person. *Journal of Philosophy* 68 (1): 5–20.

1987. Equality as a Moral Ideal. *Ethics* 98: 21–42.

2000. The Moral Irrelevance of Equality. *Public Affairs Quarterly* 14: 87–103.

Fraser Nancy. 2009. *Scales of Justice*. New York: Columbia University Press.

Fraser Nancy and Axel Honneth. 2003. *Redistribution or Recognition? A Political-Philosophical Exchange*. New York: Verso.

Friedman, Milton. 1970. The Social Responsibility of Business Is to Increase Its Profits. *New York Times Magazine*, 13 September.

Fuller, Steve. 2006. The Public Intellectual as Agent of Justice: In Search of a Regime. *Philosophy and Rhetoric* 39 (2): 148–57.

Gabbatiss, Josh. 2017. Plants Can See, Hear, and Smell. *BBC*, 10 January. Available at www.bbc.com/earth/story/20170109-plants-can-see-hear-and-smell-and-respond.

Gabizon, Sascha. 2016. Women's Movements' Engagement in the SDGs: Lessons Learned from the Women's Major Group. *Gender and Development* 24 (1): 99–110.

Gardiner, Stephen M. 2006. A Perfect Moral Storm: Climate Change, Intergenerational Ethics and the Problem of Moral Corruption. *Environmental Values* 15: 397–413.

2011. *A Perfect Moral Storm: The Ethical Tragedy of Climate Change.* Oxford: Oxford University Press.

Gelbspan, Thea. 2017. Interview. Civicus online. Available at www.civicus .org/index.php/media-resources/news/interviews/3027-even-the-most-progres sive-un-agencies-have-become-vulnerable-to-the-threat-of-corporate-capture-fortunately-there-are-precedents-of-the-un-tackling-this-kind-of-challenge.

Gellers, Joshua Chad. 2016. Crowdsourcing Global Governance: Sustainable Development Goals, Civil Society, and the Pursuit of Democratic Legitimacy. *International Environmental Agreements: Politics, Law and Economics* 16 (3): 415–32.

Gendler, Tamara. 2018. Imagination. In Edward N. Zalta, ed., *Stanford Encyclopedia of Philosophy,* summer 2018. Available at https://plato .stanford.edu/archives/sum2018/entries/imagination.

Girard, Charles. 2015. Making Democratic Contestation Possible: Public Deliberation and Mass Media Regulation. *Policy Studies* 36 (3): 283–97.

González-Ricoy, Iñigo and Axel Gosseries, eds. 2016. *Institutions for Future Generations.* Oxford: Oxford University Press.

Goodin, Robert E. 1985. *Protecting the Vulnerable.* Chicago: University of Chicago Press.

1986. Laundering Preferences. In Jon Elster and Aanund Hylland, eds., *Foundations of Social Choice Theory,* pp. 75–101. Cambridge, UK: Cambridge University Press.

1996. Enfranchising the Earth, and Its Alternatives. *Political Studies* 44: 835–49.

2007. Enfranchising All Affected Interests, and Its Alternatives. *Philosophy and Public Affairs* 35: 40–68.

2017. Duties of Charity, Duties of Justice. *Political Studies* 65: 268–83.

Goodin, Robert and John Dryzek. 1980. Rational Participation: The Politics of Relative Power. *British Journal of Political Science* 10 (3): 273–92.

Goodin, Robert E. and Kai Spiekermann. 2018. *An Epistemic Theory of Democracy.* Oxford: Oxford University Press.

Goodin, Robert E. and Steven Ratner. 2011. Democratizing International Law. *Global Policy* 2 (3): 241–7.

Goodpaster, Kenneth E. 1978. On Being Morally Considerable. *Journal of Philosophy* 75: 308–25.

Gosseries, Axel. 2001. What Do We Owe the Next Generation(s)? *Loyola of Los Angeles Law Review* 35: 293–354.

Gould, Carol C. 2004. *Globalizing Democracy and Human Rights*. Cambridge, UK: Cambridge University Press.

2014. *Interactive Democracy: The Social Roots of Global Justice*. Cambridge, UK: Cambridge University Press.

Grisanti, Mary Lee and Howard E. Gruber. 1993. Creativity in the Moral Domain. In Mark A. Runco and Steven A. Pritzker, eds., *Encyclopedia of Creativity*, vol. 1, pp. 427–32. San Diego, CA: Academic Press.

Grönlund, Kimmo, André Bächtiger, and Maija Setälä, eds. 2014. *Deliberative Mini-publics: Involving Citizens in the Democratic Process*. Colchester, UK: ECPR Press.

Gutmann, Amy and Dennis Thompson. 1996. *Democracy and Disagreement*. Cambridge, MA: Harvard University Press.

Haas, Peter M. 1992. Banning Chlorofluorocarbons: Epistemic Community Efforts to Protect Stratospheric Ozone. *International Organization* 66 (1): 187–224.

Habermas, Jürgen. 1990. *Moral Consciousness and Communicative Action*. Cambridge, MA: MIT Press.

Hajer, Maarten A. 2009. *Authoritative Governance: Policy-Making in an Age of Mediatization*. Oxford: Oxford University Press.

Hajer, Maarten, Måns Nilsson, Kate Raworth, Peter Bakker, Frans Berkhout, Yvo de Boer, Johan Rockström, Kathrin Ludwig, and Marcel Kok. 2015. Beyond Cockpit-ism: Four Insights to Enhance the Transformative Potential of the Sustainable Development Goals. *Sustainability* 7 (2): 1651–60.

Haley Kevin J. and Daniel M. T. Fessler. 2005. Nobody's Watching? Subtle Cues Affect Generosity in an Anonymous Economic Game. *Evolution and Human Behavior* 26: 245–56.

Hall, Peter A. and David Soskice, eds. 2001. *Varieties of Capitalism: The Institutional Foundations of Comparative Advantage*. Oxford: Oxford University Press.

Hamilton, Clive. 2014. The Ethical Dimensions of Climate Change. Lecture to the Colloquium on 'Ethics and Policy', 13 July, Climate Change Institute, Australian National University. Available at www.youtube .com/watch?v=vbga0V0kn1g.

Haraway, Donna. 1988. Situated Knowledges: The Science Question in Feminism and the Privilege of Partial Perspective. *Feminist Studies* 14 (3): 575–99.

Harris, Aidan. 2015. Agenda 2030: Recognition for the Role of Justice and Government in Sustainable Development. *Open Society Foundations Voices*, 2 September.

Harris, Paul G. 2009. *World Ethics and Climate Change: From International to Global Justice*. Edinburgh: Edinburgh University Press.

Heins, Volker. 2005. Global Civil Society as a Politics of Faith. In Gideon Baker and David Chandler, eds., *Global Civil Society: Contested Futures*, pp. 186–201. London: Routledge.

Held, David. 1995. *Democracy and the Global Order: From the Modern State to Cosmopolitan Governance*. Stanford, CA: Stanford University Press.

Hershfield, Hal E., Daniel D. Goldstein, William E. Sharpe, Jesse Fox, Leo Yeykelis, Laura L. Carstensen, and Jeremy N. Bailenson. 2011. Increasing Saving Behaviour through Age-Progressed Renderings of the Future Self. *Journal of Market Research* 48: s23–37.

Higgott, Richard and Eva Erman. 2010. Deliberative Global Governance and the Question of Legitimacy: What Can We Learn from the WTO? *Review of International Studies* 36: 449–70.

Hobbes, Thomas. 1651. *Leviathan*. London: Andrew Crooke.

Hoffman, Matthew J. 2011. *Climate Governance at the Crossroads: Experimenting with a Global Response after Kyoto*. Oxford: Oxford University Press.

Hohfeld, Wesley Newcomb. 1917. Fundamental Legal Conceptions as Applied in Judicial Reasoning. *Yale Law Journal* 26: 710–70.

Honneth, Axel. 1995. *The Struggle for Recognition: The Moral Grammar of Social Conflicts*. Cambridge, MA: MIT Press.

  2004. Recognition and Justice: Outline of a Plural Theory of Justice. *Acta Sociologica* 47 (4): 351–64.

Hooper, John. 2011. Italian Cat Inherits 10m Euros Fortune. *Guardian*, 9 December. Available at www.theguardian.com/world/2011/dec/09/ital ian-cat-inherits-fortune.

Hopmann, P. Terrence. 1995. Two Paradigms of Negotiation: Bargaining and Problem Solving. *Annals of the American Academy of Political and Social Science* 542 (1): 24–47.

Howard, Jo, Erika López Franco, and Jackie Shaw. 2018. *Navigating the Pathways from Exclusion to Accountability*. Brighton: Institute of Development Studies.

Howard, Jo and Joanna Wheeler. 2015. What Community Development and Citizen Participation Should Contribute to the New Global Framework for Sustainable Development. *Community Development Journal* 50 (4): 552–70.

Hsieh, Nien-Hê. 2011. Global Business and Global Justice. In Michael Boylan, ed., *The Morality and Global Justice Reader*, pp. 185–210. Boulder, CO: Westview.

Hulme, David. 2007. The Making of the Millennium Development Goals: Human Development Meets Results-Based Management in an Imperfect World. Brooks World Poverty Institute Working Paper 16. Available at https://sustainabledevelopment.un.org/content/documents/773bwpi-wp-1607.pdf.

    2009. The Millennium Development Goals (MDGs): A Short History of the World's Biggest Promise. Brooks World Poverty Institute Working Paper 100. Available at https://papers.ssrn.com/sol3/papers.cfm?abstract_id=1544271.

Hume, David. [1739–40] 2007. *A Treatise of Human Nature*, ed. David Fate Norton and Mary K. Norton. Oxford: Clarendon Press.

    [1751] 1998. *An Inquiry concerning the Principles of Morals*, ed. Tom L. Beauchamp. Oxford: Clarendon Press.

Jackson, Frank. 1982. Epiphenomenal Qualia. *Philosophical Quarterly* 32: 127–36.

    1986. What Mary Didn't Know. *Journal of Philosophy* 83: 291–5.

Johnson, Mark. 1985. Imagination in Moral Judgment. *Philosophy and Phenomenological Research* 46: 265–80.

    1993. *Moral Imagination: Implications of Cognitive Science for Ethics*. Chicago: University of Chicago Press.

Kahan, Dan, Hank Jenkins-Smith, and Donald Braman. 2010. Cultural Cognition of Scientific Consensus. *Journal of Risk Research* 14 (2): 147–74.

Kahneman, Daniel. 2011. *Thinking: Fast and Slow*. New York: Farrar, Straus and Giroux.

Kamau, Macharia, Pamela Chasek, and David O'Connor. 2018. *Transforming Multilateral Diplomacy: The Inside Story of the Sustainable Development Goals*. London: Routledge.

Kanie, Norichika and Frank Biermann, eds. 2017. *Governing through Goals: Sustainable Development Goals as Governance Innovation*. Cambridge, MA: MIT Press.

Kanie, Norichika, Steven Bernstein, Frank Biermann, and Peter M. Haas. 2017. Introduction: Global Governance through Goal Setting. In Norichika Kanie and Frank Biermann, eds., *Governing through Goals: Sustainable Development Goals as Governance Innovation*, pp. 1–28. Cambridge, MA: MIT Press.

Karnein, Anja. 2016. Can We Represent Future Generations? In Iñigo González-Ricoy and Axel Gosseries, eds., *Institutions for Future Generations*, pp. 83–97. Oxford: Oxford University Press.

Kekes, John. 1991. Moral Imagination, Freedom, and the Humanities. *American Philosophical Quarterly* 28: 101–11.

Kemner, Jochen. 2011. Lobbying for Global Indigenous Rights: The World Council of Indigenous Peoples (1975–1997). *InterAmerica* 4 (2). Available at http://interamerica.de/current-issue/kemner/.

Keohane, Robert O. 2015. Nominal Democracy? Prospects for Democratic Global Governance. *International Journal of Constitutional Law* 13 (2): 343–53.

Kjørven, Olav. 2016. The Unlikely Journey to the 2030 Agenda for Sustainable Development. *Impakter*, 8 December. Available at https://impakter.com/impakter-essay-unlikely-journey-2030-agenda-sustainable-development/.

Kobrin, Stephen J. 2009. Private Political Authority and Public Responsibility: Transnational Politics, Transnational Firms, and Human Rights. *Business Ethics Quarterly* 19 (3): 349–74.

Kuper, Andrew. 2002. More Than Charity: Cosmopolitan Alternatives to the 'Singer Solution'. *Ethics and International Affairs* 16: 107–20.

Landemore, Hélène. 2012. *Democratic Reason: Politics, Collective Intelligence, and the Rule of the Many*. Princeton, NJ: Princeton University Press.

Landman, Anne. 2010. BP's 'Beyond Petroleum' Campaign Losing Its Sheen. *PR Watch*, 3 May.

Lang, Sabine. 2012. *NGOs, Civil Society, and the Public Sphere*. Cambridge, UK: Cambridge University Press.

Langford, Malcolm. 2016. Lost in Transformation? The Politics of the Sustainable Development Goals. *Ethics and International Affairs* 30 (2): 167–76.

Lapegna, Pablo. 2016. *Soybeans and Power: Genetically Modified Crops, Environmental Politics, and Social Movements in Argentina*. Oxford: Oxford University Press.

Larmore, Charles. 2001. Moral Judgment. In Ronald Beiner and Jennifer Nedelsky, eds., *Judgment, Imagination and Politics: Themes from Kant and Arendt*, pp. 47–64. Lanham, MD: Rowman & Littlefield.

Leopold, A. 1949. *A Sand County Almanac*. Oxford: Oxford University Press.

Levi-Faur, David, ed. 2012. *The Oxford Handbook of Governance*. Oxford: Oxford University Press.

Lindblom, Charles E. 1977. *Politics and Markets: The World's Political-Economic Systems*. New York: Basic Books.

List, Christian and Philip Pettit. 2011. *Group Agency*. Oxford: Oxford University Press.

Locke, John. [1690] 1960. *Second Treatise of Government*, ed. Peter Laslett. Cambridge, UK: Cambridge University Press.

Loewenstein, George and Jon Elster. 1992. *Choice over Time*. New York: Russell Sage.

Lomborg, Bjørn. 2007. *Cool It! The Skeptical Environmentalist's Guide to Global Warming*. New York: Knopf.

ed. 2010. *Smart Solutions to Climate Change: Comparing Costs and Benefits*. Cambridge, UK: Cambridge University Press.

Lukes, Steven. 2005. *Power: A Radical View*, 2nd ed. New York: Palgrave Macmillan.

Lupia, Arthur, Adam Seth Levine, Jesse O. Menning, and Gisela Sin. 2007. Were Bush Tax Cut Supporters 'Simply Ignorant?' A Second Look at Conservatives and Liberals in 'Homer Gets a Tax Cut'. *Perspectives on Politics* 5 (4): 773–84.

MacAskill, William. 2015. *Doing Good Better: How Effective Altruism Can Help You Make a Difference*. New York: Gotham Books.

McCarthy, Michael. 2017. A Giant Insect Ecosystem Is Collapsing Due to Humans. It's a Catastrophe. *Guardian*, 21 October. Available at www .theguardian.com/environment/2017/oct/21/insects-giant-ecosystem-col lapsing-human-activity-catastrophe.

MacIntyre, Alasdair C. 1984. Does Applied Ethics Rest on a Mistake? *The Monist* 67: 498–513.

1988. *Whose Justice? Which Rationality?* Notre Dame, IN: University of Notre Dame Press.

MacKenzie, Michael. 2016. A General Purpose, Randomly Selected Chamber. In Iñigo González-Ricoy and Axel Gosseries, eds., *Institutions for Future Generations*, pp. 24–47. Oxford: Oxford University Press.

McKeon, Nora. 2014. The New Alliance for Food Security and Nutrition: A Coup for Corporate Capital? TNI Agrarian Justice Programme, Policy Paper. Available at www.tni.org/en/publication/the-new-alli ance-for-food-security-and-nutrition.

Mansbridge, Jane. 2009. A 'Selection Model' of Political Representation. *Journal of Political Philosophy* 17 (4): 369–98.

Mansbridge, Jane, James Bohman, Simone Chambers, Thomas Christiano, Archon Fung, John Parkinson, Dennis F. Thompson, and Mark E. Warren. 2012. A Systemic Approach to Deliberative Democracy. In John Parkinson and Jane Mansbridge, eds., *Deliberative Systems: Deliberative Democracy at the Large Scale*, pp. 1–26. Cambridge, UK: Cambridge University Press.

Mansbridge, Jane, James Bohman, Simone Chambers, David Estlund, Andreas Føllesdal, Archon Fung, Cristina Lafont, Bernard Manin, and José Luis Martí. 2010. The Place of Self-Interest and the Role of Power in Deliberative Democracy. *Journal of Political Philosophy*, 18 (1): 64–100.

Martens, Jens and Karolin Seitz. 2015. *Philanthropic Power and Development: Who Shapes the Agenda?* Bonn: Global Policy Forum.

Martinez-Torres, Maria Elena and Peter M. Rossett. 2010. La Via Campesina: The Evolution of a Transnational Movement. *Global Policy Forum*. Available at www.globalpolicy.org/social-and-eco nomic-policy/world-hunger/land-ownership-and-hunger/48733-la-via-campesina-the-evolution-of-a-transnational-movement.html.

Mearsheimer, John. 2001. *The Tragedy of Great Power Politics*. New York: W. W. Norton.

Mele, Alfred R. 2003. *Motivation and Agency*. Oxford: Oxford University Press.

Milewicz, Karolina and Robert Goodin. 2018. Deliberative Capacity Building through International Organizations: The Case of the Universal Periodic Review of Human Rights. *British Journal of Political Science* 48 (2): 513–33.

Miller, David. 1995. *On Nationality*. Oxford: Oxford University Press.

2008. National Responsibility and Global Justice. *Critical Review of International Social and Political Philosophy* 11 (4): 383–99.

Mingst, Karen A., Margaret P. Karns, and Alynna J. Lyon. 2018. *The United Nations in the 21st Century*, 5th ed. New York: Routledge.

Montanaro, Laura. 2018. *Who Elected Oxfam? A Democratic Defence of Self-Appointed Representatives*. Oxford: Oxford University Press.

Montero, David. 2018. *Kickback: Exposing the Global Corporate Bribery Network*. New York: Viking.

Morgenthau, Hans. 1948. *Politics among Nations*. New York: Alfred A. Knopf.

Mpofu, Elizabeth. 2018. Agroecology Is Our Best Hope for Sustainable Development. *Farming Matters* 34 (1): 33.

Munnell, Alicia H., Anthony Webb, and Francesca Golub-Sass. 2009. *The National Retirement Risk Index: After the Crash*. Chestnut Hill, MA: Center for Retirement Research, Boston College.

Naess, Arne. 1973. The Shallow and the Deep: Long-Range Ecology Movements. *Inquiry* 16: 95–100.

1984. A Defence of the Deep Ecology Movement. *Environmental Ethics* 6: 265–70.

Nagel, Thomas. 1970. *The Possibility of Altruism*. Oxford: Clarendon Press.

1974. What Is It Like to Be a Bat? *Philosophical Review* 83: 435–40.

Naím, Moisés. 2009. Minilateralism. *Foreign Policy* 173: 135–6.

Narayan, Deep, Raj Patel, Kai Schafft, Anne Rademacher, and Sarah Koch-Schulte. 2000. *Voices of the Poor: Can Anyone Hear Us?* New York: Oxford University Press.

Nardin, Terry. 2008. International Ethics. In Christian Reus-Smit and Duncan Snidal, eds., *The Oxford Handbook of International Relations*, pp. 594–611. Oxford: Oxford University Press.

Newell, Natalie. 2014. How Did the Ground Level Panels Catalyse Change? In Thea Shahrokh and Joanna Wheeler, eds., *Knowledge from the Margins: An Anthology from a Global Network on Participatory Practice and Policy Influence*, pp. 30–1. Brighton: Institute of Development Studies.

Nicholson-Cole, Sophie A. 2005. Representing Climate Change Futures: A Critique on the Use of Images for Visual Communication. *Computers, Environment, and Urban Systems* 29: 255–73.

Niemeyer, Simon. 2002. Deliberation in the Wilderness. PhD thesis, Australian National University.

Niemeyer, Simon and Julia Jennstål. 2016. The Deliberative Democratic Inclusion of Future Generations. In Iñigo González-Ricoy and Axel Gosseries, eds., *Institutions for Future Generations*, pp. 247–65. Oxford: Oxford University Press.

Nixon, Rob. 2011. *Slow Violence and the Environmentalism of the Poor.* Cambridge, MA: Harvard University Press.

Nordhaus, William D. 2007. A Review of the Stern Review on the Economics of Climate Change. *Journal of Economic Literature* 45 (3): 686–702.

Norton, Bryan G., ed. 1986. *The Preservation of Species.* Princeton, NJ: Princeton University Press.

Nozick, Robert. 1974. *Anarchy, State and Utopia.* New York: Basic Books.

Nussbaum, Martha. 2011. *Creating Capabilities.* Cambridge, MA: Harvard University Press.

O'Neill, Onora. 2001a. Agents of Justice. *Metaphilosophy* 32: 180–95.

2001b. Practical Principles and Practical Judgment. *Hastings Center Report* 4: 15–23.

O'Neill, Saffron J., Maxwell Boykoff, Simon Niemeyer, and Sophie A. Day. 2013. On the Use of Imagery for Climate Change Engagement. *Global Environmental Change* 23: 413–21.

Offerdahl, Kate. 2013. Representing Youth and Future Generations in the United Nations. Discourse at the Expert Panel on Intergenerational Solidarity, New York, 9 May. Available at https://sustainabledevelopment.un.org/content/documents/3576offerdahl.pdf.

Ostrom, Elinor. 2009. A Polycentric Approach for Coping with Climate Change. World Bank Policy Research Working Paper 5095. Available at https://ssrn.com/abstract=1494833.

Page, Edward. 2011. Climatic Justice and the Fair Distribution of Atmospheric Burdens. *The Monist* 94 (3): 412–32.

Page, Scott E. 2007. *The Difference: How the Power of Diversity Creates Better Groups, Firms, Schools and Societies*. Princeton, NJ: Princeton University Press.

Parfit, Derek. 1971. Personal Identity. *Philosophical Review* 80: 3–27.

1984. *Reasons and Persons*. Oxford: Oxford University Press.

Parkinson, John. 2006. Rickety Bridges: Using the Media in Deliberative Democracy. *British Journal of Political Science* 36 (1): 175–83.

Parkinson, John and Jane Mansbridge, eds. 2012. *Deliberative Systems: Deliberative Democracy at the Large Scale*. Cambridge, UK: Cambridge University Press.

Participate. 2013. Response to the Report of the High-Level Panel on the Post-2015 Development Agenda, 6 June. Available at https://participatesdgs.org/2013/06/06/participate-response-to-the-high-level-panel-on-the-post-2015-development-agenda-report/.

Pascual, Unai, Patricia Balvanera, Sandra Díaz, György Pataki, Eva Roth, Marie Stenseke, Robert T. Watson, Esra Basak Dessane, Mine Islar, Eszter Kelemen et al. 2017. Valuing Nature's Contribution to People: The IPBES Approach. *Current Opinion in Environmental Sustainability* 26: 7–16.

Paxton, Joseph M., Leo Ungar, and Joshua D. Greene. 2011. Reflection and Reasoning in Moral Judgment. *Cognitive Science* 36: 163–77.

Payton, Autumn Lockwood. 2010. Building a Consensus Rule for International Organizations. European University Institute, Max Weber Programme, Working Paper 2010/22. Available at www.peio.me/wp-content/uploads/2014/04/Conf4_Lockwood-Payton-01.10.2010.pdf.

Pennycook, Gordon and David G. Rand. 2019. Fighting Misinformation on Social Media Using Crowdsourced Judgments of News Quality. *Proceedings of the National Academy of Sciences* 116 (7): 2521–6.

Peters, B. Guy and Jon Pierre. 1998. Governance without Government? Rethinking Public Administration. *Journal of Public Administration Research and Theory* 8 (2): 223–43.

Pettit, Philip. 1997. *Republicanism: A Theory of Freedom and Government*. Oxford: Oxford University Press.

Pickering, Jonathan. 2018. Ethical Mapmaking: The Epistemic and Democratic Value of Normative Theory in Intergovernmental Panel on Climate Change Assessments. Draft manuscript.

Pingeot, Lou. 2014. Corporate Influence in the Post-2015 Process. Working Paper. Aachen: Misereor. Available at www.globalpolicy.org/images/pdfs/GPFEurope/Corporate_influence_in_the_Post-2015_process_web.pdf.

2016. In Whose Interest? The UN's Strategic Rapprochement with Business in the Sustainable Development Agenda. *Globalizations* 13 (2): 182–202.

Pogge, Thomas W. 2002. *World Poverty and Human Rights: Cosmopolitan Responsibilities and Reforms*. Cambridge, UK: Polity.

2005. Recognized and Violated by International Law: The Human Rights of the Global Poor. *Leiden Journal of International Law* 18: 717–45.

Pogge, Thomas and Mitu Sengupta. 2016. Assessing the Sustainable Development Goals from a Human Rights Perspective. *Journal of International and Comparative Social Policy* 32 (2): 83–97.

Popper, Karl R. 1966. *The Open Society and Its Enemies*. London: Routledge and Kegan Paul.

Posner, Eric A. and David Weisbach. 2010. *Climate Change Justice*. Princeton, NJ: Princeton University Press.

Powell, Kate L., Gilbert Roberts, and Daniel Nettle. 2012. Eye Images Increase Charitable Donations: Evidence from an Opportunistic Field Experiment in a Supermarket. *Ethology* 118: 1096–101.

Rabinowitz, Aaron and Lea Heinhorn. 1985. Empathy and Imagination. *Imagination, Cognition, and Personality* 4: 305–12.

Ramsay, Frank P. 1928. A Mathematical Theory of Savings. *Economic Journal* 38: 543–59.

Rao, Vijayendra and Paromita Sanyal. 2010. Dignity through Discourse: Poverty and the Culture of Deliberation in Indian Village Democracies. *Annals of the American Academy of Political and Social Science* 629: 146–72.

Rask, Mikko, Richard Worthington, and Minna Lammi, eds. 2012. *Citizen Participation in Global Environmental Governance*. Abingdon, UK: Earthscan.

Rawls, John. 1971. *A Theory of Justice*. Cambridge, MA: Harvard University Press.

1999. *The Law of Peoples*. Cambridge, MA: Harvard University Press.

Reich, Rob. 2013. What Are Foundations for? *Boston Review*, March/April. Available at http://bostonreview.net/archives/BR38.2/ndf_rob_reich_foundations_philanthropy_democracy.php.

Richardson, Henry. 1990. Specifying Norms as a Way to Resolve Concrete Ethical Problems. *Philosophy and Public Affairs* 19: 279–310.

Rios, Mauricio. 2015. What Does Media Coverage of the SDGs Tell Us? Available at www.weforum.org/agenda/2015/10/what-does-media-cov erage-of-the-sdgs-tell-us/.

Risse, Mathias. 2005. Do We Owe the Global Poor Assistance or Rectification? *Ethics and International Affairs* 19: 9–18.

Risse, Thomas. 2000. 'Let's Argue!' Communicative Action in World Politics. *International Organization* 54 (1): 1–39.

Robeyns, Ingrid. 2017. *Wellbeing, Freedom and Social Justice: The Capability Approach Re-examined*. Cambridge, UK: Open Book Publishers.

Roche, Declan. 2003. *Accountability in Restorative Justice*. Oxford: Oxford University Press.

Rolston, Holmes. 1975. Is There an Ecological Ethic? *Ethics* 85: 93–109.

Ross, William D. [1930] 2002. *The Right and the Good*. Oxford: Clarendon Press.

Routley, Richard and Val Routley. 1979. Against the Inevitability of Human Chauvinism. In Kenneth E. Goodpaster and Kenneth M. Sayre, eds., *Ethics and Problems of the 21st Century*, pp. 36–59. Notre Dame, IN: University of Notre Dame Press.

Rubenstein, Jennifer. 2014. The Misuse of Power, Not Bad Representation: Why It Is Beside the Point That No One Elected Oxfam. *Journal of Political Philosophy* 22: 204–30.

  2015. *Between Samaritans and States: The Political Ethics of Humanitarian INGOs*. Oxford: Oxford University Press.

Sachs, Jeffrey D. 2012. From Millennium Development Goals to Sustainable Development Goals. *Lancet* 379 (9832): 2206–11.

Samuelsohn, Darren. 2009. No 'Pass' for Developing Countries in Next Climate Treaty, Says U.S. Envoy. *New York Times*, 9 December. Available at www.nytimes.com/gwire/2009/12/09/09greenwire-no-pass-for-developing-countries-in-next-clima-98557.html?pagewanted=all.

Saward, Michael. 2009. Authorisation and Authenticity: Representation and the Unelected. *Journal of Political Philosophy* 17 (1): 1–22.

  2010. *The Representative Claim*. Oxford: Oxford University Press.

Schattschneider, Elmer E. 1960. *The Semisovereign People: A Realist's View of Democracy*. New York: Holt, Reinhart and Winston.

Scheffler, Samuel. 1982. *The Rejection of Consequentialism*. Oxford: Oxford University Press.

Schelling, Thomas C. 1984. Self-Command in Practice, in Policy, and in a Theory of Rational Choice. *American Economic Review* 74 (2): 1–11.

Scherer, Andreas Georg and Guido Palazzo. 2011. The New Political Role of Business in a Globalized World: A Review of a New Perspective on CSR and Its Implications for the Firm, Governance, and Democracy. *Journal of Management Studies* 48 (4): 899–930.

Scheyvens, Regina, Glenn Banks, and Emma Hughes. 2016. The Private Sector and the SDGs: The Need to Move beyond 'Business as Usual'. *Sustainable Development* 24: 371–82.

Schlosberg, David. 1999. *Environmental Justice and the New Pluralism*. Oxford: Oxford University Press.

Schlosser, Markus. 2015. Agency. In Edward N. Zalta, ed., *The Stanford Encyclopedia of Philosophy*, fall 2015 ed. Available at https://plato .stanford.edu/archives/fall2015/entries/agency.

Sen, Amartya. 1985. Well-Being, Agency and Freedom: The Dewey Lectures 1984. *Journal of Philosophy* 82 (4): 169–221.

1999. *Development as Freedom*. New York: Knopf.

2002. Open and Closed Impartiality. *Journal of Philosophy* 99: 445–69.

2009. *The Idea of Justice*. Cambridge, MA: Harvard University Press.

Sen, Gita. 2013. An All-Embracing Development Agenda Is the Only Way Forward, 28 January. Available at www.together2030.org/archive/ www.beyond2015.org/engage-empower-impact.html.

Sengupta, Mitu. 2016. The Sustainable Development Goals: An Assessment of Ambition. *E-International Relations*, 18 January. Available at www .e-ir.info/2016/01/18/the-sustainable-development-goals-an-assessment-of-ambition/.

Sénit, Carole-Anne. 2017. Taking Democracy to the Next Level? Global Civil Society Participation in the Shaping of the Sustainable Development Goals from Rio to New York. PhD Thesis, University of Utrecht.

Sénit, Carole-Anne, Agni Kalfagianni, and Frank Biermann. 2016. Cyberdemocracy? Information and Communication Technologies in Civil Society Consultations for Sustainable Development. *Global Governance* 22: 533–54.

Sénit, Carole-Anne, Frank Biermann, and Agni Kalfagianni. 2017. The Representativeness of Global Deliberation: A Critical Assessment of Civil Society Consultations for Sustainable Development. *Global Policy* 8: 62–72.

Shahrokh, Thea and Joanna Wheeler, eds. 2014. *Knowledge from the Margins: An Anthology from a Global Network on Participatory Practice and Policy Influence*. Brighton: Institute of Development Studies.

Shapiro, Ian. 1999. *Democratic Justice*. New Haven, CT: Yale University Press.

Shue, Henry. 1993. Subsistence Emissions and Luxury Emissions. *Law and Policy* 15 (1): 39–59.

Simmons, A. John. 2010. Ideal and Nonideal Theory. *Philosophy and Public Affairs* 38: 5–36.

Sinclair, Timothy J. 1994. Passing Judgement: Credit Rating Processes as Regulatory Mechanisms of Governance in the Emerging World Order. *Review of International Political Economy* 1 (1): 133–59.

Singer, Peter. 1972. Famine, Affluence and Morality. *Philosophy and Public Affairs* 1 (3): 229–43.

2009. *The Life You Can Save*. New York: Random House.

2015. *The Most Good You Can Do: How Effective Altruism Is Changing Ideas about Living Ethically*. New Haven, CT: Yale University Press.

Skocpol, Theda. 1979. *States and Social Revolutions: A Comparative Analysis of France, Russia, and China*. Cambridge, UK: Cambridge University Press.

Smith, Adam. [1759–90] 1982. *The Theory of Moral Sentiments*, ed. D. D. Raphael and A. L. Macfie. Indianapolis, IN: Liberty Fund.

Smith, Graham. 2009. *Democratic Innovations: Designing Institutions for Citizen Participation*. Cambridge, UK: Cambridge University Press.

Solt, Frederick. 2008. Economic Inequality and Democratic Political Engagement. *American Journal of Political Science* 52 (1): 48–60.

Spangenberg, Joachim H. 2017. Hot Air or Comprehensive Progress? A Critical Assessment of the SDGs. *Sustainable Development* 25: 311–21.

Spijkers, Otto and Arron Honniball. 2015. Developing Global Public Participation (2): Shaping the Sustainable Development Goals. *International Community Law Review* 17 (3): 251–96.

Steffen, Will, Katherine Richardson, Johan Rockström, Sarah E. Cornell, Ingo Fetzer, Elena M. Bennett, Reinette Biggs, Stephen R. Carpenter, Wim De Vries, Cynthia A. De Wit et al. 2015. Planetary Boundaries: Guiding Human Development on a Changing Planet. *Science* 347 (6223): 1259855.

Steiner, Hillel. 2017. Debate: Levels of Non-Ideality. *Journal of Political Philosophy* 25: 376–84.

Stern, Nicholas. 2007. *The Economic Consequences of Climate Change: The Stern Review*. Cambridge, UK: Cambridge University Press.

Stueber, Karsten. 2019. Empathy. In Edward N. Zalta, ed., *The Stanford Encyclopedia of Philosophy*, fall 2019 ed. Available at https://plato .stanford.edu/archives/fall2019/entries/empathy.

Stevenson, Hayley. 2013. *Institutionalizing Unsustainability: The Paradox of Global Climate Governance*. Berkeley: University of California Press.

2016. The Wisdom of the Many in Global Governance: An Epistemic-Democratic Defense of Diversity and Inclusion. *International Studies Quarterly* 60 (3): 400–12.

Stevenson, Hayley and John S. Dryzek. 2014. *Democratizing Global Climate Governance*. Cambridge, UK: Cambridge University Press.

Stiglitz, Joseph. 2002. *Globalization and Its Discontents*. New York: W. W. Norton.

2006. *Making Globalization Work: The Next Steps to Global Justice*. London: Penguin.

Stock, Christian and Ian D. Bishop. 2002. Immersive, Interactive Exploration of Changing Landscapes. First International Congress on Environmental Modelling and Software, Lugano, June 2002, 130. Available at https://scholarsarchive.byu.edu/iemssconference/2002/all/130?utm_source=scholarsarchive.byu.edu%2Fiemssconference%2F2002%2Fall%2F130&utm_medium=PDF&utm_campaign=PDFCoverPages.

Stone, Christopher. 1972. Should Trees Have Standing? Toward Legal Rights for Natural Objects. *Southern California Law Review* 45: 450–501.

Suter, Renata S. and Ralph Hertwig. 2011. Time and Moral Judgment. *Cognition* 119: 454–8.

Tanasoca, Ana and Jensen Sass. 2019. Ritual Deliberation. *Journal of Political Philosophy* 27: 136–63.

Thaler, Richard and Shlomo Benartzi. 2004. Save More Tomorrow: Using Behavioral Economics to Increase Employee Saving. *Journal of Political Economy* 112: s164–87.

Titus, Zoé. 2017. The Role of the Media since the Adoption of the Sustainable Development Goals. Namibia Media Trust. Available at www.nmt.africa/uploads/5a2e5d9c4a234/TheroleofAfricanmediainpromotingandentrenchingtheethosoftheSDGs.pdf.

Tyson, Jeff. 2015. Jeffrey Sachs Is Putting 'a Lot of Hope' in the SDGs. Available at www.devex.com/news/jeffrey-sachs-is-putting-a-lot-of-hope-in-the-sdgs-85661.

United Nations (UN). 2012. *The Future We Want.* New York: United Nations.

2013. *Intergenerational Solidarity and the Needs of Future Generations.* Report of the secretary-general, 15 August. New York: United Nations.

2015. *Transforming Our World: The 2030 Agenda for Sustainable Development.* UN General Assembly Resolution A/RES/70/1 (21 October). New York: United Nations.

2017. MyWorld Survey. Available at https://myworld2030.org/.

United Nations (UN). n.d. About MY World. Available at www.myworld2015.org.

United Nations Development Group (UNDG). 2012. *Post-2015 Development Agenda: Guidelines for Country Dialogues: What Future Do You Want?* New York: United Nations Development Programme.

2013a. *The Global Conversation Begins.* New York: United Nations Development Programme.

2013b. *A Million Voices: The World We Want.* New York: United Nations Development Programme.

United Nations Development Programme (UNDP). 2012. *Post-2015 Development Agenda: Guidelines for National Consultations*. New York: United Nations.

Urfalino, Philippe. 2014. The Rule of Non-opposition: Opening Up Decision-Making by Consensus. *Journal of Political Philosophy* 22: 320–41.

Valentini, Laura. 2009. On the Apparent Paradox of Ideal Theory. *Journal of Political Philosophy* 17: 332–55.

2011. *Justice in a Globalized World*. Oxford: Oxford University Press.

2013. Justice, Charity and Disaster Relief: What, If Anything, Is Owed to Haiti, Japan and New Zealand? *American Journal of Political Science* 57: 491–503.

2017. The Natural Duty of Justice in Non-ideal Circumstances: On the Moral Demands of Institution Building and Reform. *European Journal of Political Theory* [online first]. Available at https://doi.org/10.1177% 2F1474885117742094.

Vanhuysse, Pieter. 2013. *Intergenerational Justice in Aging Societies: A Cross-National Comparison of 29 OECD Countries*. Gutersloh: Bertelsmann Stiftung.

Varela, F. G., H. R. Maturana, and R. Uribe. 1974. Autopoiesis: The Organization of Living Systems, Its Characterization and a Model. *Biosystems* 5 (4): 187–96.

Velleman, D. 1992. What Happens When Someone Acts? *Mind* 101 (403): 461–81.

Vosoughi, Soroush, Deb Roy, and Sinan Aral. 2018. The Spread of True and False News Online. *Science* 359: 1146–51.

Wallace, R. Jay. 2014. Practical Reason. In Edward N. Zalta, ed., *The Stanford Encyclopedia of Philosophy*, spring 2018 ed. Available at https://plato.stanford.edu/archives/spr2018/entries/practical-reason.

Walton, Richard E. and Robert B. McKersie. 1965. *A Behavioral Theory of Labor Negotiations: An Analysis of a Social Interaction System*. New York: McGraw-Hill.

Waltz, Kenneth. 1993. The Emerging Structure of International Politics. *International Security* 18: 44–79.

Walzer, Michael. 1983. *Spheres of Justice*. New York: Basic Books.

Warren, Mark and Jane Mansbridge. 2013. Deliberative Negotiation. In Jane Mansbridge and Cathie Jo Martin, eds., *Negotiating Agreement in Politics*, pp. 86–120. Washington, DC: American Political Science Association.

Watts, Jonathan. 2018. Red List Research Finds 26,000 Global Species Under Extinction Threat. *Guardian*, July 5. Available at www.theguardian.com/environment/2018/jul/05/red-list-research-finds-26000-species-under-extinction-threat.

Wettstein, Florian. 2009. *Multinational Corporations and Global Justice: Human Rights Obligations of a Quasi-governmental Institution.* Stanford, CA: Stanford University Press.

Wiggins, David. 1975–6. Deliberation and Practical Reason. *Proceedings of the Aristotelian Society* 76: 29–51.

Wilkinson, Richard and Kate Pickett. 2009. *The Spirit Level: Why Greater Equality Makes Societies Stronger.* New York: Bloomsbury.

Winkler, Harald and Joan Beaumont. 2010. Fair and Effective Multilateralism in the Post-Copenhagen Climate Negotiations. *Climate Policy* 10 (6): 638–54.

Wisor, Scottt. 2012. After the MDGs: Citizen Deliberation and the Post-2015 Development Framework. *Ethics and International Affairs* 26 (1): 113–33.

World Bank. 2017. *Monitoring Global Poverty. Report of the Commission on Global Poverty.* Washington, DC: World Bank. Available at https://openknowledge.worldbank.org/bitstream/handle/10986/25141/9781464809613.pdf.

  2018. *Piecing Together the Poverty Puzzle.* Washington, DC: World Bank.

World Commission on Environment and Development. 1987. *Our Common Future.* Oxford: Oxford University Press.

Yee, Nick and Jeremy N. Bailenson. 2007. The Proteus Effect. *Human Communication Research* 33: 271–90.

Young, Iris Marion. 2004. Responsibility and Global Labor Justice. *Journal of Political Philosophy* 12: 365–88.

  2006. Responsibility and Global Justice: A Social Connection Model. *Social Philosophy and Policy* 23 (1): 102–30.

  2011. *Responsibility for Justice.* New York: Oxford University Press.

Ypi, Lea. 2012. *Global Justice and Avant-Garde Political Agency.* Oxford: Oxford University Press.

Zuijderduijn, Mike, Francine Egberts, and Ella Krämer. 2016. *Outcome Evaluation of the UNDP Project: 'Building the Post-2015 Development Agenda: Open and Inclusive Consultations'.* Ede, the Netherlands: MDF Training & Consultancy BV.

Index

CPSIA information can be obtained
at www.ICGtesting.com
Printed in the USA
BVHW041720010621
608563BV00010B/107